Prison
Transformations

Prison Transformations

The System, The People in Prison, And Me

A Prison Story, 1962-2009

It is fitting to make merry and be glad, for this your
brother was dead and is alive; he was lost and is found.
—Luke 15:32

Stephen Chinlund

To order additional copies of this book, contact:
Xlibris Corporation
1-888-795-4274
www.Xlibris.com
Orders@Xlibris.com
62552

Contents

---

*   This chapter appeared in a slightly different form in the *Journal of Religion and Health.*

Acknowledgments

Countless people have helped me to write this book, each contributing in unique ways. I am grateful to them all: Assemblyman Jeff Aubry, Rev. Ed Bacon, James Baldwin, George Beeks, Chris and Margaret Beels, John Bell, John Pairman Brown, Cherie Clarke, Michael Cork, Joe Cruickshank, William Dean, Bill Gard, Marty and Roger Gilbert, Fred Dicker, Brian Fischer, Marshall Green, David and Margaret Gullette, Frederick P. Herter, Chuck Hamilton, Amos Henix, Earle Hunter and the Friends Seminary community, Judge Judith S. Kaye, Max Kenner, Kenneth Kramer, The Very Rev. Ledlie I. Laughlin, Leroy Looper, Elaine Lord, Paul McGinnis, The Rt. Rev. Paul Moore Jr., The Very Rev. James P. Morton, Sidney Moshette, Rev. Ed Muller, Reinhold Niebuhr, Rev. Clarke Oler, Jo Ann Page, Robert M. Pennoyer, Selma Price, Rev. George Regas, Jack Rosenthal, David Rothenberg, Sister Elaine Roulet, Benay Rubenstein, Jim Ryan, Hans Toch, Diana Sands. Joe Santana, Marguerite Saunders, Virginia Satir, Carol Shapiro, Roger Schutz, Elisabeth Sifton, Père Sofronius, Dorothy Stoneman, Joe Sullivan, Jeremy Travis, Baylis Thomas Senator Dale Volker, Benjamin Ward, Sam Waterston, Rev. George "Bill" W. Webber, Wendy Weil, Anne Williams, Dr. Walter Wink, Christian Wolff, and thousands of incarcerated and formerly incarcerated men and women who have shared their most intimate shame and hope and love in their transformations.

And I give special thanks for the inspiration of my parents; my three children; and my beloved, wise, and patient wife, Caroline.

Prologue

This is a story written to honor the thousands of men and women who have been locked up in prison and have emerged as people of persistence, courage, and compassion. They are the ones who have changed their prisons into places of hope and new life.

Prison has also been a soul-destroying place, revealing the depths of human cruelty. There is no deeper helplessness than that experienced by a man or a woman locked up at the mercy of others when there is no appeal. When no scream can be loud enough or long enough to reach the human ear and bring relief, then the one in pain has hit the stone floor of the bottom. The relentlessness of that despair has driven many people insane. It has led many to suicide.

However, prison has a contradictory truth. The ones who are destroyed are those who could not find a way to break out of the dark woods to the meadow that is the subject of this book. The fact is that many people have made prison into a good place—the place where men and women transform their lives for the better, in a way they themselves say they could not have found on the outside. At their best, prisons are modern monasteries—quiet, contemplative worlds—where people are able to confront the truth about themselves, come to find peace with it, and be free.

This is a dangerous story to tell because it may sound as if I am praising prison. Instead, I write in praise of the countless thousands of incarcerated people who found ways to make prison work for them.

I am an Episcopal priest, a former prison warden, and former chairman of the New York State Commission of Correction. I have worked for over forty-five years with men and women locked up inside to help them find freedom, inside prison within themselves, and after release in the community. Most books are written either from the point of view of a prisoner or of the authorities. I have worked on both sides of the street.

Bill Dean is a lifelong friend and chairman of the Correctional Association of New York. He and colleagues visit inside prisons and have done so for decades. He recently said, after his latest visit inside, "I feel as if I am watching the Pirandello play *Right You Are If You Think You Are*. I listen to one group, and they seem to be telling me about conditions as they are. Then I listen to the next group, and they give me a different and completely believable reality. It is baffling." So I admit that this book is written from my point of view. I try to show my own background in the first couple of chapters so that the reader may be informed in judging the rest of the narrative. Feel free to skip to chapter 3.

Millions of people in our country have lived lives of anger and despair since birth. They often come from poverty-ridden neighborhoods and violent families (rich and poor) where anger and despair are the norm. Finally, not surprisingly, they commit some thoughtless, desperate act and get arrested for it. They end up in a police precinct holding pen, then go to a too-rapid appearance in court, and finally land behind the doors that clang shut on the last stop—a prison where they will have to remain, perhaps for many years—frozen, incapacitated, held still.

Many people in the outside world are happy about this concrete aspect of prison; incapacitation means that the criminal cannot get at them. Prisoners are not happy about it; being locked away is a lonely, terrifying, painful experience as it is meant by society to be. It takes most prisoners a long time simply to accept the fact that there is no way out. But sooner or later, they begin viscerally to know that they are not going anywhere. They face a breaking point—a point at which they have a choice. They can become ever more committed to anger, despair, and violence. Or they can look around and take stock: three meals a day even though the food is bad; a roof over their heads even though it is too cold in winter and too hot in summer; relative safety if they watch where they are going and have some luck; minimal temptations to use drugs or alcohol (though that opportunity is never entirely gone); an absence of distractions from fancy cars, gold chains, or the opposite sex. Prison becomes a kind of enforced monastery. If a person can take advantage of confinement instead of being crushed by it, then being held still can often be a good thing.

Many do decide to use this time as well as prison allows. They seek out positive-minded friends, attend school, take vocational training, participate in drug rehabilitation workshops, and engage in anger management classes. As a result, many achieve higher levels of self-esteem than they ever had hoped to gain. They come to know the "natural high" of communicating with family; creating artwork; and discovering the intelligence, courage, patience, and talents that they did not know they had. They develop skills that will serve them well in outside jobs.

Virtually all people in prison are released from prison with a strong wish never to return. They want the joys of freedom. They just need help—usually, a lot of help—attaining the state of mind and spirit that brings those joys within reach.

For much of my adult life, I have tried to help formerly incarcerated people become reintegrated into society: to find housing, get and keep employment, reconnect with family, and maintain their positive attitudes with support groups. One of the biggest obstacles to their successful is the mind frame of citizens influenced by the distorted movies showing prison as a place of unrelieved horror, the classic "school for crime"—with gang rapes, escape plots, beatings, knife assaults, dark cells, and disease. How then to account for those who come out and make excellent employees, neighbors, and friends? Some are, in fact, better in those roles than some average citizens who have not yet learned the hard lessons of patience, forbearance, persistence, and flexibility, which nearly all formerly incarcerated people have been forced to learn. These people have risen above the dehumanizing dimensions of their confinement, transforming cells into rooms of their own.

The riots in California in August, 2009 made it clear that the movie images of the horrors of state prisons are sometime reality, not distortion. The federal courts had ordered California to release 40,000 prisoners (net) over the next couple of years. It is impossible to provide adequate supervision of triple-bunk dormitories. California needs twenty more prisons to house adequately the 140,000 people they currently confine! At the same time, New York State has closed nine prisons in the last three years. It has plans to close a couple more because the prison population has gone down dramatically from 72,000 to 64,000. So I admit that my story, in concentrating on New York State is a much more positive narrative than the ones being told in some other states.

The point is that prisons do not have to be nightmare institutions. They can be run in a professional and humane way and thereby offer the opportunity for positive change to the vast majority of those they confine.

Jeremy Travis, president of the John Jay College of Criminal Justice in New York City has made major contributions to changing public opinion about reentry. In his most recent book, *But They All Come Back: Facing the Challenges of Prisoner Re-entry*, Travis lays out—in impressive, sometimes chilling, statistical detail—the reentry issues at the heart of this book. His years directing the National Institute of Justice (and growing its work massively) are evident in the strong case he makes for focusing our attention away from revenge and toward more-effective prison and parole policy. In his current office, he has established the Prisoner Reentry Institute, launched ably by the fine leadership of Debbie Mukumal. It is attended by commissioners and superintendents, parole officers, and formerly incarcerated men and women—a tribute to the relevance of its discourse.

America is slowly turning away from prison as the only reflexive solution for criminal action. For years, we have locked up people, over two million of them, in various kinds of prisons; and that is far too many. But it is a hard reality that sometimes prison is the only possible choice; and in those cases, we simply must expand greatly the educational opportunities, vocational training, social services, and other programs to encourage personal transformation.

Parole must be significantly enhanced, with manageable caseloads, improved training and support for parole officers and their supervisors and ready access to referrals for temporary jobs and transitional housing. Most of all, we must reform the process of revocation of parole, to make sanctions (return to prison) a more efficient (initially brief) process.

Not only would more people in prison be transformed but also our society would move toward being safer, more secure, and spiritually richer. We would move away from revenge as the primary motive for imprisonment toward a clearer focus on reentry as our primary concern, with public safety as our goal.

Notes.

1. Some of the names of people in prison have been changed to protect their privacy.

2. The use of the word "prisoner" has been opposed by many of us in the prison reform movement because it seems to reduce a person to the fact of his/her incarceration. The subject of this book and the work of my life has been to make the same point in working directly with people who are confined. They are more than the crime(s) which have changed their lives. For some, the impulsive act of a moment seems to erase all that they were before or have become since that terrible moment. That is not a true representation of them and I have tried to conform my language accordingly.

3. The use of the word "ex-offender" is also abused and is wrong for the same reasons. It does, however, imply to some the belief that one can leave the past behind and lead a new life. Still, it is generally better to find new phrases.

4. The use of the word "inmate" is even more loaded. It seems to imply that there is a happy band of people inside prison, wrapped up in comfort and affectionate loyalty to each other. I have tried to avoid the use of the word because any happiness, friendship or loyalty achieved inside is won at a great price and should not be demeaned, however inadvertently, by the use of the word "inmate." However, as I explain in the book, there are many who have said that they discovered family love and personal commitment inside for the first time in their lives. They even have said, albeit ruefully, that they were "happier inside with all of you (Network members) than they were on the outside." And people, after release, have often expressed a longing for the closeness they knew inside, now gone, in the rush of life in the free world. So I am not ready to leave the word "inmate" behind entirely, though I reject any facile implications about an easy life in prison.

Chapter One

Beginnings

As I stumbled across a heavily plowed field one spring morning toward the front door of the prison in Coxsackie, New York, prison correction officers were throwing clods of earth at me. I kept on walking. One clod hit me in the back. It did not hurt, but I slowed down a little, not wanting them to think I was intimidated.

It was 1979. I was chairman of the New York State Commission of Correction, an agency that had been created six years before, in the aftermath of the bloody Attica rebellion. We were required to monitor the state's twenty-five prisons (for felons serving more than a year), sixty-four jails (for misdemeanants serving less than a year), and innumerable police lockups (for those arrested and awaiting their appearance in court). On some days, it seemed like a thankless job. On this one, it felt also fruitless.

The state's correctional officers were on strike, and these officers did not want me coming into Coxsackie, a maximum-security facility near the banks of the Hudson River. However, the commission was obliged by law to make sure that minimal safety was being maintained. Rumors were buzzing about fires, beatings, and lack of food and emergency medical treatment. I had to go and see for myself; I was asking my staff to do the same in other prisons. If it was dangerous, I should face the same dangers that they were encountering.

When I arrived, I was unable to convince the pickets that I was not a scab. I explained that I was only going in to see what was happening.

They told me I could not go through the gate. However, they said I was free to walk across the field to the front door, one hundred yards away. As I trudged along, the clumps of earth were thrown at my back. It was a low point in my years of commitment to working out some new kind of cooperation between staff and people who were locked up, to finding a new life for thousands of people in their cells.

When I got to the front door, I was admitted to the prison through a series of locked gates. Some were operated with a huge key; others were opened electronically by officers behind bulletproof glass. Posts were being covered by management and by a few officers who were about to retire, and apparently did not care what the pickets on the outside might think.

It felt strange inside. All the prisoners were locked in their cells. There was no normal movement in the corridors; all programs were cancelled and closed. About the only place that seemed to have its normal staff was the infirmary, so I found that the rumors about absent medical care were untrue. Prisoners were being fed one meal a day, one block of inmates at a time, with sandwich materials distributed for them to take back to their cells—not very appetizing, but no one was starving. The atmosphere was tense because everyone knew that there were no backup officers if some kind of trouble broke out; riot, hostage taking, and bloodshed all loomed. However, even with the threat of violence, it was still a normal New York State prison.

It was a surprise, as it always is in a prison, to see how individual each cell was, despite the regimentation that defines an institution. Some were very neat, and a few were filled with artwork. Some were real pigsties. A few prisoners were full of invective toward me and all other authorities. Others were thoughtful. All wanted to know why I was there and what might happen next.

One, named Felix, was anxious about being fed. He had no food sent in regularly from home as the luckier inmates did, and so was entirely dependent on the deliveries from the mess hall. His cell was immaculate; and his fingernails, like most inmates', were almost too well clipped and clean. I reassured him that there would be enough to eat. Another man was terrified of what would happen after the strike. He was in fact confused about the difference between an officers' strike and an inmates' strike. He remembered the bloody crushing of an inmates' strike in 1960 in the state's Green Haven prison, and he remembered the carnage in Attica prison in 1971. He was terrified that it would happen again. I tried to explain and reassure him, but with only medium success. He did not know me.

After five hours, I walked back out toward the front gate on the paved road. The officers who had denied me that route on the way in allowed me to leave without any more harassment. I told them I was as interested in their safety as they were, and we parted. I wondered, *How had I ever come to be involved in this strange business?* I felt as if I were an explorer in a part of the world for which no map had been made. And years earlier, I felt that I had found gold in that strange new land.

My journey probably began with my own parents' perennial optimism and the upbringing they gave me. I was born in the Great Depression, in December 1933 in New York City, and have lived in New York City almost all my life. My father, Edwin Chinlund, was a successful vice president and treasurer with Macy's. My mother, Helen Brown Chinlund, was self-educated after high school, but would have been a lawyer or a professor had she been born forty years later.

My parents were not religious, but they liked the ideals of the Quakers, and they sent me to New York Friends Seminary, a Quaker institution. There we were expected to attend hour-long traditional silent meetings for worship. At my initial one, in first grade, I was sure that there must have been some mistake. I was confident that someone was about to stand up and say what we *really* were going to do for the next hour. When I realized that there would be only silence for that whole sixty minutes, I felt panic. I looked at my classmates, who picked at their nails and ears, swung their feet, and pushed the borderline of permissible mischief. Somehow I allowed myself to sink a little into the silence. It was still a bit scary, but it was also different.

Over the months and years, I found it increasingly exciting, mysterious, and, as I came to realize years later in subsequent meetings, deeply peaceful. As time went by and the layers came off those dimensions of silence, it became progressively clearer to me that silence is a friend. Even today, unexpected delays (waiting for the elevator, the subway, or the doctor), occasions of enforced silence, come to me as opportunities (not always taken!) to enjoy the healing peace of silence. Silence is not just an invention of the Quakers, it is central to the lives of both monasteries and prisons as well. In monasteries, the silence is of course voluntary, welcomed, and embraced—a space within which one can discover God as well as more of what it means to be human.

My parents were strongly opposed to any kind of coercive religion and I have shared those feelings from childhood. My mother was born of Jewish parents who were not particularly observant. My mother was fifth of five children and her oldest sibling, a brother, was fierce in his demands that the family goes to temple and be orthodox Jews. She remembered many painful arguments in her home about religion. Her brother bullied her, trying to get her involved. She often spoke of the unfairness of being "born into a particular religion" when that was not true of Methodists or even Catholics. She thought she should have the right to choose and she was still deciding when I began, at age thirteen, to go to church. They began to go with me when I was about fourteen.

My father was tenth of eleven in a Swedish Lutheran family and he, also, had an oldest brother who was angrily committed to a fundamentalist Lutheranism. So my father also hated conversations about religion and I imagine that he and my mother fell in love partly because of their agreement that religion was a conversational mine field to be avoided. They were surprised and glad to discover that there was a whole other way of thinking and speaking about religion than they had known as young people. My early connection with the Dutch Reformed Church opened the door to discover a much more humble theology than they had previously encountered. I have continued all my life to abhor references to God and especially to Jesus, which appear to come from a smug, know-it-all certainty. I still believe that it is possible to be passionate about one's faith without disparaging the faith of anyone else.

When I was in the second or third grade, three ex-convicts came to speak at our Quaker meeting. I was flabbergasted. All I remember is that they seemed as if they were unusually sympathetic and intelligent people, and I wished that they would go on talking. I wanted to be friends with them. I had thought that they would be scary, even monsters, and I was surprised when they did not match the stereotype. They spoke comfortably and with humor about their past lives and, eloquently, about the need for prison reform and for employment after release.

My parents were admired as civic leaders in New York, and they gave generously to a range of admirable causes, including those that helped formally incarcerated people. My father always hoped for good things to come from political leaders he admired, especially Mayor Fiorello LaGuardia and, later, President Dwight Eisenhower, Senator Jacob Javits, and Mayor John Lindsay.

My mother was with him in all that, but she also had a special devotion to foster care. She was a member of the boards of three foster care agencies and struggled to find new ways of setting children free from the cycle of abuse and neglect, lack of education, welfare dependency, teenage pregnancy, and the resultant creation of a next generation of troubled children. The seeming obviousness of the root causes fascinated her: continuing racism, lack of job opportunities, poor schooling, lack of the kind of parental encouragement I received from my own parents, poor housing, inadequate medical care, and elitism by the very agencies she supported. This last obstacle vexed her most. She was contemptuous of the "helping professionals" who shrugged with indifference over clients who would not come on time for their appointments in the professionals' midtown offices.

As a member of the board of the Women's Prison Association, my mother sometimes visited with women who were newly released from prison. She told of one of those visits with an Irish woman who had bright red hair and a strong brogue. My mother was pressing her about her future plans. The woman was cheerfully indifferent in her vague answers. My mother became increasingly anxious on her behalf, imagining the trouble she might get into because of her poor planning. Finally, she said in exasperation, "And *then* what will become of you!" The woman fixed her with a warm, peaceful gaze and said, "Ah, Mrs. Chinlund, the likes o' you will always be takin' care o' the likes o' me." My mother told the story more than once, in my company, to various friends. It was never quite clear to me just what she took from the tale. For me, it has been a helpful refrain to get me to relax a little when talking with someone who has had a life like a train wreck, not to be compulsively and paternalistically anxious about his/her future.

My sole experience at being on the receiving end of a violent crime came when I was twelve. My brother, two friends, and I were playing baseball in Central Park. Some older boys approached as my brother, about fourteen, was batting. They asked if they could play. "No," he said. One boy then grabbed the bat from him and swung hard at him, breaking his arm. I yelled from the field, "Hey, you can't do that!" And two of them started to run toward me. I began to run away, so did my brother and our friends, splitting off in different directions. Two of them chased me down with ease, took my glove, money, and spikes. Then in what now seems like an unbelievable bit of old-fashioned courtesy, my attackers made sure I had enough money for carfare home!

A broken arm was important enough in 1945 to warrant two rides around the city with detectives in an unmarked car looking for our tormentors. We even went into a couple of schools in East Harlem. I actually spotted one of the boys on a stoop in front of a house. The detectives jumped out after him, but he ran away and up the stairs, then to the safety of the roof. There were endless exits from there. He was never caught.

For quite some time, I was afraid to be around guys who looked like the ones who had mugged us—that is, Latino men. But over the years, my fears melted as I had positive experiences with people of color who looked like the same people. That diminished the size of the incident in my mind. Later, I was with black and Latino men in school, college, seminary, church, and, finally, prison. My experiences were invariably favorable. In fact, I found them generally more spontaneous and fun than people in my own more-uptight white world. My parents had raised me to be extremely well behaved—home early from parties, never open in disagreement.

Actually, growing up during World War II, I was living in a genuinely scary world. I was terrified of the Nazis, and I did not feel that there was much margin for frolicsome behavior. I had fantasies about what I might do if I were living in occupied France. I would go around on my bicycle, delivering secret messages to the underground! Then what would I do if the gestapo caught me? How much torture could I stand before I gave them the names of the people I knew? In 1942, my father had hesitated for an unforgettable second before assuring me that we were going to win the war.

One evening, soon after the war was over, in the late summer of 1946, I was lying under a tree outside our country home in Massachusetts, thinking about the emerging stories of the Holocaust. The scent of pine was strong. I continued to be frightened by stories of the starvation, the torture, and the ovens that had burned the victims. Based on accounts I read, it seemed that neither wealth nor education had helped people to survive or to keep their sanity in the concentration camps. More useful (by some accounts) seemed to be a strong religious faith. It seemed to me that the Jews who had been able to trust in God entirely were among those who resisted in Warsaw or elsewhere or who maintained their equanimity in the face of death. That still seems true today even though we know there are many sources of personal strength.

That night, lying under the tree, I wondered what I might do with my life that would respond to a world in which even my own parents, my strong, unshakable parents, were clearly scared, deeply unsettled by the news from Europe. They and all the other adults I knew could not integrate those events into any previous understanding of what it means to be human.

At that moment, a drop of water, accumulated dew on a twig of the tree, landed on my forehead. I experienced the moment as a powerful event. I interpreted it as a sign, and then and there, I decided I would be a Christian minister. Despite my Quaker education, I had never been to Sunday school and only infrequently, with a friend, to church. I still was not even baptized. But my vocation seemed clear then, and it has never changed in all the intervening years. It never occurred to me, until it was suggested years later, that the drop of water was some sort of baptism. I do not believe it was, and I resist scenarios of divine intervention of such particularity, but I do know that I felt much more at peace from then on; I was committed to doing my own small part to alleviate human suffering. Though I was not quite a teenager, I knew rationally that the pain of everyday peacetime life could be as harsh as wartime suffering. My life began to take a form.

My parents gave me the opportunity to go to Europe one summer with my best friend, Christian Wolff, and his parents, Helen and Kurt Wolff. I was sixteen. One of the places we visited was the Franciscan monastery in Fiesole, outside Florence. The war had just ended three years before, and like much of the rest of Italy, the place had a battle-scarred exterior. I entered the cloister, which was full of wild roses and had been battered even inside by gunfire and bombs. I sat down on the low wall, leaned back against a column, and had the powerful feeling that I had come home. I immediately felt the deep peace of the place and did not want to leave. The Wolffs went off to see other places and returned much later to find me contentedly still sitting there.

I was fascinated that for centuries, men and women had lived alone, then later in communities, to give themselves to God in prayer, with only the barest minimum of physical subsistence. From the beginning, I was struck by the freedom of their lives. They were unencumbered by fixing the washing machine, paying the insurance, buying the latest jacket, or keeping up with the newest novel.

So I went the next year, 1951, at seventeen, to Mount Athos, which is technically a holy independent republic in northern Greece, on a peninsula stretching into the Aegean Sea. I visited several monasteries on the peninsula, which hosts seventeen monasteries of various sizes, saving the one named after Saint Paul to visit last. It had the reputation of being the most populous and alive. Some of them were shabby, physically and spiritually, but some were exalted. Saint Paul's, on the west side, was the best led and the most beautifully situated, perched on a cliff over the sea.

There was a story that the brothers told me that when the Nazis came to occupy Mount Athos, the monks went to gather on the dock as the German boat drew near, and one of the abbots solemnly forbade the Germans to set foot on the ground of the holy republic. Though it was then and had always been a militarily strategic peninsula occupied by successive armies, the Nazis withdrew, presumably impressed by the spiritual power of the assembled group. Many Nazis, of course, would not have taken the time to notice holy power when they met it. If the story is true, then it could have been that this particular platoon was led by Germans too "soft" for deployment elsewhere. I prefer to believe it was some sort of miracle of the monastery, high over the Aegean.

Before I left, I talked with the abbot of Saint Paul's long into the night. He explained the happiness of a life given over entirely to God, and I felt a desire to stay right there. As I stood on the ramparts that night, I held a plane ticket from Athens to Paris between my thumb and index finger and tempted God to blow it into the sea. I had to leave early the next morning in order to get to Athens on time to catch the plane. I looked up at the millions of stars in the black sky, undimmed by clouds, smog, or lights. I regretfully put the ticket back in my pocket. I was not ready for such a huge change of plans.

However, the abbot had told me to look up his predecessor, who was leading a small monastic community in a village outside Paris called Sainte-Geneviève-des-Bois. I did so immediately on arriving in Paris—and spent over two weeks listening to and praying with the wise Père Sofronius. He continued the conversation I had started with his successor. He gave me a prayer on fine paper, which I kept in my wallet and read for years until it finally disintegrated. I especially remember the first line, "Oh Dieu, Qui sonde les coeurs" (Oh God, you who explore the depths of our hearts) I was seized, perhaps because my own heart needed some deep exploring.

The name of his little community of monks was le Donjon, or the Dungeon. I did not think much about it at the time, but the monks *chose to think of themselves as prisoners of God.* The Dungeon was their place of freedom. I was becoming accustomed to the idea that freedom sometimes required choosing to limit oneself, something inimical to the American belief that freedom means living without bounds.

I stayed in Sainte-Geneviève-des-Bois at the home of the princess Meschersky, a woman who had helped found le Donjon and had created a little émigré community of Russians around it. She believed I would be interested to visit a new Protestant/Catholic monastic community at Taizé, near the historic monastic site of Cluny. There I found a monastery to which I would return again and again.

Roger Schutz, the prior, a French Swiss, had grown up on the border with his Catholic mother and Protestant father and had been living there during the war. He had started the forerunner of the community, without realizing it, when he and five friends began sheltering fleeing Jews, especially children, thus creating their own underground railway from occupied France to the safety of Switzerland. They could have been raided, tortured, and killed by the gestapo at any time. Protestants and Catholics—they prayed together, then parted, knowing each time that they might never meet again in this life. Their lives depended on the wisdom and courage of the other brothers. They became aware every moment of what they experienced as the grace of God.

There was no church building; they worked from house to house. The community was intentionally fluid in its location. Finally, they had to stop as the gestapo was closing in. After the war, they realized that they were committed to God and to each other in a way that could not be invented artificially; it came from their personal history. So they looked for a place in which they could become a continuing community and to which they could invite other men, Catholic and Protestant, to join with them. They found the tiny village of Taizé, in the rolling hills of Burgundy. On my first visit to Taizé, I stayed for a week, joining happily in the prayers and singing along with the music that filled the place. At that time, there were nineteen brothers. They could all sit around one long table in what was called the Yellow House. Pilgrims and brothers squeezed in to the twelfth-century Romanesque jewel of a chapel and sang the Psalms set to the music of Joseph Gelinau. The chapel is now consecrated to be, permanently, a place of silence. Pilgrims come there twenty-four hours a day to be in silence, confident that there will be no interruptions but the songs of birds and the sound of bells. There is a new (1980) big Church of the Reconciliation on top of the hill, of modern design.

Out of the original brotherhood of five, forged in the crucible of the daily threat of death, has grown a huge movement. It circles the globe, with young people coming to the tiny village of Taizé to pray, sing, and reflect together on the course of their lives. They sit, hugging their knees, on the cement floor that is covered by a thin carpet; there are no pews or chairs. One individual's knees almost touch the back of the person in front of him. People are respectful of each other as they clamber through the process of standing and sitting again. The prayers and music, which come three times a day, for two hours, weave together. One sleeps on a hard bed, and eats what I can only call pea paste (lukewarm), and bathes in bad showers. In recent years, the accommodations have been somewhat improved, but the young pilgrims do not come for the physical comforts. There is a small charge now for the meals and lodging, but there are no solicitations for donations. In fact, donations are refused, unless someone who has actually gone there wishes to give something out of thanksgiving. The community is supported by the pottery, the tapes and CDs, and, most of all, the sale of the books of Brother Roger. There are no sermons; there are no strategy meetings about how to become more relevant. Young people come by the thousands every year from all over the world, mostly from Europe, but now also from Asia, Russia, several African nations, and China—and a few from the United States.

Why do young people travel to Taizé? They come even though many of them are immersed in a culture that prizes sex, drugs, money, and power, to be guided by monks, who are living their lives without any of these, under the traditional vows of poverty, celibacy, and obedience. That contrary set of values is, of course, strongest in the United States, but it exists all over the world. And still they come, embracing a way of life that embraces the opposite.

Many times I have voyaged back to Taizé, since that first visit in 1951, to find new inspiration, in seasons of my life both fair and foul. Visitors are welcomed to be reconciled to each other, not to "join Taizé." You cannot become a "member" of Taizé; instead, you are only directed back to your church at home. For me, Taizé has always been nourishing and sustaining. It is physically uncomfortable; but I always feel myself lifted by this noncompetitive Christianity to new levels of mercy, joy, and peace. I have often wept during the prayers at Taizé. When I went, years later, with my daughter (she was sixteen), she was understandably concerned about me.

The Taizé brothers seemed to me to be a peaceful, joyful band who had voluntarily given up that which controls much of the rest of the world. With all the beauty of the hills of Burgundy around them, with obvious intelligence and energy within them, they nevertheless had chosen a life that was sharply circumscribed. Like the inhabitants of the Dungeon, they were voluntary prisoners, and they seemed happy and freer than any group I have ever known. I am overwhelmed there by the hopefulness and inclusiveness of all nations and tongues coming together in trust in God.

I tell the Taizé story because it came ultimately to inform my hopes about the way men and women might live in prison, perhaps more free in their confinement than many of us in the free society.

That Taizé summer bridged the period for me from Friends Seminary to applying for college. Though I did poorly in school, failing tests and then learning the material afterward anyway, I was surprised and delighted to do well on my SATs.

The moment is still clear in my mind. It was 1951, a spring day, as I stood at a public phone in the Metropolitan Museum, calling home to find out if the envelope had come from Harvard. When my mother told me I was in, it was all I could do to keep from shrieking with happiness.

Taizé had taught me that it was acceptable to want to be totally given to God, free to do whatever God wanted me to do. But being admitted to Harvard made me feel that I had a place in American society. I had not been sure about that before.

Still doubting that I was smart enough to do the work, I had a strong continuing fantasy, in the first weeks as a Harvard freshman in Weld Hall, that a knock would come on my door and I would be told, "I'm sorry, there has been a terrible mistake."

I had intended to major in philosophy. But when I realized that the department was in the grip of professors who wanted to study language rather than life, I switched to history.

At the same time, I was changing my thinking about church. Having started to attend the Dutch Reformed Church (I had a crush on my sister's best friend, who sang in the junior choir), I was increasingly moved by the physical dimensions of worship in the Catholic and Episcopal churches. I sometimes attended Roman Catholic services with my own best friend, Christian Wolff. It seemed as if they were connecting with realities that could not be reduced to words. The action of the Mass—gathering the bread, blessing it, breaking it, and then giving it to the members of the congregation touched me in a way that was more than I can explain verbally.

So I began going to the college group meetings at the Episcopal Church in Cambridge. It was there in the fall of 1952, my sophomore year, that I heard Paul Moore speak. An Episcopal priest working in Jersey City, he radiated enthusiasm about his ministry. It was, for the Episcopal Church of that day, an unusual mix of high theology of the Eucharist, advocacy in the political arena on behalf of the poor, and strong engagement of those living near the church itself. I began to attend church there whenever I was in New York City for a vacation.

Moore and his wife, Jenny, opened the rectory to the neighborhood. I loved sitting in the kitchen and talking with Jenny about Dorothy Day (founder of the Catholic Worker), Charles Williams (lyrical historian-theologian), and the beginnings of the civil rights movement. Boys and girls came through the door all day, some helping themselves to soft drinks from the refrigerator. Jenny or one of the clergy was likely to engage them in challenging conversations about school, work, or attendance at church. It was all managed with devotion, style, and, most of all, humor. I loved it and wanted to have a ministry just like theirs.

For my honors thesis, I was permitted to do a study of the amazing variety of ways different people can perceive the same particular event in history—an idea that has stayed with me and helped me to do work with groups of individuals.

I chose to write about the French invasion of Italy in 1498. One account, by a Frenchman named Andre de la Vigne, paid attention to the wonderful new cheeses and beautiful women he was encountering as he marched along with King Charles VIII and the invading army. Another Frenchman, Philippe de Commynes, a member of the king's court, explained in detail how everything the French did was part of the grand design of divine providence. The king, he said, had been chosen by God to be the liberator of all the kingdoms of Italy. He had trouble explaining the disorderly French retreat, but he held to his unifying theme. An Italian named Francesco Guicciardini, a colleague of Machiavelli, described the invasion in terms with which we would be entirely comfortable today: as the *realpolitik* of the fifteenth century, the struggle for power or riches. Except for one thing. He writes that, at one point, everyone in Florence knew that big trouble was coming "because the statues were seen to perspire, several women gave birth to monsters, and soldiers were observed flying through the air." For me it was a memorable lesson in the fact that people, no matter how educated, perceived reality very differently from one another and differently than we do today.

It is a lesson that also works behind bars. What an inmate sees as an assault by the "police," an officer may see, honestly, as a guiding hand. What one officer experiences as harassment by a prisoner, the prisoner sees, honestly, as simply asking a question. On a deeper level, one prisoner experiences his cell as his coffin or torture chamber; another experiences it as his "house" or even as his "monastic cell." And each is correct, from his perspective.

We contain contradictions within ourselves. The true painted portrait of any person often contains a "hard" eye and a "soft" eye. Look in the mirror as you cover one eye, then the other. One eye may look shrewd, the other feeling compassionate. Both sides are parts of ourselves. We are complicated.

But we still often think that we can trace the causes of an act by an individual or by a nation as if there is only one side to the motivation. We say that poverty led to desperation and, in turn, to suicide. Or that harsh parenting led to serial murder. On a national scale, we might find the same explanations for revolution or mass murder. And maybe the explanations are true. But the reasons are almost always more complicated.

What Andre Gide called *l'acte gratuis*—or act of freedom, unmotivated, something freely done for good or ill—seems always to intrude. Even when the thrust of the drama is very strong, we find ourselves hoping that Othello or Romeo or Anna Karenina will stop and think it all over and decide to be patient, waiting for a better time or a better way to act. That is what makes the drama absorbing. Freedom *could* assert itself at any time, and reason *could* triumph over jealousy, sexual obsession, or the blind drive for power.

I experienced this insight as a liberating truth. I realized I could commit myself and my life to whatever I chose even if my parents or my world thought that my decision was eccentric.

Chapter Two

Commitment Tested: Priesthood

Since I faithfully attended Grace Church (Van Vorst) in Jersey City every Sunday I was home from college (and I worked there in the summertime), it was logical that I be confirmed there, at age nineteen, even though I was a Manhattan resident. Bishop Benjamin Washburn was the one who opened the doors for the new ministry in that parish, part of his diocese. Paul Moore and his fellow priests Kim Meyers and Robert Pegram (it was another minicommunity) lifted it from being only a big building of mostly closed doors to being a vital, bustling parish. Many visitors came to experience its extraordinary blend of high church ceremony—incense, genuflections, reserved sacrament—along with a ministry of social justice, petitions, picket lines, and demonstrations for racial and economic justice. I loved the combination of holiness (still very new to me) and muscular social action. I wanted to embrace the same as a priest myself someday.

Bishop Washburn laid his hands on my head very heavily when he confirmed me. I can still remember the gravity of the moment and his voice, which was like deep, low thunder. "Defend, oh Lord, this thy child, with thy heavenly grace." I suddenly had a whole new and much bigger family.

I had been in love since my freshman year at Harvard. I had gone back to check out the new girls at Friends School and found the woman who was to be my first wife, Gay Sourian. She was a serious Presbyterian. We corresponded, and she laced her love letters even more heavily with biblical texts than I did. Four years later, during my first year at the General Theological Seminary, I wanted to be married. Bishop Benjamin Washburn was not only my bishop, but also the president of the board of trustees of General Seminary. He urged me to wait. It was then a rule at General Seminary that you could arrive married or wait until you were graduated, but you could not marry in course. The rule was a historical accident. Before the war, it was assumed that a man would wait until he was graduated from seminary, ordained, and settled in a parish before getting married. Then after the war, there was a group of returning veterans who were not about to wait three years to marry. So the seminary said that you could arrive married or marry after seminary, but could not marry in course. I said that I had known the woman I wanted to marry for over four years, that this was not an impulsive act. They said no, housing was a problem. I responded that my parents were willing to help me find a little apartment, so that would not be an obstacle. Well, marriage was distracting, I was told. I replied that I thought it even more distracting to be unmarried.

Subsequently I realized that they were really inviting me to shack up, to just do weekends and vacations. I didn't get it. I really believed in the teaching of the time (1956) that there should be no intercourse before marriage. I was committed to the happy prospect of giving myself heart and soul to my wonderful woman forever. I was a very restless virgin groom. So I asked Bishop Washburn, "Will you still be my bishop if I marry?" In an unforgettable moment, he said, "You make your decision, and then I'll make mine." I was in serious conflict because I loved him and wanted him to be my bishop. But I said, "I cannot imagine going through more than two years without being married to Gay." Two days later, he said he would continue to be my bishop.

Then it was a question of choosing which seminary to attend next. The choice was between the Church Divinity School of the Pacific (Episcopal) and Union Theological Seminary (nondenominational) in New York City. Washburn told me he preferred that I go to Union "where I can keep my eye on you better." So I happily went to Union, and all the great faculty were there except Paul Tillich (who had just gone to Harvard): Chris Becker taught New Testament; Samuel Terrien, Hebrew and Old Testament; Daniel Day Williams, theology; and John Bennett, ethics—a stellar lineup of excellent, challenging faculty. Most of all, I had the immense good fortune to sit at the feet of Professor Reinhold Niebuhr, who taught social ethics. He was a great pastor, theologian, preacher, and author. He was, in my eyes, the conscience of the nation. He is the person who authored the famous Serenity Prayer:

> God, grant me the serenity to accept the things I cannot change,
> The courage to change the things I can,
> And the wisdom to know the difference.

It is widely used in twelve-step meetings around the world. I was one of those naive students who wanted to win arguments with the great man. Niebuhr, on the other hand, was all humility and compassion, finding a way to turn even the most pompous, foolish question into an opportunity to lead a student into a new understanding. There was steel in his humility, and he showed, in class after class, how important he knew it was to help students *discover the truth for themselves* by the skill of his questions. He trusted the sequence of inquiry, communicating a confidence that the greatest value lay in simply going forward with the education process, letting it take on its own life rather than imposing it. He taught the joy of embracing complexity as much by the way he was, as by the questions he asked.

I was ordained an Episcopal priest in Grace Church, Manhattan, on December 13, 1958, at Broadway and Tenth Street. My first child, my daughter Sarah, was born seven months later. Her birth raised the level of my commitment even higher. Looking at her, awake or sleeping, holding her in my arms filled me with a ferocious determination to provide for her.

My bishop wanted me to go to a "regular parish" before going to the slums, where I wanted to be. So I went to Grace Church, where I had been ordained, just ten blocks from my childhood home. I was immediately concerned about the stream of homeless people who came through the church door looking for money. Since virtually all of them were alcoholics, I knew that giving them money would not help. There was a strong AA program in the parish hall, so I encouraged them to attend. I was then only twenty-five years old and had walked to school hundreds of times along that same street, under the old elevated train, passing many such alcoholics. I had always wanted to help them, but could not, and now my big opportunity had come.

One day, a man came in who moved me in a way others had not. Tall, black, well-spoken, he had a sad story, which I no longer recall. I took him upstairs to my apartment, offered him a shave, a shower, some food, a little money, a clean shirt, and a blue suit that was old, but which I still wore. We had a long conversation, prayed together, and he seemed to me to be on his way to better things.

I saw him again the next day in the spring sunshine, still in my shirt and blue suit, spread-eagled in the middle of the sidewalk, so drunk I could not waken him. His body was warm, which was the only way I knew that he was not dead.

The foolishness of my optimism has remained with me, fifty years later. Even now, I sometimes tend to imagine that problems that have taken a lifetime to build up can be resolved more easily than, in fact, is possible. It is still a challenge for me to understand that when I talk with someone who seems only to need some encouragement, help with a job, or a place to stay, I can be dead wrong.

I served two years at Grace Church, most of the time under Dr. Louis Pitt, a grand old gentleman of the church. We got along very well even though he was quite old-fashioned (could not believe that the mother of a new child at Grace Church school had greeted him at the door of her home in purple pants. "I was there on time for a 5:00 PM appointment! You better take charge of visiting the new parents.")

Then there was an opening at Saint Augustine's Chapel of Trinity Church on Henry Street on the Lower East Side. Under Father Kim Meyers, they had had a ministry to young men in gangs and to drug addicts. The main church was at the head of Wall Street, but Saint Augustine's, one of the "chapels" of the massively wealthy mother church, was located in a poor part of town with street gangs and a flourishing neighborhood drug trade. I wanted to do that work. But Meyers had left, and though the replacement clergy said that they wanted to continue his work, they really did not. I became as much a frustration to the priest in charge as he was to me.

At last I was working with the people I felt called to be with, and I was a happy man, even more so when my son Nicholas was born. He was energetic from his first day on earth, and I felt my life was complete. I was ready to give my all to God, my family, and my work.

It was from Saint Augustine's that I was able to make my first visit inside prison. It was 1962, and as part of my ministry, I volunteered to help at the Lower East Side Information Center—a euphemism for *drug treatment center*, then an almost unmentionable term.

I was drawn to it out of my sadness at seeing drug addicts barely able to stand in the street, out of curiosity about how they could fall so low, and out of my eagerness to help them stand up and be themselves. Like everyone else, I was a volunteer. Part of the program involved visiting neighborhood addicts when they went to prison, usually for possession or sale of heroin. We kept a list of people we knew, and if someone disappeared, we inquired on the grapevine if they had been arrested. More often than not, the answer was yes, so we called the authorities and found out where to visit.

Most ended up at Rikers Island, New York City's huge infamous complex of prisons. I took a ferry across the East River to Rikers—this was in the old days, before there was a bridge—and boarded an ancient shuttle bus. There, right in front of my window, a long line of prisoners filed past, a sort of urban chain gang. On the way to the administration building, I could see their faces, one after another, barely five feet away as they walked by. That was a turning point in my life.

I was embarrassed to recognize my first impression: "They look like regular people." I thought immediately of the wives and children in my parish who needed these men—longed for them to be the sensitive, intelligent people that they appeared to be through the bus window. Then I thought of the men I had heard speak at Friends School years before. The dancing red ponytail of the office worker seated ahead of me on the bus accentuated the cruelly wasteful deprivation of prison. Women on the outside miss the men. The men on the inside miss the women. That red ponytail spoke of all that is soft, lovely, sexy, and playful missing from the life inside. My heart beat faster as we approached the gate.

Rikers was noisy, dirty, and disorganized. It took a long time for us to clear the front gate. Then it was a long wait until I could meet the first of the twelve parishioners who were on my list to see. Typically, prisoners had not been there long; so some were still in withdrawal, badly nourished, and often with serious underlying health problems. Each of them, six husbands and six sons, was a real individual; and I was struck by the uniqueness of each. One was tall, grizzled, stooped, and depressed. He only wanted "to get it over with. Get me out of Rikers. Send me upstate or send me home." The next was young, restless, full of energy, wanting me to "talk to the judge." Another was still in withdrawal and could not make sequential conversation. Then I especially remember James Samuels, with steel-rimmed glasses, a man I was to see later in prisons upstate. He was well built and well-spoken. He had been nicknamed the Bedroom Junkie because he had figured out (until his arrest) how he could sell drugs from his bedroom. His wife, Nettie, equally as intelligent and attractive, was devoted to him. He loved his family, but he was a serious drug addict. He could not stop using.

I continued to visit on Rikers Island. Most of the prisoners had awakened from their heroin high and their withdrawal low and were on the way to improved physical health despite the grimy conditions there. For them, in some ways it was better than the street. They were all eager for news from home, all embarrassed about my seeing them in prison, and all understandably distracted by the details of their individual legal problems.

For those still living in the street, the Lower East Side Information Center offered detoxification at home. We arranged for a doctor to give people medication (an early form of what was later called methadone) for five days while a family member or a friend made sure that they did not leave or return to drug use. That person had to feed them and be ready to call the doctor if there were some unexpected reaction to the pills.

I remember taking one new client, Eduardo, to the center to see Dr. Ann Shearman, a highly competent, generous physician who had agreed to see our people free of charge and prescribe medication. Eduardo was very thin and uncommunicative. After Dr. Shearman examined him, she said, "This man needs major dental work. If he were not high, he would be in physical agony." She asked Eduardo to open his mouth. It was painful to look inside at his mass of rotting teeth. It was a big challenge, but we managed to get Eduardo through detoxification, then through some dental work. To little avail. He went back to drugs—another person drowning in the depths of the drug pandemic.

Another man, Nick, maybe eighteen years old, seemed ideal for home detoxification. One of the first studies of addiction had been published saying that addicts typically were raised in homes with weak or absent fathers and seductive, capricious mothers. Nick had come in with his mother. She was straightforward, businesslike, and seemed to be an exception to this new "rule." We explained the importance of giving the food and water regularly. We told her Nick should be constantly supervised to keep him from running out to get high halfway through the protocol. When it was about time to conclude the interview, the mother turned to her son and said seductively, "Just think, Nick, you and me together, five days!" They went through detox successfully, and we never saw them again. I wish I could believe that was a sign of his continuing abstinence.

Part of my work on the Lower East Side included pastoral counseling, and some of it went outside the parish lists because neighbors had heard from parishioners that I might be helpful with some who were very far from going to church. Tony, sixteen years old, and his mother, an old-time Lower East Side Italian mama, came to see me. She told me that she was beside herself with worry about her son. "I've tried everything to make him go to school, but he refuses. I went to my parish priest, and he told Tony he would go to hell for disobeying his mother. I went to the precinct and got one of the officers to talk to him. He told him he was headed for a life in prison, and Tony told him to go to hell. Excuse my way of speaking, Father Chinlund. You are my last chance! He won't listen to me."

I said that I doubted that I could help after all those heavy hitters had struck out, but that I would be glad at least to visit and try. So I went to her tenement apartment and found Tony slumped in a corner of the kitchen, his filthy shirt and pants holding his bony body like the pieces of a boy in a bag. He was monosyllabic, at best, in his replies to my questions. In despair, his mother said, "All he cares about is his goddamn pigeons. Excuse my language, Father."

"Pigeons?" I asked.

"Yes, he's on the roof any chance he can get. All day if I would let him. Filthy place."

"Tony, what do you do with them?"

"Fly them." (Barely audible.)

"What do you mean?"

"I make them do patterns." (More audible.)

I asked if he would show me.

"Don't encourage him, Father. Don't go up there. You'll really get dirty."

The pieces of the boy came together, and Tony was standing, ready to show me.

Up on the roof, he had built a coop using one wall of the entrance shelter and pieces of scavenged material. As soon as we got there, he picked up a twelve-foot pole with a rag attached to one end and ran straight to the roof's edge and jumped up on the cornice. I was terrified that he was going over the top, six stories over the street, but he stopped just in time, waving his giant wand as he looked up. "There they are, those are mine. See them go where I wave?" There were indeed pigeons flying around the building, but I could not tell if they were his. "Want to see me bring them down?" He waved the wand, and in a moment perhaps, two dozen landed on the roof. I could hardly believe my eyes. He continued to flirt with death on the edge of the roof as he sent them up again and waved them in all directions. "Want to see me get some more?" He then merged his flock with another one, and some from the second flock came toward us and landed. I had no trouble showing my fascination and admiration for his skill.

We agreed to meet on the roof the next day. After another show, we talked. I asked him what he wanted to do with his life. He began to crumple again. I asked if he would like to fly his own plane. He clearly loved the idea, but did not know how that could ever be. I told him that with the kind of innate aerial skill he had, if he would commit to his studies, he could eventually get into the air force and learn to fly. If he didn't like the military, he could retire and fly a commercial airplane. He was cautiously interested, but it all seemed unreal to him, far removed from this Lower East Side rooftop.

In the following weeks, I brought him recruitment literature. He devoured it, but he still would not necessarily show up at school.

One day, I went looking for him on the roof and found him sitting mournfully next to his coop, nursing a bloody, battered-looking bird. During aerial maneuvers, he had "taken" pigeons from another young man's flock; he was not the only kid in the neighborhood playing this game. He figured it was the other man who had come and plucked many of the feathers from this pigeon and left it dying. He was trying to feed the bird and get it to drink some water. He was inconsolable at that moment.

The bird died, but Tony somehow absorbed this by deciding to finish high school and join the air force. He and his mother continued to fight, but she was delighted that he was back to school. He stopped going to the roof and was no longer filthy. He had given up the pigeons because he needed all his time to catch up in school.

Tony managed to finish high school, and he went through on his decision to join up. One day, he came to see me in his air force uniform. He was taller and looked proud and happy.

Tony's transformation was inspiring to me. *If he could make it, anyone can make it!* I thought. I was ready to start visiting prisons, imagining that the people locked up there could learn to fly and help others to fly.

In retrospect, the early 1960s solution to the "drug problem" was naive. We really believed that all an addict needed was painless withdrawal, a job, a prayer, and a pat on the back. We screened out the pain of dysfunction in the family, the handicaps of poor education and housing, substandard medical care, poor coping skills, and the burden of racial prejudice. The truth was that for many drug addicts, race was the final crusher on the list of burdens.

It was at Saint Augustine's that I met the writer James Baldwin. His play *Blues for Mister Charlie* was scheduled to go into rehearsal in a month, and Baldwin was still working on the text. It was 1963, and the Freedom Riders were making history. Baldwin needed to stage a scene in which a group of young black men was being trained in the techniques of nonviolent protest. I volunteered to collect a dozen young men from the parish and get permission to create the scenes in the basement of the church, where there was a stage at one end. Baldwin sent someone to check out the arrangements, and the day came.

The young men were introduced to the play and given minimal rehearsal. The scene was blocked and ready to go. It was powerful theater and still would be today. It depicted people attempting to integrate a lunch counter and the brutality they had to endure. As I watched, totally absorbed in the world being represented, I realized more deeply than ever that I would never fully know what it meant to be black. My tender nerve endings, reaching into that endlessly complex world, were scorched by the cruelty not only of the worst of Southern racism, but also by the naïveté and presumption of Northern racism. I felt as if I had turned a corner that allowed me to look into a whole other world, one I had thought I knew a little about, but now realized would always be closed to me in its endless nuances. I understood just a little bit better why Baldwin said that "to be black and male in America is to be in a constant rage."

It was a heady experience to meet James Baldwin and feel that I was, in a very small way, contributing to his creation of a Broadway play. He was opening a little wider the window on the reality of life in black America.

I had begun to visit Rikers regularly, and the Baldwin play helped me realize that the racism experienced by minority prisoners was a daily, hourly burden, marking every single contact with the white world. It was a yellow star that could never be removed, seeming to invite the disdain and violence of the dominant race, which had more guns, police, judges, bankers, opportunity, and money than they would ever have.

When the rector of Trinity Wall Street fired our assistant sexton shortly before Christmas, denying him his regular 10 percent bonus, I was angry. He compounded that problem by preaching and printing a sermon on stewardship that I felt called for my response. He had said that it had come to his attention that some parishioners were pledging as little as twenty-five cents per week—remember, this was 1962, when a quarter was worth something—and that he "trembled for them as they would one day appear before our crucified and risen Lord and give account of that fact." I knew some of those people who pledged twenty-five cents per week and greatly admired them. Mostly black, all poor, they paid their pledges at genuine sacrifice of food and comfort.

So I wrote to the rector, referring to Jesus's commendation of the widow who gave her mite out of her tiny purse. I said I believed that the people who gave a quarter would "fare better facing their crucified and risen Lord, the One who had walked barefoot through Galilee, than either you, in your chauffeured limousine, or I, in my little Hillman Minx convertible."

The rector called me in immediately and scolded me for my lack of respect. He warned me, "Never ever send a letter like that again. I am keeping the letter." I said that I stood by what I had written, felt strongly about it, and was prepared to discuss the substance with him. He was furious. I left his office feeling dangerously peaceful.

The fact was I loved working with the people of Saint Augustine's. Especially the Militants, a group of almost all women, almost all black, who had lived in the neighborhood for years. They loved the church, and they were in fact the real leadership, not the clergy. I was thrilled that they had let me into their circle, let me listen to what they called their nigger talk. Their honesty and laughter was, for me, an experience of the Body of Christ ultimately matched only by the experiences awaiting me in prison. It was the Militants who organized and paid for four buses to go to Washington DC on August 28, 1963, for the March on Washington, during which the Reverend Martin Luther King Jr. gave his "I have a dream" speech.

We were up before dawn that morning, and everyone was there on time. We sang freedom songs on the way down, too excited to sleep. When we reached the edge of DC, we were by then in a long line of buses headed for the Lincoln Memorial. Black people lined the way, waving, weeping, and clapping. We were weeping too, seeing this spontaneous outpouring of support. Our bus driver parked in a makeshift parking lot, and we all climbed off. Something new was happening. Something big that had never happened before, and we were part of it. But the day was hot, and as the hours passed, the euphoria was beginning to fade. I remember saying to Bishop Moore (we had ran into each other down there and were standing side by side), "King better be good. People are starting to leave."

Martin Luther King Jr. was, of course, not just good; he changed history. From his first words, he had the whole mammoth audience in the palm of his hand. Electricity crackled as many felt that this was the moment we had lived our whole lives to experience. Many were crying as his words reached their crescendo. Strangers were embracing (long before people did that). Nothing mattered: how to find the bus, how to get a little food, even how to find a toilet. We were soaring above the pain of individual lives, flying into a beautiful new future.

Three weeks later, on September 15, 1963, four little black girls in their Sunday best—frilly pink, white, and blue dresses—were blown up by a bomb in the basement of a church in Birmingham, Alabama. I said Mass in the basement of Saint Augustine's Church that night as word of the service passed by word of mouth. It was packed, and I was choked with tears trying to say the names of the little girls. The air was thick with the swirling incense of hatred of those who had killed the children. This was mixed with love of God, apprehension that there could be a nationwide race war, continuing hope that we had entered a new more-tolerant era, and confusion about what we should do next.

The wonderfully loving African American secretary of the parish said that she had wakened that morning and found that she hated all white people.

On November 22, President John F. Kennedy was assassinated.

On November 26, I was fired.

Chapter Three

Learning by Going Inside

I decided to raise money for my own salary and start a parochial mission out of the Church of the Holy Trinity on East Eighty-eighth Street. A parochial mission is a new parish launched by another parish; it is not permitted in the Episcopal Church simply to start a parish on your own. The Reverend Clarke Oler was the rector there, and I will be forever thankful that he was willing to take me under his canonical wing so I could move to East Harlem, fifteen blocks north of the mother church, and continue with what I wanted to do.

In the early 1960s, drugs were a new and deepening problem in New York City, especially Harlem. Everything about drugs exacerbated the poverty and racism that already plagued that part of the city. I had seen drug addicts staggering around the streets of the Lower East Side, lost in a maze that seemed even deeper than that suffered by alcoholics. The newspapers continually talked about the drug epidemic; hospitals, police precincts, courts, and prisons were faced with a rising tide that threatened all their regular work. But here, in the ghetto, the plague was truly pandemic. I was tantalized by the seeming ease of the solution: get people off drugs, and everything would be all right. I was hardly alone in this belief.

At first we talked about opening a regular storefront ministry that would reach out to anyone in the neighborhood and bring in addicts that way. There would be an emphasis on helping men just released from prison, to connect them with jobs and to offer them a support community. I raised money for my salary ($6,300), and we were on our way.

In the process of making these plans, Clarke and I recognized that it would give me more of a supportive framework to join the East Harlem Protestant Parish (EHPP), a group of clergy from various denominations who agreed that none of the staff, including themselves, would receive more than the average wage of those working in the community.

The EHPP had been started soon after World War II by Rev. George "Bill" W. Webber and Rev. Norm Eddy, clergymen with the idealism and determination of my mentor, Bishop Moore. They offered a ministry that strengthened individuals spiritually, but even more, they were politically involved in the community, trying to improve schools, housing, and employment opportunities. Tackling the drug monster was a big part of the ministry.

The assistant directorship of the EHPP Narcotics Committee was offered to me. The Reverend Lynn Hageman, a Dutch Reformed minister, was the director of the office on 103rd Street between First and Second avenues. The program at that time was largely religious—pastoral counseling, Bible study, and prayer. Lynn was a real scholar, a weight lifter with a huge chest and arms and a strong interest in Karl Marx. In the little office on Sunday mornings, we held Bible study with all the recovering addicts, followed by Holy Communion.

First, a passage was read from the Bible, and then "the guys"—there were no women yet—would retell the passage in the hip lingo of the day. The story of the life of David was especially rich since it had plenty of sex and violence. "So David peeped this broad, Bathsheba, naked on a roof, and he really dug her. But first he had to figure out how to off her husband, Uriah."

It was January 1964. I had enough for two years' salary. I found an apartment on the fifth floor of a tenement and moved in with my wife, daughter, and son, who were then four and two. Our neighbors were friendly. I took up layers of linoleum from the floor, built a double bunk for my children, made a new top to cover the bathtub in the kitchen-living room-bedroom, and we were ready for our new adventure.

As part of the East Harlem Protestant Parish, I worked with others to start a rehabilitation center called Exodus House, named as a reference to faithful people going out of "slavery" into "the wilderness," seeking "the promised land." We emphasized the troubles of wandering in the "wilderness" as we discovered the challenges of simply leaving the slavery to drugs. We all agreed quickly on the name as having great meaning for us. But looking back, we underestimated the challenges of the "wilderness," for there was no "promised land" free of trouble. Robert M. Pennoyer, first chairman of our board, helped raise money from foundations and individuals—$400,000—to build a handsome modern four-story building with rooms for ex-addicts and classrooms. In those days, there were many fewer hurdles like environmental permits and community approvals, and private money was easier to raise for this new problem. We just raised the money, built the building, and opened up. It has since become the East Harlem School and continues to offer a way out of the troubles of East Harlem.

In the 1960s, many of us were chasing a receding horizon—"sufficiency of care"—which we believed would turn ghetto addicts into taxpaying citizens. Once we got someone off drugs, we believed getting them a job would be enough. So we found them jobs. But often they failed to go to the interview and actually take the job. And if they went, they did not stay. Soon, more often than not, they were on drugs again, breaking into cars, mugging people, and burglarizing apartments to support their habit. In other words, on their way back to jail. It quickly became clear to me that a lot more was necessary.

That was when I visited a program run by psychiatrist Dr. Efren Ramirez in Puerto Rico and was much impressed by his sophisticated concept of "stages" of rehabilitation. Addicts came in for detoxification and lived in phase 1, dressed in diapers (literally) to emphasize that they were babies—focused only on themselves, psychologically very needy. The diapers also helped prevent AWOL departures. Now these practices are long discontinued, and they have disturbing echoes in the scandals of the United States prison in Iraq, Abu Ghraib, though the residents in Puerto Rico were voluntary. They moved on up to intermediate stages, taking a year or two to become "grown up." The whole structure of the undertaking acknowledged that there was no fast track to curing drug addiction. Other agencies that later became big names in the field, including Synanon and Daytop, were coming to similar formulations at the same time, though minus the diapers.

It seemed clear to the board and staff of Exodus House that there was no quick fix; it had to be a process. Without process, we were aping the problem exhibited by addicts themselves by seeking a simple, speedy exit from complex problems. So we tried to implement our own version of the Dr. Efren Ramirez process.

After a year, we stopped fruitlessly sending men who were not ready out on jobs and insisted that they first have a period in a sheltered workshop that included group discussions. I started a woodworking shop (stretching for one of my own earlier dreams to be a cabinetmaker). I found commissions through friends, enough to keep us working. I did not actually have the level of skills to run the place; so I was fortunate to recruit Jay Wenk, a superb craftsman and a thoughtful, caring man, who was a freelance cabinetmaker. The shop, we decided, was there to teach the *process* of building something as well as the woodworking skills involved in creating cabinets and shelves. We were teaching a trade, but more important, we taught good work habits—coming on time, showing respect for coworkers, and understanding the basics of running a legal business.

One of the most colorful characters in the shop was known as Cholo, at twenty-four a relatively young member. We were making one of our more-expensive pieces, a cherry kitchen cabinet, for the actress Barbara Barrie, then famous for her role in the movie *One Potato, Two Potato*. To install the shelves under the counter, we cut grooves, and all was going well until Cholo realized he had put in one of the center dividers upside down, so the shelves could not connect. In his distress, he literally fell over flat on his back into the sawdust of the shop floor as if he had passed out. When I told him that we could fix the problem, he did not believe me. Then we started the actual process of filling the wrong cuts with splints and cutting new grooves with a router. Cholo was amazed. We all talked about it later. Virtually everyone in the shop said that they had almost no experience of "fixing" a mistake. For them, a fix was a shot of heroin to transport them away from the problem. Finding a physical way of solving a problem was a new experience—one I hoped could be repeated. The very concept of "process" was a revelation to them, and it was a pleasure to watch them get it. That was what we were there for.

But we ourselves still had a lot to learn. The day for delivering the cherry cabinet arrived, and I suggested that all six of the men then in the group help deliver it. I assumed that they would like to see the cabinet in the place it was designed to fill and that they would be proud to show off their work to Barbara Barrie, who was then appearing in TV shows like *Dr. Kildare*. But not one single man came to work that day!

Maybe they could not manage success at that level. Maybe they were reluctant to part with something on which they had worked so hard. In any case, I knew I did not have everything figured out. I took a picture of the cabinet, resting it on top of the row of garbage cans outside the workshop on 103rd Street even though it was not surrounded by the smiling faces of those who had made it. I delivered the cabinet with a couple of new recruits.

So when Mary Lindsay, the wife of Mayor John Lindsay, commissioned a walnut corner shelf, I made sure that the men and I had long talks about the feelings of parting with a beautiful treasure, of feeling proud of having made it, and of believing that we had a right to be visiting in Gracie Mansion, where New York's mayors dwell. This time, everyone showed up to deliver that handsome piece, and Mary Lindsay served tea and cookies, chatting comfortably with our tongue-tied group as if she offered tea every day to ex-convict drug addicts.

Tony Rodriguez was another person who taught me a memorable lesson. We were having a group session one afternoon, and he was silent, obviously upset. When pressed, he pulled a wad of bills out of his pocket and said, "I saved all this money, $63, and I am supposed to give it to my landlord. All my life, some woman paid the rent, my mother or some other woman. I worked hard for this money." He had. He was a good worker. "I can't see just *giving* the man this money. I only live there! He doesn't *do* anything for me!" Tony had a little gray hair, and he was not as stupid as these remarks made him seem. It was not intelligence he was lacking; it was experience. No one had ever succeeded in making clear to him how the world of housing worked. We got through only by saying that someday *he* might save enough money to buy a building with a down payment and use the rents to pay the mortgage. Finally, he said, "No sonofabitch better try to beat me for my rent!" Then he laughed at himself.

Part of the work at the office on 103rd Street included visiting the prisons upstate, which I started doing in 1964. After Rikers Island, I was entering a completely different prison world.

Rikers was a place of perpetual transition. Prisoners there always had their eye on the door because, technically, Rikers was not a prison but a jail—a place where people were held pending trial or serving out misdemeanor sentences of less than a year. If they were waiting for trial, there was always a chance they'd get off; if they were serving time, they knew for sure they would be out in a matter of months. Consequently, it was a big challenge for them to be attentive to each other in a group setting.

State prison was something else. People there were doing five, ten, twenty, twenty-five years. This was serious. Yet when I met inmates doing real time, I was struck by their sense of humor and their loyalty to their families. They no longer had their eye on the door as they had on Rikers Island. They were not under the influence of drugs or drink and had not been for some time. They looked a lot healthier than the guys at Rikers because they were. For many months or years, they had been eating and sleeping with some regularity and had at least minimum medical care.

But I had begun to realize that these same men seemed to vanish once they were released back to New York City. Like leaves dropped near a whirlpool, they were quickly swept back into the downward spiral, and they returned to drugs. They seemed to give up quickly on the possibility of achieving a sober, crime-free life. They often showed up at the Narcotics Committee of the East Harlem Protestant Parish after a new crime, arrest, incarceration, and release. Then soon enough, they would disappear into the whirlpool once again. I was shocked and baffled that anyone who had unearthed such treasure buried inside him while in prison would throw it away as soon as he was free.

When the men I had enjoyed visiting in prison fell to the distractions and temptations of the street, people said to me, "I'm glad you're finding out what they're really like." They meant, of course, that they were really only junkies, and the serious earnest people they had seemed to be while they were in prison. I chose to believe the reverse: it was in prison that those men were showing their real selves. There, they could be their best. Outside, utterly crushed by temptation and severely limited opportunities, they fell to pieces.

I began doing a regular circuit: I would start at Sing Sing, travel north to Coxsackie, Comstock, Clinton, then west to Attica, turn back east to Elmira, Eastern, and Green Haven, seeing half a dozen men at each stop. It would take several days before I headed home.

Sing Sing, less than an hour out of New York City, had been built by prisoners, with stone quarried on-site. Overlooking the Hudson River from a bluff, it was shaking with all the violence of an old-time James Cagney movie. Its famous yard and four-tiered cell blocks constituted the set for a constantly unfolding drama of pain and despair. Guards beat inmates, inmates sometimes attacked and killed other inmates, some inmates committed suicide.

On my first visit, holding the list of people in prison who were known to us in our little East Harlem office (husbands and sons of people in the neighborhood), I entered Sing Sing. The 130 years of history fairly dripped from the walls. The visiting room was immediately on the right after entering the big gate, so it was not as oppressive in its first impression as some that would come later. I visited the list of prisoners in the old visiting room, which you entered through a low, swinging wooden gate. Inmates came into a U-shaped area to approach their visitors, who were waiting on the other side of a wire mesh barrier. A table separated them farther, and neither prisoner nor visitor was allowed to touch each other through the mesh, under threat of losing the visit.

I vividly remember one inmate concluding a visit with his wife, then going to the low door. We were the only ones in the visiting room. The officer looked the other way as they kissed each other. I remember her brightly colored silky dress as the kiss continued for a long time, each of them squirming with longing. Finally, the officer cleared his throat, and they parted with difficulty, touching fingers as long as possible before they staggered to their respective exits.

That kind of unspoken understanding between officer and prisoner in Sing Sing impressed me because it seemed as if it would have been impossible at Rikers Island. Prisoners did not stay at Rikers long enough for officers to get to know them. At Sing Sing, the prisoner clearly knew he was getting a break and should not push the limits. I was in an entirely different kind of institution here—slower, more intense. Life was deeper. I was eager to learn more about this complicated new world.

The next stop as I continued on north was Comstock, its stone walls breaking the softness of the rolling hills. It was a shock (and still is today) to drive through the gentle, soft landscape of upstate New York and come upon the outcropping of concrete, which is the prison. Then and now, I have the impulse to pray, "God have mercy on them all, prisoners and staff, locked in together. Help them to a new place of peace where they can really see each other and feel close to you."

Comstock housed only young prisoners, up to twenty-five years of age, and had a reputation for being particularly tough. There were frequent confrontations between officers and staff since the youngest inmates were the most likely to rush into fights.

Even then, there were stories about the gladiators at Comstock, a group of officers who would challenge an inmate to fight with fists. They would go to the basement, and one of them would strip to the waist to fight the prisoner. If the prisoner chose not to fight, he would still be beaten up by the officers. If he fought and won, he would then be beaten up by the officers. There were variations on that theme, but it was a tale retold for decades—a long sad chapter in the book of macho mania. Bones were broken; prisoners were killed. This was partly about sadistic revenge, fueled by public acceptance of the belief that prison should be hell. There was little thought about the consequences when prisoners are released other than to hope they learned their lesson.

I should not have been surprised by the warden at Comstock, Joseph Conboy. I had written to him, requesting permission to visit and including my list of inmates (those known to us at the EHPP Narcotics Office). I was a little late because I had remained longer than expected at Sing Sing. It had been hard to break off interviews at twenty minutes each. The officer at the Comstock gate told me the warden had left word for me to go see him when I arrived.

When I walked into his office, I extended my hand, but he just glowered. "Sit down!" he shouted. I sat down. "Who the hell do you think you are?"

"I'm Stephen—"

"I know what the hell your name is!"

"I realize I'm late and—"

"You're goddam right you're late! Do you think we are here to wait on you!"

"No, sir. I'm ready to stay over and come back tomorrow."

"This is a fucking tough place to run, and I don't need jerks floating in from New York City to make my life more complicated."

"Yes, sir, I understand, so I'll wait."

"You're goddam right you'll wait, maybe forever!"

"Yes, sir. I realize I'm here only if you—"

"I don't know what the hell good you think you're doing visiting this human garbage in here. They aren't worth the powder it would take to blow them all to hell!" He was standing, glaring at me, waving his arms.

"Their mothers, sir, have given me—"

"I don't think they have mothers, these sons of bitches, and you make me as sick as they do!" I started to get up.

"Sit down! I didn't give you permission to leave!"

"Yes, sir." I sat back down.

"You call yourself a minister."

"Yes, sir."

"What about all the good people you're supposed to be taking care of? What are they supposed to do while you're here wiping the asses of these rotten guys?"

"Sir, it's part of my job to—"

"I don't want to hear your bullshit."

I remained silent and let him go on talking. Slowly, he calmed down. Then suddenly, he said, "OK, you can see your list. Get the hell out of my office."

What had just happened? Did he need to determine if I would be sufficiently obsequious, or did he just need some personal ventilation while the three o'clock shift settled in and was able to pull out the inmates on my list? Maybe it was a visitor's version of the "greetin' beatin'," then still being given as a warning to some prisoners tagged as troublemakers when they arrived on the bus handcuffed and shackled from another institution. The beating would be concluded with a warning: "That's for doing nothing. Don't find out what happens for doing something!"

After that first visit, Warden Conboy always asked to see me when I came to Comstock, and he never duplicated the invective of the first visit. But he remained an angry man. He apparently operated on the philosophy that it was better to have inmates and staff more frightened of him than of each other. In some ways, it is a sound philosophy, but only if the person at the top is reasonably sound himself.

One of the inmates I got to see on that first visit was William Eldridge. We had his name because he had come by our East Harlem office occasionally. He had not seemed seriously addicted, but he had been using drugs when he was arrested. He often seemed to be homeless. He was only nineteen, slim, short, with huge brown eyes; and he spoke so softly that I had a little trouble hearing him. He reminded me of a deer looking up from grazing. Like almost all the prisoners, he seemed very glad to see me, eagerly poking his fingers through the wire mesh to approximate a handshake (as I said, those rules weren't always enforced). He asked anxiously about his mother. Unfortunately, I had no news of her. We talked about East Harlem, and I asked how he was making it inside. I was anxious for him because he seemed to me to fit the stereotype of someone who might be raped in prison. But he said he was "doing OK" and seemed to mean it. It seemed inconceivable that this person would be capable of committing a felony. Finally, I said, "I don't usually ask guys about their crime of conviction, but it seems hard to imagine you committing any crime."

He looked down shyly and said, "I never was in trouble before." He hesitated and then said, "Homicide." He sighed heavily, put his hands together, and went on, "I was in a bar. I hadn't even had anything to drink . . . A guy called my mother a whore. I got mad and said he shouldn't say that. He asked if I was going to stop him. He was a big guy, but I was ready to . . . Another guy slid a gun down the bar to me. I never had a gun in my hand before. I grabbed the gun and shot him dead." He looked down sadly. He didn't say anything that conveyed the wish that he was expecting me to do anything to reduce his sentence: twenty-five years to life, the longest possible. He had made a full confession and had presented no mitigating circumstances to the judge. I later learned the sad truth: his mother was using drugs and probably *was* a prostitute, at least part-time, to support her habit. William's anger surely came from the simple, helpless shame at being confronted with the truth. He had no father in his life and no other family, so it would take way above-average courage and resourcefulness for him to make a life on the streets, never mind shrug off insults like that. I was sad when our time was up. I knew of no clear road to freedom for the Williams of the world to follow.

As I got in my car to drive on to Coxsackie, I could not stop thinking about William. It seemed a terrible waste to send such a gentle, lost young man to prison for twenty-five years. Ironically, I thought maybe he had a chance at life, not in spite of the fact that he was in prison, but because he was there, since life had been so cruel to him in the streets.

In Coxsackie, I met a young man named Tyrone, sentenced to five years for armed robbery. He was soft-spoken and, I thought, of below-average intelligence; and he made perfect sense as we talked mostly about how bad he felt at having let his mother down. He made no excuses about the armed robbery he had committed, but the road to that robbery was similar to those I heard about many times in the years that followed. Tyrone had been struggling to stay in school, trying to please his mother and graduate from high school. He was having trouble because he needed extra academic help, and the school could not provide it. One evening at dusk, he was standing with others on a street corner. An unmarked police car pulled up. Everyone ran, or tried to, except Tyrone. "I wasn't doing nothing bad," he said. According to him, one of the others dropped a couple of bags of heroin before he ran. The police took Tyrone and one other young man to the station house and slapped them around, trying to get the names of the other boys. Tyrone refused to cooperate and vehemently denied to them, as he did to me, that the heroin was his.

The district attorney had offered him a bargain. If he wanted to plead guilty to the lowest-level felony—attempted possession of a controlled substance—the DA would ask for two years' probation, and Tyrone would never have to go to jail. Tyrone did not know what any of it meant, but he thought he understood the part about not going to jail. Legal aid was as overworked then as it is today, so no one really explained, in a way he could understand, that he was making a devil's bargain. Tyrone took it. He pleaded guilty and was sent to jail because he would not give up the names of the others.

Tyrone now had a felony record. He went back to school, but the principal gave him a hard time about his record. He dropped out and tried to get a job, but that record haunted him. Then he fell in love and got in real trouble. His girlfriend wanted to go someplace nice on a date. That cost money Tyrone did not have and would not get in the normal course of his life. So he borrowed a gun and tried to rob a gas station. He was caught.

From what I could see, it all might possibly have been avoided by a little more help at school and good legal advice at the very first arrest. Racial profiling hurts most when the first "crime" is not a crime, and the plea bargain leads to the second crime, which then is a real one. Tyrone's story is familiar—guilty of the crime of conviction, but the innocent victim of the "crime" that got him started.

Next came Clinton prison in Dannemora, New York, near the Canadian border, a visually dramatic location. Nicknamed Little Siberia, the prison is in the heart of the small town, its enormous wall running for half a mile along Main Street. The entrance through that wall leads to a long walkway to the prison itself. That entrance has always had a reputation as a "tough gate," meaning that there they go by the book. It was a time before metal detectors, so I got a serious frisk, all pockets opened out, shoes off and shaken, shirt pulled out. I had tried to arrive an hour before the appointed time to allow for those procedures. I was finally put into a room by myself, an "attorney's room" as contrasted with the regular visiting room. So there was no bulletproof glass, no telephone or wire mesh. It was a good feeling to be able to sit and talk without too much to remind us of prison.

The inmate there I most strongly remember, Cedric Harrington, was striking in both size and intelligence. He was 6'7", physically fit, had dark skin, and wore steel-rimmed glasses that looked as if he had made them himself. He had been "away" for four years, and his family had stopped writing and visiting. As I sat wondering what to say, he leaned forward and asked the most utterly unexpected question, "Father Chinlund, have you, by chance, read any S. I. Hayakawa?" His cultured voice and grave, direct gaze communicated immediately that he was serious.

By sheer coincidence, I actually had read enough Hayakawa in the not-too-distant past to be able to hold up my end of a conversation about the philosophy of language. This clearly delighted him. When we had to part, he shook my hand warmly as he thanked me for coming and said, "Father Chinlund, I cannot find words to say how much this human conversation has meant to me."

As I drove away, I discovered those words coming back to me, and I reflected on what they implied. Cedric believed that he had no one with whom he could have a human conversation. But other inmates I had seen also seemed to me men who would be grateful to have a human conversation. Their language was devoid of profanity or even rough talk (though it was clear that at least sometimes they were deferring to me because of my clerical collar). Now I was driving away, and it would be three months before my next visit. Why could those men not somehow all meet together and have a human conversation?

Some others must be isolating themselves like Cedric, I thought, and reading books in every minute of free time—not in itself a bad choice. Others were probably just joining in the endless banter about past injustices, current complaints and engaging in random macho bravado. This kind of talk seemed to have a generally corrosive effect since there was rarely any constructive dimension to it. I thought that if they could only have human conversation, they could be freer for a time, lifted out of the pain of the always-present fact of being in prison. Just listening to them had been mysteriously uplifting to me. I felt strongly that I was where I was supposed to be.

The shape of my work in prison was slowly beginning to take a more realistic frame. The men I had met inside appeared quiet and centered to the point that it was easy to imagine them being helpful to each other. They were respectful toward me; but I was sure that they would be more lively, honest, and usefully tough in a group of their peers. It made sense to organize group discussions just as we had at our sheltered workshop, but at that time, there were no such groups in prison, except for a few AA and Gamblers Anonymous meetings. If I wanted any such thing to happen, I would have to get groups going myself.

I decided to try at Green Haven, a maximum-security institution in Stormville, a little town an hour and a half north of New York City. It was much closer than either Clinton or Attica—eight hours north and west, respectively—and there were half a dozen inmates on our East Harlem Protestant Parish list at Green Haven.

On previous visits, I had met with the warden Harold Follette on my way in and on my way out. I had sat in his huge office (now divided and again divided into small cubicles) as he probed my purpose in coming, asked if there was anything that I discovered that he should know, and asked if I had any ideas to share. He weighed over three hundred pounds, and his balding head was buzz-cut. At the time, I did not know his background and was later glad I did not because I would have found it challenging to work with him.

Follette had a reputation for being vicious. He had been the principal keeper, otherwise known as deputy warden, at Dannemora; and the prisoners were aware of his ferocious actions. In fact, when he arrived at Green Haven, they went on strike by staying in their cells in the hope that they might somehow make him go away.

An inmate strike is a serious matter. The longer it lasts, the harder it is to end it. Pressure to maintain unity is excruciating. There is no mess hall, garbage piles up, tension festers. To break a strike, Follette chose the only method he knew—brutality. He had the officers form a gauntlet on each side of the corridor on one cell block. Then they pulled the inmates out of their cells one by one, forced them to strip, and made them crawl naked down the line oinking like pigs as the officers beat them with nightsticks. Then the officers went to the next block and threatened the same treatment. The strike ended. Though I did not hear this story until after Follette died, it was not hard to believe.

But I did not know that then. Follette seemed to trust me and was intrigued by the new, but escalating problem of drug abuse. Since I saw him before and after each set of individual visits in Green Haven, I had the opportunity to raise the question of meeting in groups in the normal course of conversation. It was better than trying to negotiate through a formal letter, which would surely elicit a formal rejection.

In those days, there was much anxiety that inmates would hatch plots to escape or to take over the prison—a fear that continues to this day, but which is handled in more sophisticated ways. Inmates were not allowed to speak to each other except in the yard and from cell to cell when they were locked up. They were required to be absolutely silent in the corridors. They walked single file on the right side of a yellow line. The yellow lines are still there, but silence is no longer imposed. In the few basic education classes that were held, inmates could speak only to the teacher. Group discussion of any kind was viewed as dangerous.

However, I was by then going once a week to Green Haven and had had several conversations with Follette. I proposed that I be allowed to meet with several inmates at a time. He said that we would have to have an officer present during all the meetings. I readily agreed. He said he would check out my list of prisoners to see if there were any "troublemakers." Again, I agreed. To my surprise, Follette then said I could proceed with the group meetings; but first, he insisted I get permission from the commissioner himself.

Commissioner Paul McGinnis was like many of the wardens—a gruff man given to quick, harsh judgments. Once while I was in his office, he took a call from his deputy and talked with him about what to do with a prisoner who had hidden a very small tin can up his rectum, which could not be retrieved. Could he be transferred to the prison hospital? He laughed as he ordered that the can be removed as best it could. Presumably the inmate had inserted it with drugs inside, brought by a visitor. If his rectum went into spasm, removing it without hospitalization would cause tearing in the rectum and possibly lead to infection or blood poisoning. But the commissioner was unmoved, laughing during the brief conversation. I struggled to control myself from challenging his pointless brutality.

On this visit, I simply told McGinnis that I thought the groups were beneficial, that an officer would always be present, and that Follette had approved. McGinnis was sizing me up. He apparently decided I was not a bleeding heart and approved my request. Just that was a huge concession. But then I had to go back to him in later months to get successive approvals: first, because I wanted people who had been in prison to come back inside to participate; then for someone still on parole to come inside; and finally, again to get permission for people who had been in prison to lead groups alone—the only way we could involve sizable numbers of inmates.

Each of these moves, going up another notch in the level of perceived risk, was an adventure. I always feared that I was asking too much too soon. I was anxious that McGinnis would grow weary of my importuning and, in a fit of pique, roll the program back or abolish it altogether.

During one appointment, before I could speak, he threw in my lap a copy of an anti-Vietnam War pamphlet called *The Seven Last Words of Christ*, featuring photographs of the ongoing conflict matched with the seven phrases of Jesus as he was dying on the cross. I particularly remember one photograph, then circulating around the world, of an American soldier seated on top of a huge tank, looking back at the body of a Vietnamese being dragged by a rope. The caption was "Father forgive them for they know not what they do." I could feel myself flushing with anger and shame; I was sure McGinnis knew I was passionately opposed to the war, just as I knew he was a particular kind of devout Roman Catholic who thought people of my persuasion were cowards and traitors.

I turned the pages slowly though I had seen the booklet before. I asked myself what would be the honest thing to do. I wanted with all my heart to work in the prisons. I felt called by God to be there, and I knew McGinnis would probably be commissioner for years to come. I could not change his mind about the war; and if I drew a line in the sand, I would be out the door, program eliminated, inmates abandoned by one more person trying to make a human connection. I also did not want to lie about my convictions. It was an issue I would face again and again with wardens and even officers. I found myself handing back the pamphlet, looking him in the eye, and saying, "That really is something!" I had ducked. He hesitated and changed the subject.

The last time I saw him in his office, he had returned after an illness of several months. I shook his hand and said, "You certainly look fully recovered!" He twisted my arm until I was literally on the floor of the office on my knees in the doorway, and he said, "I guess I am in good shape!" Much laughter. I saw him in the years after his retirement, eating dinner in the local Howard Johnson's, first with his wife, then alone. He always greeted me warmly, always asked about the program. The last thing he said to me was, "The whole system's going to hell. No balls."

I still marvel that these tyrants acceded to my requests when they could just as easily throw me out. But they did agree, I believe, because even they had their own buried treasures. Deep down, they wanted to believe that they too had more gifts of mercy and fairness than they revealed on the surface. They were, in effect, prisoners too; I was giving them an opportunity to be good people for a moment.

Back then, the distinction between staff and inmates was even greater than it is today. There was a deep racial divide as all-white staff from rural upstate confronted an ever-higher proportion of minority prisoners from New York, Buffalo, Rochester, Syracuse, and Albany. I wanted to minimize this divide and to emphasize the fact that we were all human with human problems that differed only in size and detail according to innumerable factors—an idea that strongly contradicted the prison culture of the time.

It was not until the 1980s that there was serious and effective recruitment of minority staff, a profound change in the prison world I had entered two decades before. It was clear that prisoners felt safer with officers of their own race. On a more subtle level, many white officers began to make friends, for the first time in their lives, with nonwhite people. Back then, it was almost unthinkable—"Where would they live, out here in the country?" and "They would not feel comfortable, being African Americans on an all-white staff."

I started running the group sessions at Green Haven in 1964. The plan was to continue indefinitely, as long as the program was useful. In the beginning, I ran the group in an "open" way. We would start by my asking, "What's happening?" and members would just say whatever they wished. One inmate might say, "I haven't had any mail from home, and I'm really pissed." Another would respond, "When was the last time *you* wrote to *them*?" Or one might say, "I can't get into the school program." Another inmate might challenge him by asking how many slips he had put in to request school. But invariably this open-ended structure also brought an airing of problems that no one could do anything about. I began to shape the exchange by asking that they limit their "distress talk" to issues they themselves could address—not problems at the institution that were the business of the people running it. The warden made it clear that he would entertain no talk about such matters. I was there only to help prisoners deal with life as they found it, not to modify their surroundings.

Furthermore, Follette always said he would not allow me to meet without staff present. In a way, I was happy to agree. The officer obviously reported on what happened to the warden, but as far as I was concerned, we were only talking about being human. That included the officer, and his presence would only reinforce the truth that we are all human, even prison staff. Follette introduced me to Wayne Strack, a fine by-the-book young officer who was perfect for the assignment. He participated in the groups in a minimal way, enough to be "in," but not so much as to attract the focus of the group to himself or to reveal too much about his personal life (which was quite conventional—he was a happy family man).

Limiting the scope of our conversations was excellent discipline because it ensured that we would have sessions concerned with personal transformation rather than gripes, however legitimate the gripes may have been—and there were many legitimate gripes. One of many attempts I made to try to focus the conversation came out of inmates' feelings that they had no recourse but to fight if they were insulted. Some said that they were in prison right then because of violent acts arising from just such insults. So we talked together about the "trigger words" that would infuriate the prisoners and trap them into answering with their fists, or worse. The simple repetition of the trigger words in the group meetings seemed to reduce, a little, the power of the insults.

One inmate said that he was currently serving a long sentence because someone in the street had called him a scumbag. He had tried to kill the man and came close to succeeding. I asked him, "Would you do the same thing again if someone used the same word?"

"I'm afraid I would."

"Would you be interested in whether everyone here defines the word the same way?"

"I guess so." Then followed a pathetic attempt at definition that boiled down to three possibilities: a douche bag, a bag in a toilet stall to be used for discarded sanitary napkins, and many said they really did not know what the word meant. No one laughed.

"How do you feel about spending years in prison because of your reaction to a word of uncertain meaning?"

"I feel bad."

"Do you think you could learn to react differently in the future?"

"I could try."

"How about trying right now?"

"OK, what do you mean?"

Then I made a big mistake. We were holding our meeting in a crowded multipurpose room. Some inmates, including the one in question, were sitting on top of file cabinets. I thought we had talked about this particular trigger word long enough for it to be effectively defused, so I raised my voice and said, "Scumbag!" to him. He leaped off the cabinet, heading straight for me. Other inmates instantly intervened and wrestled him to a standstill. No one was hurt. The man, trembling with rage, looked at me with confusion. His head was telling him that I was a friend or at least a person trying to help him. His gut was telling him that I was someone who should be obliterated.

Once again, I had been much too quick to believe that profound feelings of self-contempt could be quickly and easily resolved. In prison, there was an enormous need for people to be reminded every day of their own value as human beings. That reminder runs counter to a lifetime of contrary messages: "You're stupid," "You're bad," "You should never have been born," "You're just like your father, and he's in jail where he belongs," and, of course, "Your mother's a whore." Any taunt ignites the flame of violence in the smoldering volcano of prison culture.

The ingrained belief that "I am bad" was evident in Dilly, another member of the Green Haven inmate group. He was an intelligent, articulate, and high-strung inmate very involved in the life of the group. He remarked from time to time on ways he felt he was changing. One day, he did not show up. I learned that he had been keep-locked, or confined to his cell as a punishment. When he returned to the group in two weeks, it was part of our routine for the inmate to explain what had happened. Dilly was disgusted. "I got busted for talking in line." His lip was still swollen, and one eye was partly closed. "They gave me all this too."

The group looked at me. I repeated the rule, "I cannot do anything about unjust use of force. Do any of you have anything you would like to ask or say to Dilly?" One man asked him who the officer was.

"Powell," Dilly replied.

Another said, as others chimed in, "Powell! You know he has as bad a reputation as any officer in the joint! Why you had to pull his chain talking in line?" Dilly looked down. Another inmate said, "Dilly, you've got as many *old* scars on your face as all the rest of us put together. Have you always looked for trouble?"

It was a beginning for Dilly to look at himself in a new way. A few weeks later, he told the group that he wanted them to stop calling him Dilly, that his name was really Jonathan. It was a brutal way to learn the lesson, but I was glad he had a caring group to help him learn it instead of having people like Powell pound him deeper into the ground.

The group structure was composed of three levels, designed to address the men's different needs as they progressed. The lowest level,

C, was for groups of twenty who had signed up requesting to participate and come off a waiting list. If they talked about their own personal issues and were able to listen to others, they were eligible for the next level if they requested the promotion themselves. B groups were smaller—eight to ten—the place where the real work was done. There was stability of membership in a B group, so the trust level grew strong. The A groups were for those nearing their release dates. They had different matters to discuss, having to do with jobs, residence, and family on the outside. In retrospect, it might be better to keep A groups and B groups together so those remaining inside might be even more motivated to get ready for release and the special problems that were coming.

In B groups, we tried to reach a new level of self-understanding, and I tried many ways of helping the men achieve that. One was a self-identification exercise. Each man around the circle would simply say, "I am . . ." and then complete the sentence (or paragraph) in any way he felt was honest.

Fred Clinkscales said, "I am a thief." He laughed nervously and stopped there. When I asked if there was anything more to him, he said, "No. I'm only a thief. Been one all my life. Stole from my family when I was a kid. Then from sidewalk stores. Then burglaries. This is my third bit [third time in prison]." Another inmate said, "Fred, you're also my friend." Fred agreed, but only with reluctance, to being both a thief and a friend. It was as if he was clinging to his familiar negative identity; it was all he knew. It amazed me that admitting anything else made it seem as if he was giving up something. It took me a long time to learn that he felt he was losing his freedom. As he was, he was free to be a bad dude. He liked being a bad dude. He was good at it. No one messed with him. Now if he was also a friend, he might be weak and vulnerable, and *anyone* might mess with him.

Fred helped me realize vividly the horror of committing street crimes for a living. He described waiting to mug people, standing in a doorway, saying to himself, "The next one that goes by is mine. Tall or short, thin or fat, black or white, male or female. If I wait and think about it, there is always some reason not to do it, and then I'm still broke and still strung out." He used to wait by a lamppost or in a doorway to check out who was coming, but he said that the problem was that he had too much time to think. Often there was a reason not to jump the person, Fred said, "Looks too tough, looks like my sister, might be an undercover cop. So I started waiting in a doorway and listened for the steps. That's when I said, 'This one is mine.' And I would jump." Another prisoner asked him, "How did it work for you?" "See where I am," said Fred. No one laughed.

Then he commented, "I'd still be doing it if I wasn't in prison. I'm glad I'm not doing it." He appeared thoughtful, sincere, a little surprised at himself. He still seemed unaware of the ripples of pain he had caused to the victim of the crime; to the family around the victim; to the friends of the victim who were now afraid to go out at night even if they were shift workers, for example, and had no choice. But Fred had made a beginning.

Fred was one of many who helped me understand that for some prisoners, it can almost be said that other people don't really exist—they live in a solipsistic world that served them well while they were children. During those early years of neglect and abuse, they simply retreated for self-protection into themselves. Sometimes they went into a child's fantasy world, but more often, it was a world in which they learned to look out only for their own safety. This meant not acknowledging the existence and, in particular, the feelings of those around them. Stealing from their often-abusive fathers, mothers, and sisters and brothers led naturally to stealing from others in the streets.

In prison, even with the harsh limits of those days, they had the opportunity to begin to focus on other people and make new judgments: some people are good; some are bad. Even in the cruel disorder of prison, a new social order emerged for many.

It was painful to imagine the actual crimes, which, for me, had up to now only been statistics or media stories. I thought about the boys who had broken my brother's arm years before and taken my money. Talking with human beings who actually committed those crimes made me see their side, even though in the groups, they were always so well behaved that it was a challenge to imagine them being that desperate. It hurt to recognize the truth that these men, my friends, had caused great pain to many people.

It was also during this period that I learned that most inmates had their own limits: crimes they considered beyond the pale. This came out when one prisoner admitted, "I was so strung out that I stole money from my mother." Another inmate interrupted and said proudly, "That is something I would never do. Stealing from your own mother!" The first one replied, "I have my own limits. I would never give blow jobs for money." And then the others joined in, each proudly saying what act or crime he had reserved as "impossible." Another said that he remembered, when he was living with his sister, he was doing horrible things in the street (which he would not specify), but that he would never steal from his sister. She was his only friend. In the meantime, I was encouraged that each seemed proud of having moral limits, however minimal. Honor of some sort played some role in their lives. Later I found out that this was not true of all prisoners. Some had no limits. They were the ones who were still desperadoes, ready for homicidal violence at the smallest provocation, inaccessible to any serious conversation about anything.

Chapter Four

Going Deeper

My happiness and excitement about the strengthening work in prison coincided with the time of the greatest personal sadness in my own life. I was in the process, in 1965, of getting a divorce from Gay, my first wife. Our children were six and four, and it tore me apart. I had been utterly committed to the marriage and to my children and could not believe this was happening to me.

I was trying to help others succeed; and I was, myself, failing in my own most serious commitment, to my family. Nothing was more important to me than having a stable home for my two beloved children, and now that seemed impossible. My wife had fallen in love with another man; I waited two years for her to change her mind and finally realized that I could wait no longer. In retrospect, I should perhaps have been stronger, more demanding, but then I would never have had the joys that have come (new marriage, another son, another daughter-in-law, a granddaughter) as a result of all the pain. Back then I wondered if I was a fraud. Then my own words came back to me—no one is perfect; life goes on. Even though my children were hurt, maybe they too could gain something from the painful experience. And I never felt closer to God. My prayers were all about staying faithful to him, confident that we could go through the trying time and come out of it together. Maybe my dark night of the soul is still to come; that would have been the time, in that period, for me to have one. I feel miraculously blessed that it has not happened yet. At that time in my life, I definitely felt that I was more deeply connected to the group of men in prison than ever before.

The prison groups were not intended to be therapy for me, but when the men commented that I was not entirely myself, I shared what was going on in my life. Brief as my parts of the sessions were, it was a healing experience.

I discovered the healing Body of Christ in prison. It may sound strange; but we were all broken, without pretense, vulnerable, and honest with each other. We certainly had problems of different magnitude, but we cried together and healed together. I felt I could be more fully and consistently myself in those groups than I could be in any other setting. So the Body of Christ is characterized by honesty, most of all. Many of Jesus's sayings sound as if they could have been preceded by his stating, "Don't kid yourselves" or "Don't hide behind your questions, what you are really saying is . . ." The prison code, unspoken, certainly prevented them from saying many things; and there was a universe of revelations that they did want to speak about. Nevertheless, there was trust in those groups, and there was much that was revealed. Sharing intimate and shameful histories was a significant relief; but it meant first being somehow broken, poured out, like the body and the blood of Christ. The biblical passage "Where there is love, there is God" kept coming to mind.

One of the inmates said, "You're white, good-looking, and well educated. We thought you'd have all the women and money you ever would want. It blows my mind that you'd be sad about losing *one* woman!" I believe that my experience helped them to have a different way of looking at marriage in particular and women in general. Telling them about my troubles also helped me believe that there was someone out there for me.

I was married again, a year and a half later, at the end of 1966, to the love of my life, Caroline Cross. We were introduced by a mutual friend, and I fell in love the first time I looked into her eyes. Most of the men in the group continued as members through all that excitement, and we had good talks together about monogamy and commitment.

Mostly the meetings were times of simple sharing of pain. The men missed their children and were most open about that. There was a gritty, grinding misery about missing their women. Though they rarely mentioned it, that pain was never far away. It ate away at their cores in ways they could not explain or even describe because their relationships with their women were often subverbal and one-sided: "I command, you obey." The women could withhold sex, money, connection to children, affection, and the dimly perceived avenue to a more civilized life. The men would hit or leave or both, and they did. That layer of agony was like a time bomb because it was so poorly understood that it transformed itself into constant anger that led to sudden eruptions. One man said that he was back in prison for brutally beating his woman. As he spoke of it, he seemed to imply that the crime had followed his having failed sexually in some way. He had blamed his victim for his own human limitations.

The men were amazed to learn that sex could be even more satisfying as a part of life when it has its own rhythms and was not automatic. That fit with their disbelief that one could be monogamous and committed for a lifetime and that this led to a more meaningful relationship.

We talked particularly about domestic violence. One man said, "I don't fight. I would tell her what I wanted. If she didn't do it, I hit her. Then she would do it." I was thunderstruck by the bland way he said this. In my own life, I was wrestling with layers of upset emotions, subtleties of anger, and the denial of unwelcome feelings. Entering their world, which contained little obvious nuance, helped me to be more honest with myself. I in turn tried to help them realize that there was a universe of complex interactions waiting for them. One man shook his head. "Fucking the same woman for forty years! Doesn't seem possible."

When I tried to touch on root causes, especially childhood relationships with parents, I was quickly aware that I had moved my hand close to high-voltage wires. "If I could find my father, I would kill him," said one. Another, with smoldering flames in his eyes, said, "I don't talk about my mother—ever." And another said, "I don't remember *anything* before I was a teenager." These statements were all made with barely contained fury. One man's earliest memory was of his father killing his little sister with a poker. This told me that it would simply not be possible to go through the practice of the traditional therapy of the time—discover the childhood roots of the problems, desensitize them, and live life free of neurosis. And of course, I was not a psychotherapist. But I was in another land; and it was going to be necessary to find an innovative way to touch their older pain, one in which the men could discover their own value as people first, and then begin, maybe, to address the other, deeper, problems later. They needed to believe they were worth bothering about before they could begin any serious self-examination.

Then one day, in a group at Green Haven, a member mentioned something he himself had done in which he took satisfaction. He had finally written a letter to his estranged son. "And he wrote me back!" He was delighted with the reestablishment of his father-son connection.

The whole group connected gladly with his new satisfaction. Reflecting on that moment as I drove home, it seemed very important. It was something that could be intentionally repeated in future group meetings.

The human potential movement was just getting into full swing then; and I had learned from such seminal figures as Virginia Satir, Dorothy Stoneman, and John Bell in workshops. Virginia was a leader, going around the nation and eventually the world, helping people discover the courage, brains, and imagination that exist in ourselves, covered over by our cultural training to put ourselves down in the name of modesty. I was also increasingly upset about the usual teaching of the church that we are hopeless sinners and that only the outside help of God can make us acceptable. We are trained to ignore the good in ourselves.

Dorothy and John were involved in Re-Evaluation Co-counseling, a movement started in Washington State, and were running training groups for people unrelated to the prison world. I went to learn about what they were doing. The groups met in East Harlem, where they and others had started a primary school. The training helped everyone learn to be more understanding of themselves, their children, and their parents. They began by asking each person in the group to name something they had done that they felt good about doing. Today it may sound simple and obvious, but it continues to amaze me that this basic act of recollection and declaration in a small group has such a powerful, energizing effect. It is also more difficult than it initially appears. The practice has had a transformative effect on my own life, diminishing my tendency to be relentlessly hard on myself for not "doing enough."

So at the next prison group meeting, I asked that each of us do the same thing: say something positive we had done before starting to talk about our problems. I realized that it was hard for many group members to be able to say something good that they had done. Most had to dig pretty hard to find something that they had done that was good. But through the group process, I was attempting an all-out assault on the fortress of the members' view of themselves as bad, only bad, people.

Frankie Adams, a handsome dark-skinned man who normally had a big smile now spoke haltingly, with tears streaming down his face. We were continuing the "I am . . ." exercise described above. "I am only a piece of shit," he sobbed. He placed his large hands in front of him as one would cover a cup of hot coffee in a cold room to show that he meant just what he said. Others in the group, weeping also, told him what he meant to them as a friend. He said that no one had ever said anything good about him before. He could not think of one good thing he had ever done in his life.

However, little by little, with the new exercises, the men began to get in touch with the positive small actions that knit together any more-"normal" person's life. One inmate, Michael Odett, especially convinced of his bad identity, nevertheless looked to me as if he was deep down open. I finally asked him—on a hunch, maybe out of my great affection for my own sister, Edie—if he had any younger sisters.

His face softened. "Yes, one."

I asked if he had ever defended her when she was a young teenager.

"Oh, yes. The guys knew they would have to deal with me."

I said, "So you were a good brother."

He looked very sad and said that he had let her down badly ever since then. He had even stolen money from her at the bottom of his addiction.

I stopped him from going on, reminding him that we were only trying at that moment to remember the occasions of responsible action. We had agreed that saying, "I am a good brother [or man or son]" does not mean you *always* acted well. So again, I said, "Were you a good brother?" He said, "Yeah, I guess so." I said, "*You* have to say the words without saying, 'I guess so.' It is only the truth." Finally, he said, "I am a good brother," and his face contorted into tears.

A display of emotion like Michael's was not an uncommon experience in the group meetings, but when it happened, I was always surprised by its force. After forty years, I still only understand this phenomenon partly: there is a certain kind of security—a freedom from responsibility—in an "all-bad" identity. You have no tension in your life if you are someone from whom no good can come. You can relax and just be bad. As one inmate said, "I can just go ahead and be the son of a bitch I really am." The tears of sadness may have come also from the veil being lifted on the wasted years. A life that might have been suddenly comes clearer. It made Michael wish all the more that he had been a good brother *always*.

There is a shock of surprise for one who has thought for many years that his life was set, like a chasm opening in the road. I believe also it is a way of connecting with the person we were when we were small children. We were loving and trustful if the people around us were loving even in minimal ways. Even children who have been abused or neglected continue to have powerful feelings of loyalty toward their flawed caretakers.

Finally, there is a fear. To lose, even momentarily, the shield of cynicism and hardness means that you are vulnerable to buried memories of the past—and hopes of the future. The Russian philosopher-theologian Nicholas Berdyaev said of this process that people are thus able to move "up from absurdity to tragedy." The lives of many, perhaps most, inmates seem absurd in the literal sense (away from or outside any core meaning of life: *ab* meaning "away" and *surd* meaning "whole" or "central unity"). It is a step up, but still a step worthy of tears.

We all agreed that being able to affirm our goodness, whatever we may have done wrong, was critically important for our own sense of reality. So from that time on, the meetings started that way, with self-affirmations.

The door was now open for Michael Odett and others in the group to rediscover both old and more recent positive memories. Most important, they could recognize things they did every day in prison that made life better for another inmate (even an officer!). Or for themselves: trouble avoided, drugs refused, a letter home written, a meditation discipline maintained. Some inmates were able to make lists that seemed endless, and that in itself was energizing.

Reports of the "good stuff" were never questioned. Sometimes prisoners said that they had lied in their positive reports and then decided to actually do what they falsely said they had done.

The format of the group meetings now had two parts: self-affirmation followed by discussions of problems of stress. The stress issues continued to leave the group feeling overwhelmed and discouraged. It seemed that the men continued to be as sad at the end as they were in the beginning. So one day, I proposed that we conclude the next meeting with a third part in which we would say what we planned to do in the next week that would be satisfying. One small plan of action, something that could be reported as a self-affirmation the following week. That became the third part of the meetings. Their plan had to be specific, and it had to be something that they could be sure of doing themselves. They had control.

Initially, there was resistance to this new addition. The men protested, "We're in prison. We can't make plans. All our choices are made for us." But when I asked them to consider the number of choices they had already made, just in that day since they were first awake, many of them were amazed when they recognized the breadth of their volitional circle. First, in the morning, they got up out of the bunk. They could have stayed in their bunks and been punished. Then they washed somehow. They straightened their cells. Some prayed, and many did push-ups and sit-ups. They went out into the dangers of the population and faced other inmates. They avoided fights, avoided drugs, said an encouraging word, meditated, wrote, went to classes, read in their cells. As the group members recognized moments of opportunity to choose their course of action, this third part became a successful addition and, sometimes, emotionally moving.

For example, Sam came to a meeting in a rage. He could not even participate in the first part and say anything good about himself. "Somebody beat me for my sweater!" He explained that his sister had knit a green sweater for him, permissible on the property list; and he had greatly treasured it for the sentimental value, for being something a little special, and for keeping him warm in the yard. He said he was reasonably sure that he knew who had taken it and that he intended to "hurt the man." The group gave him good feedback, especially one prisoner who asked, "How will your sister feel when she finds out that you are doing more years for felonious assault over *her* sweater?" He was still spitting with anger.

Finally, after listening to all the rest of the meeting and everyone else's plans, Sam said, "I'm going to let it go. I'm still mad, but I'm going to start reading that book she gave me, not go to the yard and be cool. Let it go." The group cheered.

We continued with the three-part form for a couple of years. It proved so dynamic, even dislocating, that the men said they were leaving the meetings "disarmed." They returned to regular prison life "too open, too fired up," as one of them said. They were vulnerable to harm "in population"—teasing, hazing, physical attack—because they carried themselves in a vulnerable way.

So we finally added a fourth part: silence. We concluded the meetings with a time in which they could take slow, deep abdominal breaths; reflect on what they had said; and pray silently, perhaps, for themselves, for others in the group, and for family members they had named. This helped them to regain their centers, become firm and determined. They were protected, ready to return to population.

Since silence in prison is present only as a chance, unexpected absence of noise, almost never as a happily made choice, I had been anxious about proposing it as a fourth part. It was, however, the way I wished, more and more, that we could end our meetings. It connected me with the silence of the Quaker meetings of my own childhood and the silence I had experienced in the monasteries at Fiesole, Mount Athos, and Taizé.

Silence in God is one key to weathering the fearsome, noisy, and brutal storms of prison life. I hoped that some of the prisoners would find in the silence what I had first discovered as a little boy and as a teenager.

I learned that a few men were already involved in using silence to fortify themselves. Some even found themselves thinking, in the silence, about surviving the worst that could happen to them. Like a child who decides that he will not cry when he is spanked, they used the silence to make themselves stronger in the face of future beatings and humiliations. Silence became a time to build their shield. It was something new for them to be in group silence even for a full minute (eternity in today's culture), and they were impressed by the power of intentional community silence. There is a unique intimacy that comes from being with people who are letting their hearts and minds wander over the full range of thoughts—pious, violent, erotic, banal, loving, penitential, and thankful. Many of the men were praying.

It was in this way that the Four-Part Meeting was born: self-affirmations, issues of stress and pain, a short-range plan, silence. Since then, the Four-Part Meeting has proved a form of remarkable endurance and effectiveness with many different kinds of participants, not just people convicted of crimes.

I have tried this same four-part form of meeting with success in New York City public schools. The children, grades 4 to 12, get it right away. They love the structure. Dr. Thom Turner, the man I recruited to lead the program, added a phrase to the beginning. Each child says his/her name and then says, "My dream is to be . . ." before going on to "I feel good about myself because I . . ." In constantly holding their dream before them, I believe, they find new determination to live it out. And I do love hearing original combinations: "My dream is to be an actress and a lawyer" or "My dream is to be a football player and a pediatrician."

I have also used the same form with elderly people. "How can I have a plan? I could die anytime," they would say.

"You still can have a plan to buy a small potted plant."

"Oh, yes. Well, I plan to call my old friend Rachel."

Inmates often said things like "I wish I could have met this way and done these four parts, every week while I grew up, during my school years. I would never have ended up in prison."

I learned a lot in those years, 1964-1968, from working, one day each week, inside Green Haven. Most of the lessons were ones I was forced to learn. Since I had been required by Warden Follette to have officers inside the circle, I found out, for one thing, that it really is possible to break the prison code and create a setting in which both staff and prisoners can learn to be more fully human. Among the (then) almost all-white officer staff, some seemed to have taken their jobs in order to be in daily contact with people they could look down upon, so blurring the lines was unwelcome. Similarly, prisoners (who by then were increasingly black and Latino) wanted to be completely different from the "police." They generally wanted nothing to do with making things better or "squaring up." Life was simpler if they could just go ahead in their accustomed roles.

But two officers helped pave the way, Joseph Keenan and Tony Pezzullo, each in their midthirties. They both were men of courage who knew how to stand up to other officers and to prisoners. Joe and Tony each had homes nearby, were committed to their families, and loved to laugh. Joe had two children. Tony had three and was a gifted craftsman; he would build a new house, sell it, then build a new one. He made flat-bottom Adirondack boats for fishermen of such high quality that one is exhibited in the Adirondack Museum. Both men also had room for change. Each was rather committed to the conventions of being an officer, which included, at that time, a cynical attitude about the capacity of inmates to change and only a minimal interest in their own development as professionals. But each was surprised to find himself saying, "Yes, what *am* I doing about my own life, my own growth as a person?" Both began attending community college courses. Joe put his name on the list to take the sergeant's exam, a bigger step than it might seem because back then, the line between correction officers (blue shirts) and supervisory staff—sergeants, lieutenants, and captains (white shirts)—was pretty rigid.

Though I was an outsider, it was clear that I brought something to the prisoners and even to the staff. The waiting list was growing. I loved going to prison.

However, the sharing by peers was always and obviously much more important than anything I myself might say. I repeatedly had the experience of saying something, drawing blank stares, and then seeing immediate understanding by the group when a prisoner said virtually the same words I had used! It was overwhelmingly plain to me that the color of my skin, my education, and (maybe most of all) the fact that I could quit my job at any time and do something else for more money, all combined to make it hard for them to hear me.

It was also clear that after one year, in 1964, our little group of eleven had pushed the whole prison a little bit in a good new direction. Up to this time, there was just one group. Yet not only did all the 1,800 men confined in Green Haven know about the program, but they also were all challenged by it because it was a little harder to hide behind their cynicism. As the program grew in strength, it was no longer easy to dismiss it as "all bullshit." There was a voice calling all 1,800 and the staff to have the courage to sign up and get real.

I would not have missed the sessions for anything and neither would the former prisoners who worked with me. Our team arrived on time in blizzards and heavy rain, coming from East Harlem like clockwork. A few officers were even angry with us because some of them had tried to give bad weather as an excuse for being late, only to be told we had made it all the way from the city on time.

One day when we were late leaving East Harlem, it looked as if we would actually be late arriving for the first time ever. I was driving a station wagon carrying five black and Latino men on parole, and I was speeding. A state trooper stopped us, and I explained the situation, all of us in white shirts and ties (uniforms I believed necessary to gain credibility with staff) headed for prison. The trooper looked inside dubiously, then carefully, while my passengers squirmed as they always did when they were near the police. Finally, he said that he believed my story, and he was real sorry, but his partner on the bridge (still in sight behind us) would never believe it. Rather, the partner would assume I had paid him off, so he would have to give me a speeding ticket—the only one I have ever gotten in my whole life. That friendly gesture was not just because of my clerical collar; I had stopped wearing it anyway after a few years of going inside. It helped in the beginning, I thought, to diminish my difference because of race and being an outsider; I was just a person, neither staff nor prisoner.

Also, I found that many prisoners had had terrible experiences with representatives of God who had portrayed that God was a tyrant akin to Warden Follette, full of wrath and impossible to satisfy. One man, Mark Shepherd, who was soon to be released, had a mother who was a storefront minister. She had believed that her son would stop "being bad" as a teenager if he would only give his life to God. He refused ever more stubbornly. Finally, she beat him repeatedly, lashing his legs with fury until the blood came. He pulled up his trousers to show me the marks on his shins, impressive scars that remained fifteen years later. I certainly didn't want to remind Mark of her. But I stopped wearing my collar mainly because it seemed to connect me with those who said, "People are bad. Only God is good." I was there to say all people are both good and bad.

When Mark Shepherd was released, he clearly needed substantial help to make the transition. He tried to follow through, looking for work, but always came up empty. He was determined not to go back to prison. But it was the same old story. He had little job experience. He had a prison record and no money. He was tall and dark-skinned, and that all combined to make him appear threatening to employers.

I had heard that there was a place one could go "to shape up," to help unload trucks in the middle of the night. Truck drivers stopped there and picked up helpers just before delivering. The spot was in Manhattan under the West Side Highway near the Washington Street meat markets, now a chic neighborhood of trendy restaurants, but then a dimly lit, out-of-the-way warehouse district. I set my alarm for 2:00 AM, put on my boots, and went to meet Mark. I had told him that he better not stand me up; I did not want to give up a good night's sleep for nothing.

Mark showed up on time, and we moved toward a group of figures gathered around a fire in a big oilcan with holes punched in the side. There was no conversation. No one looked happy to be there, and they did not seem pleased when Mark and I arrived, a distinctly odd couple of newcomers. We took our places in the outer ring, getting little benefit from the fire. Soon the trucks began to appear. The driver climbed down from the cab and approached the group. He would quickly choose one man who would go off with him. Then the next truck came.

We waited more than two hours. I was not sure how to handle it if I were picked, intending to ask the driver to consider Mark. I did not know how that would work out. But the problem never came because as dawn was breaking, Mark was chosen. He was laughing at me as he drove off.

It was not until I was on my way home to get ready to go to my actual job that I wondered whether anyone had thought about beating me up. One less man in the shape-up. But the group around the fire might have known I would not be chosen; I looked too weird.

Mark found a job; then he disappeared from my radar. I hoped that meant that he was doing well.

In the meantime, Exodus House was growing. We had raised money to build a halfway house across the street for men coming out of prison, and we prepared for our first arrivals. Then in a dispute that seemed almost endemic to the drug rehab world, the city part of our work came unraveled. The board of Exodus House decided that neither Director Lynn Hageman nor I should live in the house ourselves. I favored, instead, having three shifts of staff and no live-in directors. We needed staff to be awake and responsible, three shifts a day, every day of the year. Lynn disagreed with me, organized some of our clients into pickets, and was ready for war. I had no wish to turn East 103rd Street into the OK Corral. With immense regret, I left—and three-quarters of the staff left with me—to create a new program. This was Reality House, on 145th Street in central Harlem. It was a similar operation. The whole prison team left Exodus House and became part of the staff of Reality House. We continued the prison visits without interruption.

Then I teamed up with an amazing man named Leroy Looper, whom I knew from Exodus House. He was an ex-con and ex-addict with an astonishing gift for group work. He had shown me at Exodus House that it is possible to run an effective recovery group for ex-addicts without tearing people up psychologically as they had done in Synanon and Daytop. Leroy became the director of Reality House; I was the administrator. He was responsible for the operations while I raised money and connected to the various agencies. We established Reality House, and then Leroy suddenly left, off to the West Coast.

He arrived in San Francisco without money, friends, or connections, but quickly began to assemble the group and the funds, which have made a major contribution to helping homeless and mentally ill people there. Leroy helped confirm for me the power of group work. A 1987 *New Yorker* profile of him later described his continuing self-transformation from violent man in the street to leader at Reality House and, later, executive director of Cadillac House, a home for people who are mentally ill in California. He was a charismatic, resourceful person, destined to go farther than most of us; and he reinforced my conviction that the same efforts that had brought him out of the deep hole that had once been his life could also bring others up to the surface.

I continued to believe that there has to be a way for people to be released on parole much more easily than was then the case. The men I worked with seemed to be completely safe to return home.

Chapter Five

Opening Doors

I found in my groups that my main challenge was simply to help prisoners feel that they were worth something. Many expressed suicidal wishes. It was in fact a kind of progress when many said that they realized, after years in prison, that they had been living as if they wanted to get killed, either by fellow criminals or by the police. At least they were beginning to recognize themselves in the mirror. Many said they were tired of living such hard lives—relieved when the prison doors closed behind them.

They reminded me of fish wriggling helplessly on a hook. The economy was against them as entry-level jobs required ever more education than they had. The culture was against them. Especially, of course, racism, which continued in more subtle but destructive ways after the victories of the 1960s. You could now eat at a lunch counter, but you could not necessarily work there. Even religions seemed against them, with their inclinations toward racial segregation and their theology dividing humanity into the good and the bad.

The men and women I was working with in prison said that they believed they had the right to a good life, to be free of physical harm and the daily threat of death, free to have their own homes with a loving spouse and children. But they were not living in ways that would lead to all these pleasures. They needed a much higher sense of themselves. The "self-esteem" movements came alive in the 1960s.

There is a strong cultural prejudice that you are not a real man or, now, a real woman unless you are making more money or have more power than your neighbor. We have centuries of momentum behind this dominant philosophy that says that if you are poor, you must be doing something wrong. It goes back to the belief that God blesses the righteous with prosperity. So if you are prosperous, you must be righteous. This thinking persists in spite of the contrary, but Biblical wisdom includes the fact that the wicked often prosper in spite of being bad and that God blesses the poor even though they remain poor. Protestants, Catholics, and Jews all continue to hold these contrary views. For example, Saint Francis is revered by people of all faiths because he loved the birds and the wolves, the sun and the rain. He also loved poor people. But very few remember that he really loved radical poverty as a gift of God. He loved Dame Poverty because until his death, "she" helped him to be clear that everything of real value comes from God. If we are too worried about our possessions or making more money, to that extent, we lose our focus on God. So feeling self-contempt because we are not rich is to go a very long way from the highest ideals of faith.

Feeling self-contempt also carries prisoners away from doing much about their plight, because most of the prisoners I worked with came from poverty so extreme that they sometimes had owned only the clothes on their backs. Many rarely could remember eating three meals a day as a predictable part of life.

A second source of confusion over self-esteem comes from the challenge to be good parents in an urban world. There was self-esteem to be gained on an old-fashioned farm where even the youngest child did chores needed and appreciated by the family. There is no easy substitute for that in modern life, even on a big farm. Children felt important for the part they played in helping the family function. Gathering vegetables, mucking the stables, caring for cows and horses were big jobs. Setting the table, doing the dishes, and taking out the garbage do not seem of equal size to a child. So we need to struggle to find ways by which young people can measure their increasing skills and have the reassurance that their responsibilities are being valued.

Third, many young people do not believe that God is watching. They do not have a sense that God knows who we are and loves us as we are, that our lives and actions are important because God is watching.

God's gaze may be described in various ways, but whatever it is, one may feel important to have such attention. Certainly, there is a negative side to the feeling of being constantly watched by God. That idea has been used as an instrument of torment by preachers through the ages. The guilt it engenders has led to emotional illness, criminal behavior, and suicide.

However, without some sense that God is watching with eyes of mercy, youngsters can feel lost. They have no ritual, no repeated way to connect them with God and to the best that is in themselves. So it is necessary to create a simple ritual that will connect one with one's own best self and with God's loving watchfulness. That was, and is, what the Four-Part Meeting was designed to do—without explicit reference to God, to connect with one's own best self even if one had once committed murder.

Such self-esteem programs have been criticized for being too vague, and to the extent that they are not achievement-based; the criticisms are sound. It is an achievement to do homework for the first time with the radio and TV off or to study for one hour without stopping or to earn a passing grade for the first time or to win a 90 for the first time or to apologize directly or to say, "I love you." I have experienced the energy that comes to men and women who can affirm themselves out of their own mouths for the first time and on a continuing basis. It is important for them to be able to do that regularly. It is needed as a ritual to balance the weight of our culture that emphasizes the success that comes from greed and power.

Our meetings were designed to create a form and ritual for achieving this balance. Part of the form is the spiritual assumption that there is One who helps us, One who is always there, giving us strength to act in the human ways that are most true to ourselves. The separation of church and state requires that we not pray aloud in public schools, and for good reason. But in prison, we can be explicit about God, or our Higher Power, taking control of our lives and making it possible to get through this one day. It may feel stiff and artificial at first to follow a sequence of steps (like the Four-Part Meeting), whether at the dinner table, in a classroom, in church, or in prison. But this process, or something like it, is needed so that we can connect with ourselves, with each other, and with God, however defined.

Ultimately, however, there is another realm beyond self-esteem. In 1977, I met a man named Bo Lozoff, with his wife, Sita, who have worked for years with thousands of prisoners all over the nation to help them learn to meditate and come to the deepest understanding of themselves and their circumstances. Creators of the Human Kindness Foundation (based in Durham, North Carolina), Bo and Sita are committed to helping prisoners find internal freedom inside prison and after release—and yet they have been critical of the self-esteem movement. Committed to the mystical elements of Buddhism, Hinduism, Christianity, and Judaism, they argue eloquently for the higher path. There the self is extinguished in nirvana or becomes one with the All, merged in the ultimate unity of all life. This is sometimes called the higher self, the self into which all individual selves are united. In the Lozoffs' view, pumping up one's self-esteem is ego-focused, contrary to their whole way of thinking. Instead of extinguishing the self, the self-esteem exercises make the self stronger.

I do not see theirs as a contrary path, just one that may be taken later, after finding a self to give up! For prisoners who regard themselves as beneath contempt, as human waste, it is a dangerous undertaking to jump immediately into meditating on their merging into the higher self. I believe it could even lead to psychosis or suicide. Bo Lozoff is a skillful and greatly experienced guide, careful to warn of the dangers for those who are fragile. Following a less-able teacher or trying to do this out of a book is perilous for many. Perhaps more to the point, it seems to me that the vast majority of prisoners (and the general public) are not able to begin meditating. They have so little awareness of any kind of inner life—even fantasies, daydreams, plans for the future—that they experience silence as frightening, confusing, or boring.

On the other hand, going *through* an enriched sense of one's own self, especially a loving self, opens the way to higher mystic possibilities. Even the simplest task is undertaken as part of God's plan. It is a first step to be glad about doing everything to the glory of God. That is the way it has been for many in monasteries as well, especially Benedictine ones. In being able to offer every act to God, even washing the dishes, to do it patiently and well, praying the whole time, has put many a monk, nun, or layperson on a road to a deeper sense of union with God.

Larry Leshan, a psychologist now famous for treating people with cancer, is also a beloved teacher of meditation, who encourages us to be gentle with ourselves in silence. He compares the process of meditation to walking on a path in the woods with a puppy who is not on a leash. As we follow the path, the puppy runs ahead and behind, to the right and the left. We call the puppy back to us, sometimes laughing at his energy and mischief. Similarly, we may continue on the path of silence in meditation while the puppy (that is our rational, verbal mind) runs all over the place. The same experience can occur as we learn to be in silence, adding little by little, as we feel comfortable.

Silent time can be an experience of melting happily into the world around us. We can feel part of the life of other people just by holding them in our silence. Yet care should be taken, and a guide is important so that we do not go too far with the melting! We can lose the sense of ourselves as distinct people and feel as if we are almost literally falling apart. In order for silence to be an experience of freedom and integration, a frame is needed. There are many such frames: the Jesus prayer; the Psalms; simply repeating deep vowel sounds; thinking of what I am thankful for, sorry about, and hoping for. Under them all, we need some sense of the all-inclusive frame of the mercy and love of God.

Upon going into a prison at any time, especially in the early years, I often thought, *What right have I to be doing this work?* But my nervousness would evaporate when I heard myself saying, "It is all because of God. Take me, God, take the work. Lead me." And then the peace had always come.

Prisoners have often seemed to me to be unusually open to the experience of being filled with the presence of God. More so than people on the outside—and unfortunately, often more so in prison than they themselves are after they are released.

Saint Paul was put in jail for challenging the authority of Caesar. He almost certainly wrote his two most closely reasoned and joyful epistles, the letters to the Romans and to the Philippians, in prison. He had been locked up as one who was preaching an alternative to the worship of Caesar and so was seen as a revolutionary against the state. In prison, he had plenty of solitude, and so the full orchestra that plays through the closely developed sequences of the book of Romans surely echoes to us the long moments he had in which to cross out, insert, and rework the passages that are a map of the grace of God.

Boethius, a fifth-century theologian writing after the sack of Rome, was imprisoned by the conquering hordes from the north and somehow persuaded them to give him enough writing materials that he bequeathed to the world a classic tract on the Trinity. Saint Thomas Aquinas wrote from a cell when he produced his *Summa Theologica.*

Between the times of Boethius in the fifth century and Thomas (1225-1279), the two great streams of monastic tradition evolved. The first grew out of the early desert fathers, true monastics in that they were "mono"—living alone as hermits on minimal food, water, and shelter. They flung themselves on a radical dependence on God, living sometimes in ecstatic states, nourished by hovering starvation. The hermit tradition has continued through the ages—in the caves of Mount Athos in Greece, in the deserts of Egypt, around Mount Sinai, and in India. Almost incomprehensible to the modern secular mind, these monastics have "accomplished" nothing.

The second stream of monasticism grew from the first. As hermits sometimes clustered near each other and surely occasionally helped each other, they developed multiple hermitages or monasteries, more properly called cenobitic communities (from the Greek *koines*, the same root word as for "ecumenical"). Cenobitic communities like the Cistercians and Trappists have maintained this initial focus on the "mono" in monastery, keeping each monk in maximum individual solitude. Other orders, such as the Franciscans and Jesuits, have tended to focus more on vocations in the world, on their members going out from the monastery.

They too evolved further as they began to recognize the value of a life of devotion in community. As they became less strictly monastic, they found they could sing the praises of God in more beautiful and complex ways. They could copy Holy Scripture in ever more elegant, eloquent, and elaborate, illuminated manuscripts because the community was big enough to support the artists to do their work full-time. And surely not least, they could create buildings—architecture expressing the austerity and transcendent devotion of their lives.

These communities received many infusions of life and inspiration, none greater than the *Rule of Saint Benedict.* It was first formulated in about 530, drawing on other rules that had begun to emerge, but adding Benedict's genius for combining firmness with tenderness. He outlines a way that men could live together peacefully, resolving their differences, praying, and working in harmony. The rule remains a foundation document for thousands of groups of people who have been called to live in community. These voluntary prisons keep the world out. They keep the monks and nuns in. For the inmates, spiritual and psychological confinement deepens as the years go by. The world outside becomes less attractive for many; and they yield, ever more deeply, to the cycle of prayer, work, and the other daily details of the lives they have chosen.

Those living in cells voluntarily seek an undistracted life and are self-imprisoned to achieve that end. From literature, we know that even monks sometimes misbehaved, and there is even considerable documentation of prisons inside monasteries with monks as the prisoners.

Yet many of us today are amazed by those who chose to live apart. At their best, they seemed entirely fulfilled. They were indifferent to comfort or even physical life itself, concerns that are of central importance to most of us. They seem free. Thus, writings from monasteries are all, understandably, devotional books. Saint Ignatius, The Cherubinic Wanderer, Meister Eckehart, Tauler, Suso, Saint John of the Cross, François Fénelon, on to present-day figures like Thomas Merton have given us writings refined in monastic life. Their greatness comes not from the fact that they had nothing else to do, but from the unique concentration that emerged from their wholehearted consecration to God every day and night.

Then there is the large number of people thrown into prison for political reasons—or, in too many cases, for something of which they were innocent. Not all these are like a typical inmate at Green Haven or Sing Sing, but some of them have achieved feats in prison that are perfectly applicable to my thesis that prison can be a place where healing work is done, which would otherwise never have happened.

Benvenuto Cellini, the great Italian sculptor and goldsmith of the sixteenth century, led an adventurous life that included time in prison for assault. He was a man of fiery temperament, and he seriously threatened the lives of people who disagreed with him or who tried to marry his mistress. By his own admission, prison saved his life. He learned to dedicate his work to God and even designed a complex Resurrection frieze while he was in a dungeon. In spite of the restraint he claimed to have learned in prison, he continued to be a wildly impetuous man who was nearly killed several times in fights he initiated. But without that centering experience, he might have challenged one too many people to answer to his sword, and died without giving his gifts to the world, from the exquisite marble *Nymph of Fontainebleau* to his autobiography.

Oscar Wilde wrote *De Profundis*, his most serious work, plumbing new depths of reflection on the meaning of life in spite of the fact that his time in prison was hardly undistracted. He had been convicted of homosexual activities and was tormented by his jailers and other authorities.

Fyodor Dostoyevsky, Boris Pasternak, and Aleksander Solzhenitsyn—all wrote important work while locked up in Russian prisons or exiled in Siberia. Dostoyevsky, in particular, learned to love the serfs, had a conversion experience, and surely deepened his monumental narrative gifts during his time in Siberia. Pasternak and Solzhenitsyn both suffered in Stalin's prisons. Dietrich Bonhoeffer, an early pacifist minister, preached in Germany in the 1930s against the rise of Hitler. Finally, he participated in a plot on Hitler's life and ended up in prison, where he was ultimately executed. He wrote *Letters and Papers from Prison,* later published as a book, a moving picture of a man in tension between devotion to the God of peace, love of family, loyalty to his nation and hatred of Hitler. Because of being in prison, he was able to describe the interplay of those forces with a clarity that might have been impossible to achieve outside.

Even Jawaharlal Nehru, prime minister of India after Mahatma Gandhi, had gone to prison in 1922, long prior to becoming the head of his nation. As war loomed between India and Pakistan in late 1947, he became despairing about the future. He wrote, "I am afraid I have had no peace whatever for an age and I think rather longingly sometimes of the quiet days I had in prison."[*]

---

*   Alex von Tunzelmann, *Indian Summer* (Henry Holt, 2007).

Gregory Corso, the American beat poet who died in 2001, served time in Clinton prison back in the 1960s for selling drugs. It must have been a hard time, but he himself said he never would have read Shakespeare, Keats, or Tennyson and become a disciplined poet himself without those three years behind bars.

Malcolm X was a pimp and a drug dealer in Detroit, but after he went to prison in February of 1946, he transformed himself from petty criminal to a mesmerizing leader with a wide-ranging mind. In his autobiography, he described his own decision to advance himself academically and make himself someone to be reckoned with during his time there. His ultimate embrace of Islam also had its roots in experiencing the dignity of the Muslim community he encountered in prison.

Martin Luther King Jr. wrote his classic "Letter from Birmingham Jail," which still commands the world's conscience, while locked up for engaging in civil disobedience against Jim Crow laws. Much that King has written comes close to the eloquence of that letter, but nothing quite matches its compressed challenge to the people of America and of the whole world. His voice, from the crucible of that dangerous jail, especially on the subjects of global vision and the poison of unrestrained greed, will continue to be admonitions from which future generations will learn.

The Indonesian writer Pramoedya Ananta Toer was arrested at the age of forty-one in 1965 and sent to a penal camp on Burn Island, 850 miles east of Java, where he spent four years. Pramoedya has written many books, but the one he wrote there, *The Mute's Soliloquy*, made him an author of worldwide acclaim. While he was in prison, fellow prisoners recognized his narrative gifts as so remarkable that they did his manual work for him so that he could spend time on his writing. They also constructed a space for him so that he could have some quiet. The irony of the book's title reflects the irony of his freedom in captivity. When he was set free from exile and house arrest in 1979 and began to receive the acclaim he deserved, he was asked about his current work. "Oh, I could not possibly write now," he said. "There are too many distractions."

One of the greatest transformations is the one achieved by Nelson Mandela. According to his friend and colleague, Archbishop Desmond

Tutu, Mandela went to prison at age twenty-five on December 5, 1963, "an angry young man." He was reacting as a young prince, as Mandela has always believed himself to be, to the oppression of his people. He reacted as virtually all-white Americans would have reacted: with feelings of hateful vengeance. So began twenty-seven years of prison. Think how you would feel to be deprived of twenty-seven years of your life at any point. We would almost all feel that this was a soul-destroying experience. Breaking rocks on Robben Island, South Africa's penal colony for political prisoners and those convicted of crimes, was a brutal way to do time.

But there were brothers. A community was forged in that crucible that ultimately brought the apartheid government to its knees without violence. People on Robben Island created a university and taught each other. They determined to live in hope and planned what they would do *when* they got out, not *if* they got out. Dignity became one of their greatest weapons. Ultimately, Mandela and some others were released on February 11, 1990. By the time he was freed, Mandela had actually been confined in a special house, a sign of the unprecedented respect in which he was held by his captors.

Finally, of course, he was elected president of South Africa, a member of the race that had been beaten, tortured, killed, imprisoned and, almost worst of all, segregated.

With bloodless liberation, their former tormentors now lay at the mercy of the black leaders. It is hard to imagine any group of whites not taking vengeance in some way if put in a similar position. The world has paid too little attention to the unprecedented miracle of the South African Truth and Reconciliation Commission (TRC), created to respond to the horrors of apartheid. It offered reconciliation to anyone who committed crimes, even murder, if he would come forward and confess, facing the victims and survivors of his crime. Though inevitably imperfect, the TRC brought miraculous healing to South Africa. The TRC had no clear antecedent in human history. In it, Mandela and Tutu created an example of human behavior in which vengeance was set aside to create a wholly new way of responding to violence.

A more lurid example is one given by Khosrow Sinai, an Iranian film director, lionized in his own country. He said in a conversation when I visited Iran in March 2008 that he had tried to do a documentary film about some men who were in prison for killing their sisters. They had believed the women guilty of some indiscretion, like talking to a man who was not a member of the family. They had thereby disgraced the family and had to be put to death according to their tribal custom. The family "honor" is preserved by the killing of the woman. However, the law of the Islamic Republic supersedes tribal law when they are in conflict, so the men had been arrested and put in jail for murder. Sinai obtained permission to interview the men in prison and realized as he came close to the gate of the institution that he "expected the men to be raging monsters. I was amazed when I found them all to be quite bent over in their remorse. They felt wretched about what they had done. While they were in prison, reading and reflecting upon their lives, they realized that the tribal practice was horrible. One of them said to me, 'While I was living outside, in my tribe, I was free, but my mind was in prison. Now I am in prison and my mind is free.'" Sinai wants to do the film to show that Iran is moving away from such tribal customs and is "embracing modernity."

Of course, some might argue that the "freedom" afforded by being in prison is purely circumstantial—and more often than not, by many, frittered away. There is validity to such a claim. Soap carvings, matchstick buildings, overworked paintings, and tinfoil sculpture are only a few of the endless ways prisoners pass time. Nevertheless, I believe that the experience of prison is actually embraced by many people who go deeper within themselves, think seriously about the meaning of life, and keep going.

People of conscience imprisoned by narrow-minded authorities are the opposite of the rough-minded children of chaos who end up in places like Green Haven. The high-minded ones *enter* prison already endowed with a well-developed sense of their own mission and a ready discipline to begin immediately to use their solitude to good purpose. However, the differences blur when we note that many ordinary people also rise to new heights of moral strength, personal discipline, and cultural achievement by the way they choose to accept their involuntary confinement.

Notably, this group includes perfectly innocent people wrongly imprisoned and sometimes later released when courts are finally confronted with the miscarriage of justice through DNA evidence or other belated revelations. The behavior of these individuals is astonishingly consistent. Almost without exception, they express little bitterness upon release. They are pushed by the media to lash out at false witnesses, overzealous district attorneys, corrupt police, or lazy defense counsel. Nevertheless, they almost invariably focus on their happiness to be free, their gratitude to the attorneys who worked for their freedom, and their eagerness to begin a new life. Surely that is part pragmatism: why dwell on an unhappy past?

However, I believe it is more. Prison has worked its refining fire on them too. They have become people less likely to be distracted by thoughts of bitterness or revenge than many of us who have been privileged to live lives of freedom.

People who actually are guilty sometimes seem to have a more challenging time. Their guilt sometimes reflects a whole life outside the law, a vacuum in their minds when it comes to self-examination and relationships of serious trust. Inside, many prisoners seem alive, healthy with a good sense of humor and a capacity to make friends with other prisoners. After release, all too often, that brightness fades; and they look burdened and harassed. They feel humiliated to admit that they miss the camaraderie and predictability of life inside. Furthermore, they are embarrassed to admit that freedom does not solve all problems as they had expected. For many, the challenges of the street, with the added permanent ball and chain of a prison record, are too profound.

A tough, cynical Jewish inmate who was sick in the infirmary in a federal prison once wrote to me, "There are some real heavy dudes of whom books are written and movies made, but in here they seem different. On the street you would never go near them, but in here they seem human."

I continue to think the alchemy of transformation comes from the crucible of the cell. Though it is most obviously a place that keeps the prisoner inside, it also, to a great extent, keeps the whole rest of the world from entering. Thousands of prisoners have been able to create their own world where they read, write poetry, and paint. Some enter a fantasy world so real that they cross the line into psychosis, but many make it their place of education. They read books that take them to other lands and, other times, more thoroughly than books can transport someone who is simultaneously wondering about which train to catch, which movie to see, which friend to call, what to have for supper. Most of all, they face themselves and learn about inner freedom.

Looking through the cylinder of a paper towel roll makes the circular scene at the end quiver with light and color. So it has been for many who have been able to focus on a shaft of light with an intensity and penetration impossible on the outside. A political prisoner in South Africa spoke of the unrelieved gray colors of the floor, the walls, his uniform, even his blanket. One day a bit of bright blue ribbon blew in the window at his feet. He said it was as if he had been hit, physically. The ribbon seemed indescribably beautiful, glowing, as if it carried the whole outside world in to him. He began to cry. Now he is free, and he wonders at what he has lost because there is no experience on the outside equal to that one in simplicity and power. Granted, he had the human gift to *see* the brightness of the blue. Not all prisoners would.

These inmates are like people who became blind and discovered music or those who became deaf and learned to paint, those who had strokes and achieved a whole new perspective on the joys of being simply alive, more alive with their narrowed focus. Cells come in all sizes, shapes, and varieties.

Many prisoners recognize the benefits, indeed the need, for holding still. Another man who had done twenty-five years in New York State prisons, released in 2000, told me that while inside, he knew there were times he had to "lock in"—spend as much time in his cell as eating, showers, work, or programs permitted. Like a time-out for grownups, "locking in" is a time to pull ourselves together when we feel bombarded by too many distractions. Cells are coveted over dormitory space because of this very relief. "When that cell door closes, I heave a sigh of relief. No one can get at me. In a cube, in a dorm, you never know when someone will crawl in for mischief, sex, or a fight," the formerly incarcerated man told me. So that man now says sometimes to his wife that he "has to lock in."

He goes to another room and just sits, letting himself center down and be at peace. It isn't easy. "What's wrong? I haven't said anything to make you mad," she says. He answers, "I'm not mad. It's not about you. I just have to lock in for a little while."

Seemingly the most obvious difference between a prison and a monastery is that a monk or a nun has the legal right to leave. But even that difference is not so clear in real life. A religious person who has begun, perhaps as a teenager, the process of preparing for final vows and then has lived for a long time "inside" cannot go quickly over the wall. He or she knows that "God will find me wherever I go," and sometimes they are more surely lifers than actual prisoners. Many suffer from belief in a harsh, pursuing, vengeful God. Some fear mothers or fathers who marked them early for the cloister and who might pursue them physically or as ghosts if they gave up their vows. Many are made anxious by the noise and turbulence of life outside and the challenge of earning a living, paying rent, or having intimate relationships with other people.

Once a man or woman enters even a semicloistered life and experiences the safety, quiet, and security of life inside, the option of leaving often recedes. When they leave for a week or two to visit family or embark on some special study, they tell me that they are usually relieved to return back inside the walls, "free from the crazy life out there."

But a religious brother or sister has not been sentenced and punished by society. They chose to enter even if the vocation came partly through guilt or harsh treatment at home.

No one would choose to go to prison. When friends of mine have gone into prison with me to visit for a day, they often shudder as one set of heavy iron doors after another clangs shut behind them. They say that they would never be able to stand to be confined. Yet all of them, all of us, have chosen some sort of confinement, a constraint, a frame that shapes our lives and sometimes imprisons us: perhaps an impulsive, passionate moment leading to pregnancy and the birth of a child, with all the restrictions of parenthood; or a determination to make money the value that overrides all others, with its attendant long hours of work; or a desire to live in the country and have a job in the city, requiring the commuting, which is a twice-daily forced march. All these choices involve doors closing on other possible pathways in life. The closing of some doors is, of course, intended to open others.

Like the Benedictines, who have their own cells but who work and worship in groups, the members of our group meetings went back and forth between being seriously committed and wanting to give up.

At Green Haven, we of Exodus House started calling our gatherings network meetings, referring to the network of needs prisoners have to achieve new caring for themselves, new stronger connections to their families, new patience and persistence, new vocational skills, higher academic achievement, firmer arrangements for living after release, new support groups to replace their old "friends," new commitments to sobriety, new spiritual life within a faith community. All these new qualities constituted a network of resources to respond to the network of challenges: harsh childhoods, poor schools, bad housing, street violence, and racism.

The 1960s were a time when several important prison reform programs started. One was right in Green Haven, started before mine by the Reverend Ed Muller, the chaplain. He called it Exodus and modeled the curriculum on the story of the Hebrew people moving from slavery under the Pharaoh into the wilderness and, finally, the Promised Land. They saw the time in prison as a mix of slavery and wandering in the wilderness. The program continued for decades, including an outside part in East Harlem, which started about 1990 and continues to this day.

A much bigger one, the Fortune Society started in 1966, under the brilliantly creative leadership of David Rothenberg. It grew out of a theater production of a play written by a formerly incarcerated man, called *Fortune and Men's Eyes*. The title was taken from William Shakespeare's "Sonnet 29," "When in disgrace with fortune and men's eyes / I all alone, beweep my out cast state." The play portrayed the brutal conditions in prisons at that time and created a sensation. David involved newly released men to answer questions after the end of the play, and audiences were amazed and moved. It helped in a major way to push forward a public concern for improved conditions. The Fortune Society continues to thrive under the leadership of Jo Ann Page, who has added the Castle to its impressive portfolio of services. The Castle is a building bought and beautifully renovated on Manhattan's upper West Side, housing sixty formerly incarcerated people. She has now added another big building next to the Castle. She has been a miraculous fundraiser for these costly endeavors, but no less remarkable is the warmth of the community embrace. That area had been very reluctant to accept the Castle when it had been first proposed, but they had been thrilled that it had added to the property values of the area because it is so well run, and the residents are an asset to the community. It is for that reason that they were happy to add the new building for more formerly incarcerated residents. David continues to be very actively involved and recently launched a new production called *The Castle*, with men and one woman telling their stories.

One man entered Network to check it out. He stayed in the program to change his life. His name was George Beeks, and I met him in Green Haven prison in 1963. George was a former hit man, short and muscular with small eyes and a thick neck. He said that he "should never have been born." His mother had told him that she had tried repeatedly to have an abortion when she was pregnant with him. "The world would've been better off if she'd pulled it off. All my life I done nothing but cause people pain. I've never done one good thing in my life," George said. He joined the group in Green Haven partly because its existence was beginning to affect his prison schemes. George was selling contraband drugs, homemade booze, and gambling for contraband cash; but now old reliable schemers were, in small numbers, turning away because of the Exodus House program.

Watching George reminded me that monasteries also made an impact on the secular life of the nearby towns. The fact that the monks were *there* praying was reassuring to the people of the town. Wealthy owners of land bordering on the grounds of the monasteries were moved by their holy neighbors, sometimes surveyed the wickedness of their own lives, and decided to give pieces of land to the brothers in exchange for the promise of their prayers. This happened at the Benedictine abbey of Sénanque, forty kilometers east of Avignon. After its founding in the twelfth century, various parcels were given in this way until the monks owned the entire valley and some fields beyond the hills. People of wealth and power wanted to benefit somehow from the goodness and divine strength of the monastery. But sometimes, surely, they found that prayers could not simply be bought, that they had to change their lives as well.

So too with George, who infiltrated the group with the intent of learning its game so that he could incorporate that knowledge into his schemes to deal in cash, drugs, or other contraband. He came at first saying "everyone" in the prison knew about the group. Like the lords near Sénanque, he wanted to benefit from the community without submitting to its discipline.

However, George soon was seriously involved and committed. He, like the others, was starving for the human exchange, the safety, and the trust that existed within the circle of the group. It was becoming a sacred place where it was the norm to be honest. I believe he was hungry, deep down, for the discipline.

He told us how his father had "trained" him. His earliest memory was of lifting his arms to his father to be held—and then his father hitting him in the face. His father explained that George had to "learn to be tough to make it in this tough world." George did learn; he became a vicious young man, a hit man, who did violent jobs for pay.

George soon said he had become confused by the group program. It opened a whole new way of thinking to him. He said that everything he used to think was right now seemed wrong and vice versa. He started wondering about the harsh values of his old world, not so much because of anything I said, but because of conversations with his peers who had grown up as he had and had hurt people as he had. Now they spoke of the happiness of looking forward to being loyal to their wives and being good fathers to their children. He was eager to hear more, like a child asking for a nightly bedtime story.

Finally, George decided to leave the contraband business forever. His fellow inmates were amazed.

Our waiting list grew. We added more leaders from former prisoners we knew in the East Harlem neighborhood who had started new lives. We added more groups until I was driving a van of six leaders, who had all done serious time inside, to Green Haven from East Harlem once a week. They would colead their groups or sit in mine until they felt ready.

George now had a new problem. "I thought all my pain came from being bad. I was certain that if I stopped doing bad things, I would be happy. This whole thing is a gyp. I thought about going back to my old life, but I know I would feel even worse after all I've been through," he told the group one day. He was experiencing all the aches that all the rest of us feel.

Then followed one of the rare, explicit theological discussions in prison I can remember. One man said he felt comforted by the cross.

"I'm not a Catholic, but I found a plastic thing of Jesus on the cross, and I hung it in my cell. When I was in the life, the cross didn't mean nuthin' to me. I thought Jesus was a chump for getting busted for nuthin', but now I look at it a lot, and it makes me feel kind of smoothed out."

Another man said, "Before, I felt like being in Network was a really bad joke. When I hurt, it was pain about getting beat for my drugs or not having any more ways of getting stuff. Now my pain is about not getting a letter from my son or them canceling a course I'm taking in school. It's like a higher pain, but it still hurts."

Somehow George was able to appreciate the value of trading a life of absurdity in exchange for one of tragedy. He realized that he was living life on another plane. He chose to continue.

George helped other people change, and he wrestled with his own new problem of being a "toothless tiger." He told us that some of the people he had hurt in the old days were in the prison yard. Back then, he had allies, his reputation, and his own menacing manner to protect him. Now for the first time in his life, he admitted that he was scared. It is hard to imagine how monumental that step is for anyone who has never been behind bars. I admire George greatly to this day. I greatly doubt that I would have had his courage if I had had the burden of his childhood and violent early career.

George felt trapped because he felt he could not go backward. Finally, he drifted into a strange peace that came from accepting the inevitability that he was vulnerable whether he was in prison or in the street. But he was never hurt in prison. In fact, he recruited others into the program who were impressed by the stark self-transformation of George.

George was paroled in 1982. It was a time when our transition groups in New York City were not as strong as they were later. He chose not to come to the groups we ran on the outside because he wanted to avoid his old "crimies." He wanted a whole new life—new friends, a new job, money for clothes, and an apartment. But he needed a whole network to help him achieve these goals. He never found the support he had had in prison, and eventually he drifted back into the life he had known too well.

I still had much to learn about the depth of the needs of a man like George at the time of his release from prison. My old friends at Reality

House told me that he bravely tried to make it in law-abiding society. However, ten months later, the relentless pressure of no money, no home, no friends, no job, little education, and no plan took their toll; and he yielded to the temptation to sell drugs. He could not adjust to low-paying jobs and could not establish a regular home. People who knew him from before welcomed his ruthless old self as an asset. All his prison progress must have seemed to become unreal as he stumbled back into the world he knew from childhood. He was doubly at risk: from his old gang, who still wanted revenge for his hit man days, and from his new world of square people, who seemed to have no room in the civilized world for him.

One spring afternoon, as George sat in the sun on a bench in East Harlem, someone came up behind him and shot him dead in the back of his head.

George's courage, and the almost-trancelike grace with which he lived the last couple of years I knew him in prison, stayed with me. I now had my own eyewitness experience of a man's capacity for transformation. That man did not have to be a saint, a world leader, or an innocent person snatched off the street. Whatever happened at the end did not alter the fact that George had really changed.

"A room of my own" was the primary wish of the young Virginia Woolf. When she got her space, she bloomed. She was no nun, but she was capable of making excellent use of her writer's cell. Probably almost all good writers have a space, a special chair, a desk or table where they can write and ride through the dry times and the wrong turns. Of course, the cells in prisons and monasteries are different because in prison, the exit is closed. But for many, it has been possible to exist, even thrive in that small space and make it productive, perhaps holy.

I admit that my hunger for silent courage when I was a child has stayed with me and has possibly colored my thinking about prisons in a naive way. But there is no question that many thousands of people in prison have discovered the healing power of solitude, even in unwelcome confinement. Prison isolation is not "better" than life outside in the crazy world, but it has been put to the service of high transformation by countless brave men and women locked inside.

Silence in and out of the cell has been well described by Bob Hausrath, for decades a champion of college inside prisons in the western part of New York State. He believes that he learned from inmates about "the gift of the subtlety and power of silence. The silence of that place of inner stillness that reaches out and welcomes all that stands before—this is the silence of conception that creates and brings into our lives new possibilities for being. It is a silence that affirms the vision that we are always more than we know and sustains us as we grow in the procreative light of learning. It is a silence that is self-reflective and enables us to recognize ourselves in all of creation. It is a silence of love where we learn our capacity for giving that which can never be possessed. It is a silence of reciprocity where we discover we are loved."

Hausrath goes on to quote the journal of an inmate, "'Currently, I am no longer afraid to enter the silent spaces and know the power of silence. Now, I actually enjoy silence and escaping my confused and frightened states and experiencing the liberated state, being open to new possibilities. In the silent inner place of self, there is peace, bringing with it healing, freedom and love. It is only here that I am not separate or superior or different, but part of the world of people and life. It is here that I share in the reciprocity of the world's Being and becoming.'"

Chapter Six

Manhattan Rehab

Increasingly, I was pushing superintendents and others in authority in the prisons to make changes that seemed obvious to me, changes that I thought would allow people like George to make it further than he had. I wanted more programs that would help people in prison to face themselves and look hard at new possibilities for their lives. I wanted more school and college inside. They would push back and tell me I should just try to run my own place. Warden Follette said, "Then you'll see how tough it is."

Then opportunity fell into my lap.

I had been recruited in 1966 to do consulting work for the newly established Narcotic Addiction Control Commission, an agency created by Governor Nelson Rockefeller and the New York State Legislature to respond to the drug epidemic. It had in haste bought and staffed six buildings in greater New York City in which to lock up addicts. The addicts were supposed to be treated, but no one confidently knew how to do that. Others' experiments still seemed new. I had already helped start two drug programs, so I was the one-eyed man in the land of the blind, and in 1967, the NACC hired me.

I went to five different institutions every week, one day in each place. I loved the work, driving my red Ford to each in turn. They nicknamed me Mission Impossible. Directors and staff welcomed me warmly, sharing the problems involved in running a secure place of confinement for drug addicts, most of whom wanted only to leave and get high again

as soon as they were detoxified. I had the opportunity to offer a frame
of experience from the Network program that included confinement,
postrelease supervision, and possible reconfinement if necessary.

In 1966, the first Rockefeller drug laws applied shaky new thinking
in a detailed way to drug addicts, requiring their confinement on the
determination that they truly were addicted to heroin. It was a daring,
controversial—and ultimately discredited—adventure in public social
policy. The original Rockefeller legislation provided for committing
people to an inpatient program for three years on a criminal commitment
if they were in possession of drugs or on a civil commitment if they
were simply addicted. They were released after a year or so to try their
wings, report regularly to staff on their employment, housing, and
family situations. They would be returned to confinement if they
returned to heroin abuse.

It is, of course, a slippery slope for the state to lock people up for
"victimless" crimes like heroin addiction. It is especially wrongheaded to
confine people on a civil commitment. But in some cases, it saved lives.
Some people's lives actually were transformed. Some few only needed
detoxification, a time of being held still postdetox, a chance to find
out that they had some brains, an opportunity to reconnect with their
families in a controlled setting, a chance to deal with horrific family
relationships, the opportunity to think about what they really wanted to
do for a living even though it would not pay as much as prostitution or
selling dope, a chance to think about God in a setting where there was
no pressure to believe a certain way. Social engineering is a dangerous
game, subject to grotesque abuses, but if the program had continued
and had been held to high standards by a good monitor, it would have
rescued many who have lived in their own hell.

The place with the most problems out of the five rehab centers I was
visiting was the Manhattan Rehabilitation Center. In the early 1950s
and 1960s, prostitutes had sometimes worked in the old Congressional
Motel on Tenth Avenue and Forty-first Street. Most had been heroin
addicts. So it seemed fitting in an ironic way when New York State
bought the motel and turned it into a place of confinement for female
heroin addicts. The prostitutes who had once worked there were not
amused to find themselves locked up inside. They put four women in
the double rooms and two in the single rooms.

The director was a man with two PhD's, but with no previous experience running an institution. He had minimal management skills and was the only director who refused my suggestions. Staffs were demoralized, the women were angry and acting out, confusing and contradictory memos were issued from the director's office, arson was common.

On June 28, 1968, I received a call from the deputy commissioner for the NACC, Dr. Seymour Joseph, a psychiatrist, asking if I would take over Manhattan Rehab Center immediately. During the previous week, the fire department had been there three times to put out blazes. The place was a disaster. The women confined there had threatened the biggest fire on the Fourth of July, warning that MRC would "go up like a firecracker," in the words of one inmate. I was to take over on July 1. Looking back on that day, it seems like an act of hubris that I really did not think carefully about accepting the position. I knew some of the staff well, and I knew that they had failed to employ commonsense practice. Nevertheless, on July 1, 1968, I was confident that I could manage a staff of 325 with 300 residents and 400 outpatients; and I looked forward happily (if a bit anxiously) to the challenge.

When I began working there, I discovered that the women were relatively easy to engage in counseling, both group and individual, compared to the men I had worked with. The women in Manhattan Rehab seemed to me, in other respects, similar to men in prison. Like the men, they had poor self-images, but were more intelligent and resourceful than they realized.

However, the women were more inclined to say quickly how they felt, both about themselves and the institution. This was of course a great advantage in the counseling process.

Another aspect of Manhattan Rehab: many residents and staff were lesbians in a day when there still was little open conversation about this subject. I attribute that in part to the fact that many of the women had had violent abusive relationships with fathers, stepfathers, uncles, cousins, and boyfriends. Rejecting men for the affectionate companionship of other women was a natural response, if that was all one knew. I did not clearly know then about sexual orientation being a fact, not amenable to "treatment," but common sense seemed to say that there was much more to being lesbian than mistreatment by men.

On my first day at work, I made rounds and discovered two residents naked to the waist, having lunch with forty-eight others in the cafeteria on their floor. This was obviously condoned, even enjoyed, by the officers on duty, who were all female. I returned immediately to my office and fired off a memo saying that residents were to be fully clothed at all times, including at night. I ordered that the changing of clothes be restricted to bathrooms. Several staff and residents thanked me for helping in this way to deflate tensions. When life became a bit more formal, it helped cool the atmosphere.

In the groups that I ran with men, homosexual alliances existed too—it is a common occurrence in prison—but the men never openly acknowledged this. However, in the hundreds of group meetings I would eventually hold with women, I found that they would openly refer to another resident as my man or my husband. Even when they referred to someone as my friend, there was a transparent clarity about the meaning. Back then, for many of us on staff, that was a new way of speaking.

Unfortunately, the issue surfaced mostly not in group discussions, but in fights. Triangle relationships were endlessly changing and given to violent eruptions of jealous feelings. Aside from the purely sexual aspects, the women seemed to like the drama of threats and counterthreats; they also enjoyed beating the system, which forbade sexual encounters. But most of all, I think they craved the same acceptance and embrace involved in any primary relationship, the joy of being "the one" to someone else.

There were secret weddings. One day, my staff brought me a beautifully lettered invitation to such an event. It was elaborate in its preparation, with a blue ribbon attached to friends of the groom and pink ribbon for friends of the bride. I sent a memo to all residents saying that I wanted to explain my opposition. I said it was wonderful to make commitments as friends and even as sexual friends, but that a woman could not be a groom inside a place of confinement. There are too many coercive pressures inside to make a clear commitment to a person locked up with you even for a few months. I wanted them to wait (none were there more than a few months) until they were released to be sure that their love endured in the free world.

I also was lucky to help calm down the place by replacing the dysfunctional discipline board. It is important, in any institution where people are locked up, to have some system for managing disruptions so that people with short tempers, angry about their confinement, are not allowed to make life miserable for others who are also unable simply to leave. The discipline board had six members, so arranging meetings was hard. Disruptive residents either continued to be disruptive or they were locked in seclusion rooms for much too long a time. There was no obvious way to maintain traditional prison discipline in what was, architecturally, still a motel. In a prison, where there are cells, a man or woman could be locked in his/her own cell until he or she calmed down; but we had no such possibility available to us. Fights were frequent.

So I ordered the line officers to remove any disruptive resident to seclusion (a regular room, but without windows; the only room in the place that could house a disruptive resident) without saying how long she would stay. The officer was then to report immediately to the charge officer what had happened. The charge officer was to write up the incident (also immediately) and determine how long the resident would be kept from her floor. Normally, the residents would be immediately returned after having had time to cool off, usually an hour. Officers felt empowered to take immediate action, and residents felt protected from each other. There was relief through the whole institution because routine temper tantrums and scuffles could be handled fairly and quickly. None were confined more than one day.

All good prison superintendents make rounds every week or even daily. I made rounds in person to all floors at all hours of the day and night. In the early period, I often encountered residents who said, "If I could just get hold of that fucking Chinlund, I'd kick his ass!" I would then introduce myself and say I was available to sit and talk right then and there. And we did. They were usually disarmed, and though they often had fierce objections to being locked up there, they were reassured that the MRC at least had courteous, respectful leadership. Officers liked it too; I was dealing with the same tantrums they were. As importantly, it gave me an opportunity to take the pulse of the place and to keep on improving our work.

I made a particular point of talking with staff at all levels. This meant that the formal structure of the place was less likely to be undercut by some informal structure. Every institution has both levels, but the closer to each other they are, the more peaceful the place. Much can be learned directly that would never surface going through the channels. The result of it all was that in three short days, the residents chose not to "blow up the center like a firecracker on the Fourth of July." In fact, we did not have a single fire serious enough to require the fire department in the five years I was there.

My years at MRC, 1968 to 1973, were particularly happy ones for me. My third child, James, was born in 1971, a continuing joy.

And working with women, both staff and residents, was new; but it seemed quite free of some of the drawbacks I had always heard about in the prisons. Men generally spoke of women as difficult, touchy, and quarrelsome; but I found them easier to talk with and more open than men.

During these years, I had my best opportunity to pay close attention to the effects of confinement on a great variety of people. Some of the residents were as young as thirteen, and one was seventy-two. There were many grandmothers in their thirties, and one great-grandmother who was forty-nine. Quite a few women were there at the same time as their daughters, and three or four with their granddaughters. At one point, we briefly held three generations simultaneously: a girl of sixteen, her mother of thirty-three, and her grandmother of forty-nine. There was much talk in the center about this phenomenon. It motivated many residents at the time to work so that the same familial misery would not be their own. All the women were wriggling to be free. It was upsetting to connect, as I did, with their pain and feelings of being treated in a subhuman way simply because they were locked up. So we made special efforts for the sixth floor, our intake floor, to be as hospitable as possible. When I went on rounds, I tried always to include the sixth floor so new inmates could express their discontent directly to me if they wished.

I often asked the women what they would do if they were suddenly free to leave immediately. Almost all said that they would get high. When I asked about the money to do that, they would almost invariably describe the alternatives: borrowing money from people who had already given them a lot of money, prostituting themselves for money or directly for drugs, shoplifting. No matter how miserable the scheme was, the chance of getting high one more time seemed to justify it. When I let them know that the whole staff and I wanted to help them find a new alternative to drugs, they would often be angry and frustrated.

To them, holding still (being unable to leave the building) seemed like torment. But after days and weeks of being held still, some of them changed. They were amazed that life could have a predictable pattern: day followed night; there was breakfast, then lunch, then supper. For many, this was their first experience of such a routine. Most people cannot imagine a life as devoid of structure as theirs had been before confinement. I still find it impossible to put myself entirely there in my mind.

But I could see that this new structure provided time for reflection and growth. We introduced small potted plants into the place. There were hardly any residents who had experienced the growth of a flower from a seed or a bulb. They were fascinated. Some were excited, and a few identified so passionately with their plants that someone having a quarrel found that destroying the plant of their enemy was the ultimate hit. Learning that the plants should have sun, but not too much, water, but not too much, that they had their own rate of growth that could not be accelerated—all these were lessons that became metaphors for their own lives. Even those who had given birth had often been too high during their pregnancies to have learned from their own much more spectacular life-giving experiences.

Still, it was hard to recruit good staff to keep all this going. I had to fill the position of head of a three-person Department of Psychology. It required a PhD and had to be filled from a civil service list. I was obliged to interview the three who had achieved the highest civil service scores who wanted the job. If after the interviews they still wanted placement at Manhattan Rehab, I had to choose one of them. Going farther down the list or hiring off the list was not allowed.

The first candidate seemed depressed, barely able to answer questions. He almost staggered in and out of my office. The second looked like the stereotype of a scholar: absent-minded, preoccupied, and lost. He seemed at home only with books. He talked about the emerging literature of addiction, but was unable to discuss any of the issues he would face in the work.

The third candidate was a conventionally attractive, but extremely nervous woman. When I asked what she would say to a resident who wanted to have a sexual relationship with her (we had so much of this, I felt it was unfair not to ask the question), she became red in the face, apparently lost the power to speak, and got up to leave. "I still want the job," she said as she fled.

There was another way I could proceed: I could lower the qualifications for the position and reduce the salary. The form to effect this change was a PR-50, and it became a verb in the lingo of state service. So I "PR-50'd" the position to the next rank, which did not require a PhD, and went through the process again. Ultimately, I hired Irving Abramowitz, an energetic, cheerful man who helped my then associate director, Marguerite Saunders, and me figure out how to recruit, train, and supervise staff to work with the residents.

At that time, it seemed to me that a PhD in psychology or other human service fields was often more disabling than enhancing. The heavy emphasis on statistics at the core of the PhD process seemed to destroy the very sensitivities we were trying to foster in our residents. Either one had to reduce human behavior to quantifiable data—drug relapses, fights, rearrests—to the point where conclusions would be obvious, or one had to rely on "anecdotal" material, which was regarded as worthless by the newly minted social "scientists." Since seeing the individuality of each person is one of the continuing lessons of my life, it seemed to me that statistics generally were not worth much.

Early on I found that the individuals most helpful to the women were not necessarily the professionally credentialed counselors (though they were often important change agents) but rather the best officers, whose civil service requirements were just a high school diploma, a civil service test, and an interview.

There are many who are deprived of a good formal education who have grown their natural gifts of wisdom, sensitivity, and good judgment. There were many such people at Manhattan Rehab. Some were able to respond creatively to the challenges of daily life on the floors. The best had an uncanny ability to defuse difficult situations with just the right blend of humor, authority, and firmness. There is a fascinating quality that some supervisors simply call It, which the best officers possess, which enables them to get residents to do what they need to do next. It is a mixture of confidence in themselves, patience, good energy, humor, and an absolute certainty that what they are asking for is reasonable and should happen. No matter how long one might lengthen this list, there remains an intangible ingredient beyond definition. It is the personification of effective authority.

I selected a small hardworking group of officers who had these qualities and called them informally narcotic correction officer therapists, or NCOTs, though there was no such title authorized by the bureaucracy.

These officers were much better than almost all the counselors at running groups. The counselors were dedicated, so much so that I required them to sign *out* because they tended to stay too late. They were a remarkably able group, many of whom went on to distinguished careers. But they lacked knowledge of the streets, and they were almost all white while the officers were almost all African American, like most of the residents. Though being the same race as your client is no guarantee of skill, it does mean you are more likely to engage them in the challenging work of self-transformation.

The NCOTs reminded me of a time (while I was working in Grace Church) when I was called in the middle of the night by a mother whose daughter had tried to commit suicide. The young woman had been taken to Bellevue Hospital and admitted to their psychiatric ward. I had put on my black shirt and clerical collar and was quickly admitted. While I waited to see my patient, another woman wandered out into the corridor and quietly lay down on the marble floor. A doctor passed by, looked down, and said, "You are not permitted to lie there. You must get up and go back to your bed." The woman did not budge. Moments later, a nurse came by in her cap and uniform. She too looked down and said, "It is against hospital rules for you to lie there! Get up and go to your room." The woman did not move. A few minutes later, a nurse's aide came along and spontaneously knelt on one knee next to the woman. She tenderly took her hand and touched her gently on the shoulder. "Mary," she said softly, "it is cold out here. Let me take you back to your room and put you in your warm bed." The woman slowly stirred, looked at the aide, let her help her up, and then slowly went off to bed. Almost sixty years later, the scene remains vivid for me as a lesson in the importance of intuitive skill and caring. The best of the officers were just like that wonderful aide.

I was not rejecting academic work; I encouraged all my staff, in every place I worked, to continue their education. It seemed the ideal place and time since we were still just beginning to learn about treating drug addicts. It was also a positive coincidence that Manhattan Rehab was right next to the Vorhees Institute, which at that time offered day and evening classes in both academic and technical subjects. I pressed members of my staff to take a class before or after coming in their shift. I especially encouraged the night staff to take evening classes, then come to work at midnight, and study during their shift when the women were supposed to be sleeping. It meant that my own staff was more likely to be awake and that they would simultaneously be advancing their education.

Marguerite Saunders showed just how far not only inmates but also staff could come. She was dignified and quiet, an extraordinarily able woman who started on the staff as a narcotic correction officer. She had recently begun working again after a time on public assistance, which she had accepted in order to raise her two small sons. When they entered school, she was free to work. Her first job was in the city welfare department. Then she came to Manhattan Rehab. From the beginning, she quietly distinguished herself as a person able to see the big picture. Diminutive of stature, she was large in spirit, caring for staff and residents.

Twice I recommended Marguerite for promotions, though it meant she would leave Manhattan Rehab. My staff was upset with me for recommending her because they missed her when she left to become a charge officer somewhere else. She then came back to be promoted to tour commander, and again left to become chief of security at another institution. Finally, she returned to become my associate director—and later succeeded me as director. She was always coming up with new ideas, challenging and supporting the staff—a practical idealist. She steadily worked on her education, earning her BA and MSW from Fordham, growing visibly in confidence and competence. Marguerite ultimately became the commissioner of the whole agency (by then called the Office of Alcoholism and Substance Abuse Services) and served with great distinction, winning respect on both sides of the aisle in Albany.

The job of Narcotic Correction Officer Therapists (NCOTs) included leading groups and engaging in individual counseling sessions. The NCOTs were teamed up with the regular counselors, who had more formal education but less experience. These partnerships were mutually beneficial; both types of counselors flourished.

The NCOTs were the heart of MRC, the primary bridge between staff and residents. They loved their work and were utterly devoted to it. I tried to get them higher salaries, but everywhere I turned, I was rebuffed. "Changing the rules to let those people with lower qualifications do the work would screw up the whole system" was the most common response, though usually stated in a more bureaucratic language. To give the NCOTs higher salaries seemed to run counter to the civil service system, which rested on three measurable credentials: academic degrees, length of service, and a written multiple-choice test. None of the three adequately measured my NCOTs. So I quietly encouraged them to sue me for working them out of title. They did so and ultimately subpoenaed me to submit a description of their work for the past couple of years. I wrote an accurate, full account of their activities. The commissioner was furious when they won a financial settlement. The new title of narcotic correction officer therapist was formally established as a civil service title.

There were success stories at Manhattan Rehab among the inmates too. One was Julia. An angular, angry African American, she was persuaded to join (only reluctantly) in the group circle. She insisted on sitting with her back to the group. When it came to her turn to speak, I tried to get her involved, encouraging her to try out the process. Finally, she turned toward me, eyes blazing, and screamed, "Will that bring my baby back?" Her infant had died in his crib while she was heavily addicted to heroin. It was never determined if it was a "regular" infant crib death or if the baby had died in some way from Julia's neglect. She was never formally charged with the death of the baby. Little by little, Julia increased her participation in the groups. Then she discovered a Harlem Pentecostal church, the Soul Saving Station. She continued to live at Manhattan Rehab, but increased her time away, deepening both her self-understanding and her involvement in the community of the church. She grew over two years, in one version of the way we hoped many others might be transformed. She became radiant, beautifully self-assured. We hired her to run the switchboard, which she did for years, living a happy life. She was an example of someone who was brought to the threshold by being held still in a safe place and encouraged to find her own next step. Her religious conversion catapulted her to a new place of acceptance of the death of her baby and a commitment to sobriety. She is one of a few people I have known for whom religious conversion was dramatic and lasting. I know that there are many others and that for many, coming to prison affords the opportunity to consider more seriously a spiritual commitment.

The conversions to the Muslim faith are an example. Especially at that time, but still today, there are many who move away from Christianity and a "white Jesus" to embrace a new faith, a new name for themselves, and a new kind of worship: listening to the Koran being chanted in a powerful, liberating, hypnotic way. And there was special confidence coming from the solidarity of the community: at that time all African American.

The fact that I have not helped many prisoners find their faith makes me sad because I have found strength and confidence coming from God. Even in the active process of leading a group, I have often felt that Christ was right there, mysteriously present in the circle. I have wished that I could find a way to be more explicit about my faith, but whenever I tried, I felt as if I was walking on scorched earth, the way of faith having been destroyed by others who came before me.

Another success story was that of Marie Blendon, a tall blonde woman, who came to us mute. She would not speak a word or even nod her head to signal the accuracy of our information. She upset the staff and residents by this refusal to speak and most of all by her bizarre behavior, taking off all her clothes and lying on her bed with her legs in the air as if waiting to be diapered. Her eyes told us that she understood most of the time what was being said to her. She followed instructions. I hoped that she would slowly get better if people were not mean to her, and I asked our psychiatrist if he agreed. Despite her abnormal behavior, he not only agreed but also interceded and provided counsel to staff and residents, who continued to be bothered by "the bug" (as prisoners label people who are mentally ill). After a while, she settled down and began to nod or shake her head in response to questions in the group.

Marie stepped up to saying yes and no and finally participated with brief but adequate involvement. She ultimately began to laugh and speak sometimes and showed herself to be quite intelligent. She continued to be extremely shy, but within a more normal range. She had individual sessions with the psychiatrist over a long period. He was appropriately professional about the content, but later told me that she had been subject to repeated sexual abuse from an early age and had used drugs as the only way to escape her pain. When she found herself in a safe place, she began to heal. Marie started working as a volunteer in our business office, was ultimately hired on staff, and moved on to a higher-paying accounting job outside the center.

Not all the stories were successes. One woman committed suicide. Sadly, I remember only that her first name was Barbara and one of the very few from a Jewish background. She had been with us for only two days. When everyone went to lunch, she hanged herself in the bathroom. When I heard what had happened, I raced to the floor with our medical staff, moving her from the bathroom to a bed where we tried everything to revive her. I remember the police were very angry with me for moving her and said I could face criminal charges. They never did charge me, but it added to the emotional tornado of the day. She was well educated, upper middle class, and had said she was terrified that her family would find out she was locked up in drug rehab.

After that tragedy, we intensified our efforts to encourage people to talk with someone about everything, including feelings about the suicide. All the residents knew instantly about Barbara's death. We were able to get many, including staff, to talk about suicides in their families, their own suicidal feelings, and the fact that mainlining heroin is a suicidal act: death can come from a "hot shot" (too-strong heroin in a poorly mixed dose), from poor diet, or from falling asleep in the cold. Barbara's death was a terrible price to pay, but we responded to this tragedy by trying to go deeper.

During the time that Marguerite Saunders and I were colleagues, she helped to shape a plan to "unitize" Manhattan Rehab Center. We turned each floor of fifty women into its own floorwide community, with subgroups meeting to provide mutual support. Residents continued to participate in facility-wide programs, including schooling, but they also began to compete for the reputation of being the best floor. When the residents and staff could focus on fifty other residents instead of three hundred, it made life more human for them. On the units, I encouraged residents to take advantage of their few months at Manhattan Rehab to think carefully about the future and the kind of friendships they wanted to have. I further expressed hope that they would see themselves as growing, no matter what their age. I asked, what are the qualities you want in a partner? Sexual excitement, understanding, reliability, loyalty, sense of humor, children, capacity to earn a living—and then I encouraged them to add to their own lists for when they could leave this little world of ours.

That unit concept was to be the groundwork for an idea I later developed: that it might be possible to create monasteries or communities of faith inside the prison system. I imagined that people might be allowed to sign up to be with their own faith community, pray together, sing together, and be healed together. A few years later, I had the opportunity to propose that plan, but it was immediately obvious that the faith communities were unable to restrain themselves from drawing the boundaries around themselves in a negative way. Many of the participants would have claimed that their way was not only the best way but also the only way, and that would have created potentially violent friction within the institution. Ultimately, the Manhattan Rehab experience helped me to create a peaceful secular version of the monastery vision.

I believed that coed activities would be good to introduce into the program at Manhattan Rehab. From my first visit to prison, it had seemed to me counterproductive to exclude the opposite sex from prison life. I believe in coed prison, though I do not know if it has ever been tried over a long period of time. I asked for permission to have some weekend program involving men, perhaps a dance. Permission was denied. I offered to take personal responsibility for everyone's safety. My request came back again, this time with NO! handwritten in giant letters by the deputy commissioner.

Nevertheless, I had the opportunity to give the coed program a brief test. The circumstance that made it possible was a slowdown of intake. Suddenly we had one empty floor, at a time when facilities for men were overflowing. At a meeting of all the facility directors, we were wrestling with the problem. When I offered to take fifty men, my colleagues could not believe I was serious. They thought it would be impossible. "The men will cut holes in the floor or ceiling to get to the women!" said one of the directors, who were all male at that time.

I said I would take personal responsibility for the safety of them all. It had been my experience that drug addicts were basically shy, underconfident people, particularly anxious around the opposite sex if they did not have the tranquillizing effects of heroin or marijuana. Permission was granted because the other directors were desperate, but on the condition that there be no mingling.

When I came back to MRC, my own staff was also incredulous, but morale was good, and they were ready to give it a try. They wanted to know how I planned to keep the men and the women separate since the elevators and stairs could not be dedicated to particular floors without creating bottlenecks. The men were to arrive in July 1971.

I suggested that we use the opposite strategy and arrange for the two sexes to meet by strict adherence to the rules of the center. It was time for a fire drill anyway, so I proposed that we give them two days' warning and have the drill in the afternoon. That meant that they would all have to be together in the closed outdoor courtyard, the designated place of evacuation. I did say that I wanted to continue to house the two groups and hoped that they would behave.

When I made rounds in the morning of the fire drill day, the women were all primping, preparing for the big encounter. The men were all shaving and showering. When the bell rang, the floors emptied out into the courtyard, the women all going by choice to one side and the men to the other. It looked like a high school dance in the 1950s.

There were no incidents of any misbehavior between floors in the ten months of this experiment.

We were soon able to run actual coed groups following the same format used with the women. As far as I know, there had never been such groups. We asked for volunteers so no one would be forced to attend, and there was no shortage of takers. Our women were much more comfortable in their group involvement than the men were, but the process was highly structured, so participation was not too uneven. Both the men and the women were surprised and humbled by the issues raised by the opposite sex. Usually the women were appreciative of the way men felt that they had to take responsibility for making enough money to support a family—and that they did not have the education or skills to achieve that goal. Men, in turn, were surprised by the depth of the emotional and physical vulnerability that the women described. The women talked about feeling unsafe alone with men they did not know, the pressure to "give it up" (meaning agree to sexual intercourse), the fear of unwanted pregnancy—things that seemingly had never occurred to the men. When each had to sit still and listen to the opposite sex, new worlds opened up.

Back in their own groups, the men spoke of how hard it must be to be a woman. One said, "This is all new to me. I never really talked to a woman before even though I've got four kids. Even my wife. When I was off drugs, working, I would come home, eat supper, watch TV, bang my wife, go to sleep, get up the next day, and do it all over. We never talked about nuttin'." One woman with a very tough appearance returned to report to her all-female group, "Hey, we think *we* got problems? Those guys *really* got problems!"

I was sorry that we could not continue those groups. Space for the men reopened in regular male facilities, so we were required to end the experiment. My supervisors had always been nervous about it and thought I had just been lucky that nothing wild had happened, which may have been partly true. The commissioner may also have been anxious that the press would hear about our program, resulting in headlines like DRUG DEALERS HAVE DANCING PARTIES IN REHAB! Fortunately, reporters never showed up. I believe that a significant number of men go to prison partly because they cannot manage daily relationships with women.

Therapeutic communities like Daytop, Phoenix, and Project Return have had coed group sessions for decades. The residents are all voluntary, unlike in the prisons, but they have the problems one might expect, including sexual relations that are not supposed to happen until residents are released, and there is sometimes a tendency to play up to members of the opposite sex instead of dealing with their own issues. We were on the cutting edge at Manhattan Rehab, but were not destined to sustain the coed program.

In the big world outside, other events overtook the system before the men even left: a bloody rebellion at an upstate prison called Attica.

Chapter Seven

The Horrors of Attica;
Becoming a Superintendent

Even before the Attica tragedy in New York State in September 1971, there was a groundswell of public and legal opinion around the nation that a prisoner should not lose all rights once he or she entered prison. There was increasing concern that it made no sense to imprison people only to release them as desperadoes, more angry coming out than going in. Reform groups had begun to push for more job training and education even if simply as a form of self-protection for law-abiding citizens. But these programs were reaching New York State in pathetically minimal ways. My Exodus House program, along with a few others, had been cautiously introduced in a few prisons—then sometimes yanked back because wardens would get nervous about plots being hatched in the meetings. School and vocational training were being enlarged, but only slowly.

On a more basic level, lawyers, and soon federal judges, started saying that you could not be handcuffed to the bars of your cell and beaten just because you were serving two years for auto theft. Prisoners were not supposed to be deprived of adequate medical treatment or food or crammed into spaces that drove people crazy and made them sick. It was "cruel and unusual punishment," prohibited by the Constitution's Eighth Amendment. Even the American Correctional Association, a trade association made up of prison professionals, not political liberals, began issuing commonsense standards, demanding that beds have mattresses, sheets, and blankets, that inmates receive mail, and that visits be possible.

The vengeance motive was slowly yielding to the public safety factor.

But right into the 1970s, when I was still running Manhattan Rehab, the prison experience was characterized by tyrannical wardens like Harold Follette and commissioners like Paul McGinnnis. There was no check on their power. As long as they were not spending too much money and inmates were not escaping, they could largely do as they wished. The doors were closed not only to escaping inmates, but also to visits from the public. Inside, life festered. Inmates and staff committed murders of other prisoners with only minimal investigations or consequences.

In 1975, what seemed like a vast sprawling prison system in New York State consisted of only twenty prisons. Now there are sixty-six. What we had then may now seem simple and small, but the system was often profoundly and gratuitously cruel. I knew this not only from talking to inmates but also from overhearing conversations among the staff themselves. There were "goon squads" made up of officers who routinely beat inmates in their cells for real or imagined infractions. There was an arrangement called the Box—a block of cells in which troublesome inmates were isolated, usually with minimal light, little food, and more beatings. Black inmates—at this point a fast-increasing proportion of the population—were routinely called nigger by the all-white staff.

Inmates lived in fear of the officers, who in turn lived in fear of the warden or his deputy. Wardens lived in fear only of escape or riot, which would lead to their losing their jobs.

Wardens were the fortunate few who had survived their time as principal keepers, or PKs, the ones who actually ran the prisons. Wardens themselves worked short hours and led comfortable lives. In most prisons, prisoners worked as white-uniformed servants in the wardens' homes. This was demeaning to the inmates, but those jobs were regarded as better than the alternatives inside the prison.

There was a riot in the Attica mess hall in 1957, which was put down with tear gas. It was followed by a sit-down strike the same year, quelled and punished by massive force. Another strike came in 1962, and later, a two-day work stoppage. A new unity was being forged among prisoners who were black Muslims.

The violent desperation that comes from utter hopelessness is impossible to contain for long in a prison. Most prisons are very securely built and have none of the possibilities of action-movie-type escapes. Digging tunnels is impossible. Fires become all too common and horror-filled for both staff and prisoners since there is not *supposed* to be any way out; to escape the fire cannot mean that you escape the prison.

A few prisoners tried to win favor and better conditions by informing on others who were making booze in their cells or smuggling drugs or money. Then as now, if it became known who the snitches were, they could be hurt, maimed, or killed. Aside from the fact that no one wanted to be "snitched out," there was a deeper motivation for this violence. Informers broke the solidarity of the inmate group. Incarcerated people were greatly strengthened in their spirits by being a unified "us" against a seemingly monolithic "them." Neither group was, of course, as unified as they struggled to portray themselves. That made any visible breaking of rank all the more serious and in need of punishment.

Imagine how you would feel if you were one of half a dozen officers on duty in a yard full of hundreds of inmates, carrying just a baton (guns are never allowed near inmates). Many of them hate you simply because of your uniform. If they wanted to kill you, your fellows in the guard towers would not be able to intervene with their guns quickly enough to save you. Incarcerated people themselves were sometimes "piped" (bludgeoned) in the yard, sometimes with the heavy rods available for weight lifting. Everything momentarily screened from view—no witnesses—only a body lying dead as prisoners drifted away. As University of Chicago criminologist Norval Morris noted, ultimate power belongs to the staff since inmates cannot get out. But immediate power belongs to the people who are incarcerated.

I have walked in the yards in Green Haven, Attica, Clinton, and Sing Sing; and I have always felt vulnerable to an angry, spontaneous attack by a single prisoner out of the hundreds who were there. I have foolishly believed that (because of my good intentions) I would not be assaulted, but back then, it was not a sensible chance to take.

Changes that the bureaucracy could not control were already underway. The caprice with which each level of the power system treated the level below became increasingly unbearable through the 1960s, a time when the prison population was growing. In 1960, there were 11,000 inmates in New York; in 1970, 12,000; in 1976, 20,000. The population has continued to grow; in 2004, there were 66,000. Attica was built to hold 1,600 prisoners; in 1971 (the years of the tragedy), it held 2,250. At that time, 54 percent were black; 9 percent Latino. Almost two-thirds had been convicted of violent crimes. There were no black officers, and there was exactly one Latino. As the system grew, the use of goon squads became more dangerous. The Attica inmates in greater numbers began to feel that they wanted to take guards down before the guards killed them for nothing. Assaults on officers, almost unheard-of before this, began to increase. At this time, there were inmate strikes and riots in Auburn and elsewhere.

These events were taken more seriously as time went on, but never in a way that worked significantly to correct the horrors. Governor Nelson Rockefeller had wanted to build up the state mental hospital system and the state university campuses and felt that he could not do those two and also modernize the prisons. The public had little interest in prison reform. So as with a developing volcano, the heat and pressure grew slowly greater.

On August 21, 1971, George Jackson, a hero of the black liberation movement, was shot and killed at California's San Quentin prison. The story explaining his death (that he was trying to escape) was not believed by other incarcerated people.

On August 22, there was an eating strike at Attica. All inmates wore something black to honor George Jackson, and the mess hall was entirely ominously silent. The pressure continued to build. On August 29, the sick call tripled its normal number. An inmate group, the Liberation Faction, sent a list of demands to Commissioner Russell G. Oswald. On September 2, Oswald went to Attica, an almost unprecedented step to take; but he was aware of the increasing heat. Among other things, prisoners were asking for two showers a week instead of one, more vocational training, more minority staff, and recognition of an inmate grievance mechanism. Oswald had already lightened censorship of inmate mail, but he begged for more time on the other issues. He really did want to make big positive changes.

On September 8, there was a fight in the yard. Larry Dewer, an inmate, punched Lieutenant Richard Maroney, who was known as a serious disciplinarian. This was a major infraction. Another inmate, named Lamorie, came to Dewer's aid while Lieutenant Robert Curtiss tried to help Maroney. More prisoners joined in, and the officers retreated, but reinforcements arrived, and order was restored. After supper, when all the prisoners were in their cells, Superintendent Vincent Mancusi ordered Dewer and Lamorie to the Box. When officers went to get Dewer from his cell, he put up a fight, heard throughout cell block A. Dewer was finally cuffed and carried off by four officers. Lamorie went quietly. As he was escorted out, a prisoner (one named William Ortiz was later charged) threw a soup can at one officer and hit him in the face, causing a cut, which later required four stitches. The night was uncommonly silent as rumors spread that Dewer had been beaten in the Box and was dead. (Dewer was in fact alive, in spite of his beating.)

At that point, an inexperienced officer named Gordon Kelsey neglected to lock down the ancient levers that operated the cell doors in cell block A, so an inmate was able to pull the lever for cell 17, releasing William Ortiz. He was the prisoner identified as having thrown the soup can the night before. He had been ordered to be confined to his cell. Superintendent Mancusi heard of the glitch and ordered Ortiz to be returned to his cell.

The next morning, many inmates were headed toward "Times Square," the intersection of all four main cell blocks, and Lieutenant Robert Curtiss walked alongside as a prisoner yelled, "You no good motherfucker!" Instantly Curtiss was hit on the side of the head. Other officers tried to intervene, but they were beaten, and they ran. Curtiss tried to reach the phone in the A block offices, but prisoners overtook him and ripped out the phone, taking his keys. They opened the A block cells.

Both groups were stunned by the events. Prisoners surged back toward "Times Square." Officer William Quinn, whom *New York Times* reporter Tom Wicker called "an amiable young guard who had a reputation for overlooking minor rule violations" controlled the "Times Square" gates.

There was a defective bolt in the ancient gates, and they gave way under the pressure of the rampaging prisoners. Quinn was assaulted, his skull fractured in two places, and left for dead.

Prisoners then opened the doors in cell blocks B, C, and D. More inmates poured out, arming themselves with sledgehammers and other pieces from the metal shop, and baseball bats. They set fire to the school building, the chapel, and other structures. A thick cloud rose over the prison as sirens sounded, audible through the town of Attica.

Many officers were badly beaten. Some were forced to run a gauntlet, naked, as the prisoners once had been. Some inmates tried to talk their fellow prisoners out of committing the beatings, and some simply hid in their cells. A respected prisoner, Richard Clark, persuaded other inmates to help him carry Officer William Quinn to the front of the prison where he could receive medical attention. With reinforcements from outside, officers soon recaptured A and C blocks as well as E and C yards; and prisoners were isolated in D yard, about 1,280 of them, roughly half of the total population. This part of the riot took only a few hours. When the dust settled, inmates had control of D yard, and forty-one officer hostages were being held. Now the standoff began.

Over the course of the next two days, Richard Clark and other prisoners drew up an initial list of demands. Negotiators were chosen by Commissioner Oswald and Governor Rockefeller, and a process was launched. Some agreement still seemed possible.

Then news came of the death of Officer Quinn, and everything changed.

Russell Oswald had been commissioner of the Department of Correctional Services since January 1, 1971. Named to succeed Paul McGinnis, he was part of a belated vanguard of change, the first real professional to head the department. He was an intelligent, warm man capable of eliciting loyalty in those around him. I had been delighted with his appointment, having known him from his days as commissioner of Parole.

Immediately, an inmate negotiation committee was formed and a new list of demands drawn up. The inmates asked to see Oswald himself; and after consultation, Oswald, who had gone to Attica on September 2, bravely went into D yard. There was also an impressive list of other citizens who went in before and after him. Oswald agreed to many demands readily since they were part of his own improvement plan. But he told the prisoners honestly that it was not in his power to guarantee amnesty for anything, especially the taking of hostages and the murder of an officer. The inmates then called for Governor Rockefeller himself to come.

Some criticize Governor Rockefeller for "not going to Attica," whatever that would have meant. But the die had been cast, years before, by his choice not to reform the system in commonsense ways. At this point, it would have been as easy to stop an earthquake as to resolve these events peaceably. It took great courage for the negotiators to enter D yard the first time and more courage for them to return for subsequent meetings. The prisoners who kept other prisoners from beating or killing the officer hostages held their authority by a thread, and tempers were also rising outside the prison.

As news of the death of Officer Quinn was absorbed, lust for revenge by state troopers, who were gathering, began to grow. Many of them had relatives and friends on the prison staff. As the hours passed and the negotiators kept going in and out, the resentment heated up among the families and friends of officers too. People began saying it was "time for a turkey shoot." Anger even focused on the negotiators themselves. Attempts to explain that they were trying to save the lives of the hostages met with stony stares.

Finally, on September 13, the troopers, who had no special training for such an operation, stormed the prison in a cloud of tear gas. Thirty-three inmates and six officers were killed—all by the guns of the state troopers, whose vision was seriously impaired by the mist of gas and their gas masks. In the subsequent reclaiming of the prison by staff, many prisoners were tortured and beaten.

I remember sitting at my desk at the Manhattan Rehabilitation Center on September 13, listening to the live radio report of the attack. The gunfire was audible to those outside the walls, where the radio report was being made. I knew the Attica superintendent, and I had visited the huge recreation yards there, including D yard. I trembled for them all as the shooting continued. I knew that history was being—made in a terrible, bloody manner and that prisons were going to be different in ways that no one could predict.

I also had three hundred women locked up in MRC, and they were listening to the same news that I was hearing. Whenever there is a disturbance in one prison, there is always a danger of trouble erupting in other prisons; a sense of solidarity with those in revolt is inevitable. I wanted to stay in my office and mourn and pray for those whom I knew were being brutalized, maybe killed. But I knew it was important to make rounds, to visit each floor, and to connect with the helplessness and hurt of the women upstairs. We cancelled regular programs so that everyone could talk through some of their feelings about the tragedy of the day and the unknown, frightening consequences in the days that would follow.

I believe that the deep, cruel forces at work in prisons at that time could probably only have been addressed by a disaster as public and bloody as Attica. Today, those forces, mostly terrible anger and the desire for revenge, have been considerably diminished because of the enormous but undramatic changes in the way prisons are run. (see Appendix C)

So the bloodshed led to progress: prison order maintained by skilled administration, not inchoate, brute force. However, the pace was exceedingly slow.

No bell rang to signal the start of a new chapter. There had always been rules, stated and unstated. However, now there was an unprecedented and generally recognized need for reform. It was time to become much more intelligent about the way we ran prisons. So the professionalism that Russell Oswald and others had sought to introduce, instead of being discredited by the Attica disaster, was dusted off and reviewed.

Officers thunderously insisted, correctly, that their own safety was at stake; and their union immediately became much more powerful. Prison programs such as school, college, vocational training, AA, and NA were recognized as the best security because inmates were much less likely to engage in assault, riot, and hostage taking if they had meaningful activity and hope. Everyone, staff and prisoners, wanted to move on.

Nevertheless, one important affirmation was made—prisons will always require the absolute power of the staff. There is a severe limit on the degree to which inmates can govern each other. There are many reasons: endemic distrust, little or no experience in governing (even in a school classroom), poor impulse control, and inclination to be too harsh in judging their peers. Prisoners live under layers of despair often covering layers of anger.

Since the staff still had to be in complete control, it became clear that someone needed to monitor the staff. In 1972, the New York State Commission of Correction was created to be an independent watchdog. Its chairman and commissioners reported directly to the governor, with no interference from the New York State Department of Correctional Services, the agency that actually runs the prisons.

Among other things, the commission was given supervisory responsibility over staff training. Many small changes were instituted to achieve long-range, major improvements. Some were minor, like the abolition of off-color lyrics in the marching cadences. A paramilitary pride in appearance and by-the-book action was promoted. Self-respect was taught as the basis of gaining inmate respect. The first attempts were made to recruit minority staff. Those were major changes.

Most important was the training now instituted for supervisors. Sergeants, captains, deputy superintendents, and superintendents had all been expected to learn on the job and fill in the gaps with informal advice from their peers. Now they were actually instructed in supervisory and management skills. Brutality was continued by officers, both verbal and physical, but it was not condoned. Officers began to learn that their own safety ultimately was endangered if a fellow officer was gratuitously harsh.

New York State started keeping order more and more by threatening troublemakers with the loss of good time (time counting toward parole or conditional release), loss of privileges or of a good job, keep-lock (being confined to one's own cell), and isolation in the special housing unit. Inmates were frequently transferred, especially if it was suspected they were about to do something harmful or about to be victims of others with old grudges. Subsequently an elaborate computerized system was developed to attempt to stay up to date on the enemies of each inmate: informers and previous enemy gang members. These methods became ever more important in the 1970s as prisons became more and more crowded.

I had the opportunity to deal with the overcrowding issue in a way not open to many superintendents. At Manhattan Rehabilitation Center, we had a capacity of three hundred, six floors of fifty women each. The program was going well, and we had a good reputation with the courts. Judges were sending women in increasing numbers. In order to keep from exceeding our limit of three hundred, we speeded up the release process. That was within our power, but we wanted to be responsible about providing real care. Finally, we felt that we were in danger of doing little more than providing detoxification services, so I said we had to hold at the current rate of release. Then I exceeded capacity by one, then two, then four per floor. With six floors, we were finally at a total of 324. I refused to take more. People were being turned away at the gate.

A judge called, saying he was sending another. I explained my problem. He said that it was not his problem. I said that I still refused. He said that there was a frail blonde sixteen-year-old in court, shivering in withdrawal from heroin. I suggested he send her to Beth Israel Hospital. He said I was in defiance of a court order. I said I understood that. He said he could put me in jail for contempt. I said I would rather go to jail for contempt than try to explain in court and to my conscience how I had allowed my place of confinement to be overcrowded and sort out the bodies at the bottom of a stairwell after a fire. He hung up. We stayed at 324. I never knew what happened to the frail girl.

My own commitment to help improve the prisons finally led me to take the civil service test, when it was first given in 1972, to be superintendent of a prison. Before that time, superintendents were all appointed by the commissioner from the group of deputies who had, almost without exception, come up through the ranks. The test had an oral part, and I remember one question: "What would you do if you had a psychiatrist on your staff who did not do what you ordered him to do?" I went through the normal steps, extra cautious because the man asking the questions was himself a psychiatrist. Finally, I had exhausted the possible remedies and said, "I would fire him." My questioner surprised me by looking pleased. I finished in the top three.

As a result, I had to be considered when the Department of Correctional Services was looking for a superintendent to reopen a then-closed prison, Taconic (in Bedford Hills), and turn it into a prison college in which all inmates would be enrolled as college students. It may seem surprising, in our present political climate, that there was ever such a thought; but everything was ready to begin in 1973. The idea had been nurtured by Commissioner Oswald, and the project went into the official state budget. I applied for the job.

Chills ran up my spine when I got the call at Manhattan Rehab that the job was mine if I wanted it. I was overjoyed, and I accepted, but I was a little scared of finally becoming a warden. Even though I would be getting the most eager, motivated, intelligent inmates, I would be part of a system that still included many staff accustomed to rule by cruelty. Civil service and the officers' union limited my ability to fire unduly harsh staff. Many inmates were going to be more intelligent and more academically advanced than many officers, and that would probably create some new tensions inside.

Timothy Healy, a Jesuit, then vice-chancellor of the City University of New York, accepted the position of president of the college. I was to run the prison itself. We had some serious and hilarious times making plans together, quickly developing a strong relationship of mutual trust. We were both disappointed when the whole scheme was torpedoed by the New York State Legislature in what turned out to be the first of many budget crises.

In retrospect, I think it was just as well that we never succeeded in opening the prison college. It would have drawn many of the most academically gifted inmates out of the rest of the prisons. That would have drained the law libraries and other informal tutoring activities. Tim Healy left, but I stayed a year to turn Taconic into the first work-release facility in New York State. I had long hoped that some sort of halfway step might become part of the prison system, so helping with the process was a big consolation.

The purpose of work release was to provide prisoners a way to ease back into the world. Imagine being released after years inside prison with $40, no job, a poor history of employment, and a family that wants to disown you. Many inmates were returning with high hopes of a good new life, strong commitment to take any job, and live anywhere in order to succeed. But to qualify for a job, an address, some sort of shelter, is a necessity. And even looking for a job requires some carfare. So if it were possible to settle into a job before release, there would at least be a steady income as a foundation for everything else.

At Taconic, the men would leave at 5:30 AM, dispersed to jobs in New York City, and meet back at the bus at 6:00 PM to return to prison for the night or the weekend. It is a sound idea, now in practice in many other states; but at that time, 1973, I was unaware of any models to follow.

It is important to acknowledge that I was the beneficiary of the discipline of other superintendents, up the line, in prisons from which my inmates had come. It had been sharply enforced that staff, especially superintendents, be addressed as sir. There was a hard hierarchical structure on which relative peace rested uneasily. It was still only two years after the Attica tragedy.

That particular point had been made to me when I was preparing to reopen Taconic. There were no inmates there yet, and I had the luxury of a long orientation period. My deputy superintendent for security, Joe Sullivan, was a seasoned professional; and we completely agreed on mutual respect between staff and prisoners, on going by the book, and having the "book" be a clear set of rules. Joe was well respected by staff and inmates, a rational leader. We developed a manual for staff and prisoners to fit our unique situation.

Staff was assigned in two groups, phased in to save money since there were no inmates yet in residence. I met with the first group of staff, and they seemed pleased with the way things were starting up. They were particularly happy that I promised that I would write a supervisory memorandum on anyone who came even one minute late to punch in at the time clock. I did this because most of the officers came from Sing Sing, where, at the time, discipline was lax. Officers chronically came to work late, which meant that the ones they were relieving had to be held over so that their posts would be covered. Those who had second jobs or home responsibilities could not keep their commitments. So they liked my new rule.

Then came the second half of my staff, and the new ones did not like my rule. They were younger, less settled in the area, and they liked getting the overtime pay they would receive if the relieving officer was late.

My rule was soon tested. An officer was four minutes late punching in, and I wrote him up with instructions that the memo be put in his personnel folder. He brought a grievance request to the union, a formal hearing was held, and the union supported me. When the officer asked for a grace period of five or ten minutes, I replied that it would again appear rigid for me to write him up four minutes after the grace period. Flat tires, blizzards, and sick children were all unacceptable excuses. I did not realize it at the time, but I gained an evanescent reputation as a tough warden that was helpful in my getting started.

As the first staff orientation was taking place, a group leader came to my office saying the officers wanted to know what to call me. I said they should call me Steve. He came back and said they did not want to do that. I said they could call me whatever they wanted to. He came back and said they wanted to call me Mr. Superintendent. Furthermore, they wanted me to make everyone else call me Mr. Superintendent. I realized that I had been flippant about a matter of importance, not just to them, but also to the maintenance of structure and order inside. It was so soon after Attica that they felt they needed every possible tool to maintain the delicate balance of order.

We were under pressure to open and to take prisoners from upstate who were eligible for the new work-release program. As a result, we received prisoners before we could recruit a doctor on staff and without a working pharmacy. Soon after the first draft of fifty arrived, I was told that there was one man who was asthmatic and needed his medication. No medication was allowed on transfer buses since staff was anxious about the presence of anything that might provoke attempts at theft or violence. I asked to see the prisoner, and he came to my office perspiring freely. A pale redhead, he stood at rigid parade rest in front of my desk.

I said, "Hello, Brendan, have a seat."

Looking at some point in the wall behind me over my head, he said, "Sir, that's all right, sir. I don't mind standing, sir." He appeared to be completely terrified even though his breathing seemed normal. I went around the desk, put my hand on his trembling shoulder, insisted that he sit, and explained that I only wanted to see him because of his need for asthma medication. I told him that I too was an asthmatic and felt a particular concern for him as a result.

He said, "Sir, excuse me, but this is all too crazy for me, sir. Any place I have ever been, only bad things happen when a guy goes to see the superintendent. And, sir, I don't want to go back to Attica"—his last stop before coming to Taconic. We continued to talk, and he began to tremble and perspire less. I asked him how much his asthma seemed related to pressure. He replied that he had always had the problem, but that it was much worse in prison. He went on to tell me he had become a practicing Buddhist while inside because it helped him to calm down and to be ready to accept whatever might come his way. We continued to talk about Buddhism and the mystic tradition in general.

I assured him that he would not be transferred back to Attica. Finally, I asked if he thought he felt calm enough to try to manage without medication.

He said he would give it a try; I told him I would arrange to have the medication available if he needed it. As he left, he shook my hand and said, "Sir, the guys will never believe that I was shootin' the shit with the warden. I'm not sure I believe it myself."

Another early problem arose, concerning the handball courts. In every prison I had entered, there were always three courts: black, white, and Puerto Rican. After all those prisoners had suffered from racial discrimination, it seemed to me wrong for Taconic to perpetuate the problem when the solution lay within my power. Why should 10 percent of the inmates (the whites) get 33 percent of the court space? So I ordered that a sign be put in front of the courts saying, "These courts are each to be used by prisoners regardless of race." A few days later, the new interracial inmate liaison committee, which I had ordered formed, asked to see me. Six of them came into my newly enlarged office, obviously nervous, and said that they wanted to do whatever I wanted ("sir") and would, of course, accept any decision I made ("sir") and that they were very happy to be at Taconic ("sir"), but would I possibly consider taking down the new sign so that they could have "regular" handball courts ("sir").

I put forward my argument. They said that none of them minded the disproportional use; it would "save a lot of trouble" to go back to the usual way. I specifically addressed the black inmates, and one looked me firmly in the eye and said, "There will be fights." I asked them to think about how this petition would be seen in the outside world. Would segregated housing, schools, or hospitals be justified in the name of peace? I got nowhere and, finally, reluctantly yielded.

To me, it showed that they were collectively unable to manage even the most minimal social compromises. The inertia of the system combined with the delicacy of the peace militated against it.

I did make one feeble new effort at understanding life on the inside by arranging to spend one night in a cell. I went in after the inmates had eaten and were also locked in their cells. I took my own toilet kit. The bunk was made in advance. There even was a wooden board over the toilet in the cell and the board had been draped with a blue towel. When the officer locked me in, he could not restrain himself from saying, "This is too crazy, sir." I slept soundly and left in the morning when the other inmates were wakened, and I went to have breakfast in town.

That was a far cry from the policy-changing adventure of the great reformer Thomas Mott Osborne. In 1913, Osborne had been warden of Sing Sing for a short time when he chose to dress in prisoner issue, be locked in a cell, eat in the mess hall, and work in industry, like any other prisoner. He did this for three weeks. There was no way that he could keep everyone from knowing who he was. Staff and inmates participated in the endeavor for the most part as if he really were another inmate.

Even though he received somewhat special treatment, as he acknowledged himself, he learned a great deal from the experience that I already knew: that the prisoners often were friendly and helpful to each other, that they valued productive use of their time, that the separation of officers from inmates was unnecessarily great, that family visits were greatly coveted and needlessly limited, that too little attention was given to preparation for release. Osborne was a great hero in the story of prison reform.

One of the greatest legacies of Thomas Mott Osborne was the ultimate creation of the Osborne Association in 1931 by people inspired by his vision. Under the dynamic, passionately committed leadership of Liz Gaines, it now offers one of the most complete range of services of the several agencies offering help to formerly incarcerated people. The Osborne Society continues to this day, a fine program for men and women inside prison and on re-entry.

The fence at the back of the Taconic prison ground was rusting, and it looked as if it could be easily knocked over by a little concerted action by several men. I discussed the problem with Joe Sullivan; and we agreed that the inmates would immediately discover it, that they would not want to knock it down because they left every day anyway, and that it would be good to let them know that we were aware of the situation. So we agreed to make it part of our regular orientation.

When the first group of inmates arrived, Joe and I briefed them on their new life. Part of that was my telling them, "The back fence is very rusty. You could knock it down. Please don't do that. If you do and you are found on the other side of the line, you will be charged with escaping, which is a D felony, and you will go back upstate." No one laughed, but there were a few smiles and rolling eyes. When it was over, Joe muttered to me, "This whole thing just stays unbelievable."

Watching the officers put the men on the buses on the first morning was a moving event. Here were men who, for decades, had devoted themselves to keeping prisoners inside. Now it was their duty to put them on buses that would just leave them in the city. Though there were staffs at the other end to direct them to their work, many of our staff were sure that there would be a half-full bus coming back. In fact, we never lost a man during that first year. We had a lot of momentum going for us. The upstate prisons were full of Attica memories and hatred, making it a "harder time" than it had been pre-Attica. The inmates desperately wanted anything but that.

However, there was one unforgettable exception—James Pennington. With a name like that, he should have been the lord of the manor, and in a twisted way, that was his problem. He had been a big-time pimp and a drug dealer on the outside. He had had a chauffeur and a limousine, two fancy apartments, many girls, and lots of fashionable clothes. Pennington insisted that he be given those fashionable clothes from his property, including his blue velvet pants, shiny black boots, and lace shirt. It was explained to him that everyone was required to wear blue jeans; a blue work shirt; and regular, not shiny, work boots. Most of the men were headed for rough construction jobs (demolition and sandblasting), and his costume was not appropriate. Pennington said that he had not been told about the costume limitations when he signed on for work release. "I cannot appear in New York City in blue jeans!" he said. He was quiet, but determined.

As with much else, this was new and got bucked up to me. I ordered him held back on the first day, hoping that his seeing the others leave and my having a chance to discuss his future with him might lead him to change his mind. I did not want what seemed like a failure on the first day. Pennington watched the bus leave. Then I tried talking with him about his future work and found him quite closemouthed. It became clear that he intended to continue to be a pimp and had no alternative plan. All my talk about trying something new, and that no one would see him in jeans, was to no avail. I told him he would have to go back upstate if he did not agree to wear work clothes. He was entirely unmoved, looked at me with his hard eyes, and said, "Then I'll have to go upstate and finish my bid." And that is what happened. Pennington went peacefully.

At Taconic, I did not get to see the inmates much since they left early in the morning and did not return (exhausted) until the evening. That was not satisfying to me, but it was the way the program had to work. So after a year in which I felt that, along with my staff, I had established an efficient program; I decided to move on and accepted a call to be executive director of Big Brothers of New York City. It was an opportunity to help young boys avoid going to prison in the first place.

A challenge awaited me at Big Brothers. The budget was in the red, the residential program was in an uproar, and the staff had just voted to form a union. I was overconfident about my skills after the successes at Manhattan Rehabilitation and Taconic. Big Brothers was a lesson in humility.

The program had begun in Cincinnati in 1903 by a group of visionary probation officers. They were seeing increasing numbers of boys in trouble who seemed simply to be lacking a father or an uncle who would provide a strong male presence in their lives. So they volunteered to be "big brothers" to a few of the boys and were pleased with the results. The program quickly mushroomed around America.

New York City's Big Brothers program had greatly expanded the scope of services and, fifty years later, provided a residence for boys who had only marginally functional single mothers and absent fathers. The movement itself had begun when the boys being admitted were young and easily tractable. Now the seventy "little angels" were neither little nor angels, and they were tearing the residence apart. It was a beautiful spacious place with a huge dining hall / auditorium and dormitories. But the architecture made it impossible to break it up into smaller units (as we had done at Manhattan Rehab), a prescription for chaos. The atmosphere was marked by angry, cynical talk and fights. Staff were trying hard to be kind and persuasive when sterner corrective action was needed. And more staff than we had were required to go one-on-one with boys who desperately needed attention. Most of all, we needed staff skilled in molding a peer culture, and that did not exist at the time. I tried but could not fix it. Reluctantly, I called for a closing of the residence, sent the boys to other foster care agencies, and sold the building. It broke the hearts of board members who had raised the money to create the residence. I have never regretted the decision; we just did not have the staff, the right balance of toughness and caring, or the right space for the institution to live up to its original potential.

That brought us back to being a traditional Big Brothers undertaking. Among other things, I started a Senior Big Brothers program in which experienced Big Brothers helped new ones get adjusted to the challenges of volunteering to help boys in need. Part of this involved training the new Big Brothers to elicit self-affirmations from their Little Brothers. The boys needed to be able to say that they were capable of doing good things at home and in school. The way to do that was to train the adults, the Big Brothers, in how to affirm themselves right in the group.

One of the men in this group had been a dazzling success at work. He had made partner at his law firm at a young age, had a lovely wife, two children, and a big house in the elegant suburb of Greenwich, Connecticut. He drove a fancy car, played excellent golf, and seemed as if he would have no trouble finding something he had done lately that he was glad he had done. No. The process came to a full stop. Finally, on prompting from me, perspiring freely, he said, "I am proud I made partner." As the training sessions went on, he was able to manage what he called the water torture of self-affirmation without sweating and realized that he had been a big success partly because for him, nothing was ever enough. Even his Big Brother involvement was partly a result of his compulsion to overachieve. He continued as a leader with us, but he made a new commitment to pay more attention to his family.

The experience reminded me that it was not only prisoners who had a need for personal transformation.

Chapter Eight

Chairman of the Commission of Correction

One hot day in August 1976, I was amazed to receive a call from Robert Morgado, secretary to then Governor Hugh Carey. Morgado wondered if I would be willing to be considered for the position of chairman of the New York State Commission of Correction. I assumed that I was one of a huge number that would make it possible for the governor to say that he had "made his selection from a long list of fine candidates." However, the governor's secretary is sometimes seen as having as much power as the governor himself, so when Morgado asked if I could come that day or the next, I realized that there might be something more to it. I got a haircut, put on my best suit, and went to his office the next day.

The Commission of Correction is technically a recreation of an early nineteenth-century agency, inoperable for decades, but revived because of the Attica tragedy. The legislature was determined to correct the problems that had led to the disaster and to create a body that would warn of any possible repetition. The commission was charged with investigating and correcting abuses both in the state prisons and county jails, providing training for officers in prisons and jails, and intervening in crises when they came up. As a last resort, it was empowered to close institutions it deemed dangerous or unfit for habitation. There were to be three commissioners, one being chairman.

Responsibility for deployment of staff fell to the chairman, but in order
for the commission to act formally, two of the three were needed for
an action to be legal.

I knew that I would be stepping into a hornet's nest. Governor
Carey's first choice as chairman two years after Attica, in 1973, had
been Herman Schwartz, a professor of law from the State University
of New York at Buffalo. Buffalo is fairly close to Attica; and Professor
Schwartz, long concerned about issues of confinement, had been one
of the first to arrive at the prison after hostages were taken. In the days
that followed, he continually risked his life as he went in and out as an
active member of the negotiating team. He particularly distinguished
himself by securing a guarantee of amnesty for prisoners from U.S.
district court judge Constance Motley. He had worked hard, driving
all over the state trying to find her, and then developed the wording
of the amnesty instrument. In a nutshell, it said that she would grant
amnesty to those who peacefully surrendered, except for those who
would be tried for the murder of Officer William Quinn.

Schwartz arrived back in Attica exhausted, but triumphant,
hoping he could save lives. When an inmate leader tore up the order
by torchlight in front of the inmates in D yard, Herman Schwartz
must have felt that his own life might be destroyed next. This strong,
intelligent man believed prison was the wrong punishment for most
criminals. He had been radicalized long before the torches were lit in
D yard, but the Attica experience deepened his convictions about the
corrosive effects of prison. His fiery rhetoric in support of this position
collided with one of the many get-tough-on-crime spasms that have
rocked the political life of New York State in the thirty-five years since
Attica.

So there had been heavy opposition in the state senate to his
confirmation. A bitter struggle ensued, and for the first time in New
York history, after two years, the senators rejected a gubernatorial
appointee. Schwartz was forced out of the chairman's hot seat—now
closely watched by the polarized groups of prison-reform supporters
and antagonists. The commission staff also wanted to close prisons and
make other dramatic changes that the commission legally could do but,
in reality, would have been blocked by the governor or the courts. With
a vacuum in the chairman's office, the commission staff tried to act on

their own. They called a press conference, to be held on the steps of Attica, on the fifth anniversary of the bloodshed, September 13, 1976. They wanted to list all the continuing ills of the system in general, and Attica in particular, and to call for the closing of Attica.

That could have been a spark to ignite new fires, and the governor was understandably anxious to get a new chairman in place quickly in order to control the staff.

I was sure that there was no real possibility of my being appointed, so I went to my interview relaxed and was recklessly outspoken. I wanted the governor's staff especially to know how I felt about Attica. This was my big opportunity to vent all my pent-up passion about the horrible conditions I had observed in my many years of work with Exodus House, then later with the Reality House programs.

I met first with the governor's aides and told them that I believed that it would have served no purpose for former governor Nelson Rockefeller to go to Attica, that nothing would be gained by calling for the closing of Attica, and that I wanted to concentrate on making reforms in the training of staff and ending the practice of ruling by beating up incarcerated people.

The next morning, I found myself back at the governor's office, meeting with Robert Morgado himself. We had another long talk, and he finally said, "There is someone else you should meet." Then he ushered me into Carey's office.

The governor looked at me cautiously, and after some conversation, he said, "How would you feel about my appointing you chairman of the commission?" Without hesitation, I found myself saying, "Governor Carey, I am greatly honored that you would ask that question of me. I would love to be chairman of the commission. However, you really do not want me for that position. You need someone who will smooth over the troubled present situation. The only reason I would be interested is if I could help change the prison system." Carey jumped from his chair, came over to me, punched me appreciatively on the shoulder, and said, "That's what I want too, and that is why I want you to be chairman!"

Some months later, I realized that he was more concerned with reining in the runaway staff and heading off their planned press conference than I wanted to admit. However, I know that he did also want to change the system because he appointed other reformers including Benjamin

Ward, the first black commissioner of the Department of Corrections, as eventual successor to Russell Oswald.

Our talk was on Thursday, and I was living in New York City. The governor wanted me to begin the next day in Albany. We compromised on Monday. The governor said I did not have to move from New York City.

It was the most pain-filled job I have ever had because I felt almost helpless to investigate properly the numerous complaints of abuse, which came from state prisons, county jails, and Rikers Island. We had great staff, but our numbers were too small.

However, it gave me the opportunity to participate in real change in the state prison system.

The first thing I did was to meet with the commission staff and tell them I was the only one who would call a press conference. I said that there would be no event on the steps of Attica and that anyone failing to follow that order would be fired. It was not the way I wanted to start; it was the way I had to start. In the weeks that followed, I did fire three senior staff people who were committed to closing prisons. I was committed to improving them, but repeated what I had told the governor's people: if the commission did succeed in closing a prison (very unlikely), it would just mean sending the inmates to other prisons and make overcrowding worse. The only answer was systemwide reform.

The staff members were bright and knew the law better than I did, but we were on almost opposing tracks. In going up against them, I also immediately incurred the wrath of the left wing in the legislature—an odd position for me to be in since I was basically on their side. We all wanted to change the system, but I was for great change slowly yet relentlessly. They dreamed of great change quickly, and I felt they were making it more difficult by being so confrontational about it. One lawmaker in particular, the late senator Stanley Fink, insisted on a face-to-face meeting with me in a memorably small room; and there he let me have it, a forty-five minute broadside in which he allowed me little time to reply. He was literally spitting out his words in rage, accusing me of murdering the commission, betraying the memory of those who had died in Attica, and destroying the entire cause of prison reform.

On top of the anger of my liberal friends, there was a rumor of an impending inmate strike in Attica. Though a few changes had been made there (a little more education and vocational training and some additional staff) and more changes were coming, Attica was a big ship, and turning it around was taking too long a time. Some officers still harbored vengeful feelings toward specific inmates, as well as inmates in general, whom they saw as responsible for the beatings and deaths of their friends. The brutality and torture in the aftermath of the uprising seemed to them insufficient revenge; their friends had been murdered. They did not want to hear that the killings had been at the hands of the state troopers.

There were also conflicts within the prisoner population. Some were angry that those incarcerated leaders who controlled D yard had not taken their chance to kill or hurt any officers themselves. Some were angry at other prisoners who had allegedly informed on those seeking more blood. The beatings and torture left behind an understandably fierce hope for revenge.

So the rumor of a strike was to be taken seriously. This was the sort of situation that the commission had been created to address. There was no question that I had to go to Attica. Several legislators and representatives of the Department of Correctional Services central office also went.

No single prisoner or even a small group of prisoners was willing to represent the whole prison population. That spot was too hot for any one person to accept. Nevertheless, there was a group of sixteen to twenty incarcerated people with whom we met. They expressed their "concerns," careful not to call them *demands*. They focused on getting more education, vocational training, increased minority staff, inmate grievance committees, and conjugal visits. We treated them with respect and promised to return each day as long as the process seemed helpful.

The meetings were an eye-opener to me. My previous experience had been primarily with incarcerated people who were the most eager and positive in the whole prison population. I had never met before with such a group of prisoners, a large percentage of whom seemed to have no interest in going straight. They had long years inside ahead of them and spoke like men with nothing to lose. They were intelligent and verbally impressive, but seething with anger. We agreed to have a morning and afternoon session each day. There was no strike yet.

I was able to have individual conversations with some incarcerated people during the breaks. One handsome man named Red, with green eyes and a café au lait complexion, seemed closest to being willing to assume leadership and a little reckless in his venturesomeness. As we talked alone, in a break, I was even more impressed by the power of his presence and asked if he had any regular visitors. He did not hesitate in his reply, "No, I don't get any visitors. I'm doing twenty-five to life, and I've got five in. My visits stopped before my first year was done." He continued without hesitation, "If I could get a woman to come visit me, I would get as far with her as I could, under the table, before they dragged me away." His glittering green eyes opened a window on a cruelty that I had rarely seen before in other prisoners. I had never heard it articulated in such a burning way. In my group sessions, I had never met anyone like Red, but I met many later in my career.

I appealed for time for the commission to work and agreed to come back in six months to assess its progress. The interim plan was to move forward on their concerns, emphasizing that changes were being planned anyway. The DOCS officials did not want to seem to be yielding to inmate pressure out of concern that further strikes might be threatened to gain new concessions. The incarcerated people seemed especially impressed by the legislators who came. The legislators' presence strengthened my own promises and those of the DOCS officials since they were the ones who would have to appropriate money for the programs. Some small progress was made on actually delivering on reforms that should have been made anyway. All of us worked well together, and there was no inmate strike that time.

Confirmation hearings for my appointment were soon set by the Senate Committee on Crime and Correction. Even more than I had anticipated, they were a rerun of the matters that had so enraged the senators, especially Republican senator Ralph Marino from Long Island, one of those who had led the fight against Herman Schwartz. He was chairman of the Senate Committee on Corrections.

"Do you believe state inmates should receive minimum wages for the work that they do?" Marino asked me.

"No," I answered. "If we did that and deducted the cost of food, housing, and security, they would owe money to the state. Better to leave it as it is."

"Do you believe in inmate self-government?" he asked.

"No. I believe most inmates have a significant challenge in governing themselves. Trying to run a prison as a democracy is impossible. It would be an invitation to the population to form strong-arm parties, which would be impossible for staff to know about. Protecting rival parties would be a nightmare."

Democratic senators were not ready simply to roll over, and they questioned me about "contact visits," which would allow prisoners to embrace their family members and sit with little children on their laps. No more glass or wire mesh separations. I strongly favored such visits even though I knew that there would be contraband drugs and money introduced through the visits. But the gains in strengthened families would offset the contraband problems.

The Democratic members also asked about "conjugal visits," which would take place in trailers on the prison grounds, giving the opportunity for prisoners to live with their wives and children for a full day without supervision. I strongly favored those as well for the same reasons. Both are now routine parts of prison life.

They also gave me an opportunity to speak out in favor of inmate liaison committees to plan special events like Saint Patrick's Day, Mother's Day, and other holidays.

Racism mixed with sexual needs in Mississippi in the early 1920s. The opportunity for men in prison to meet with women was offered: visits to take place in a hut in the middle of the exercise yard. The visits were to be for a half hour and any woman was allowed to come, wife, friend or prostitute. It is amazing that it was only offered to Black prisoners! The privilege was given and withdrawn as a way of maintaining discipline. It is said that prejudice was so heavy among white men that for years they did not even request similar privileges because they did not want to seem to be "like them."

They questioned me especially on the issue of inmate grievance committees because this seemed so close to inmate self-government. I argued in favor of the IGCs as a modulated way of providing a channel for complaints. Much work had already been done in this area by the DOCS, and it was not especially radical to favor its further implementation.

There were hoots and boos from my staff and others in the hearing chamber as I expressed myself, especially concerning inmate self-government and inmate unions. This was painful to me since I still hoped we could work together.

Maybe I sounded tougher than Professor Schwartz. Maybe the senators were tired. In any case, my confirmation was unanimously approved after I was nominated by Ralph Marino.

I let it be known that we intended to take seriously our legislative mandate to monitor prisons throughout the state. Anytime there were allegations of brutality or inadequate medical care or unsanitary conditions, we would investigate, as thoroughly as staff limits permitted, and seek improvements. These old problems never went away. "Happiness is only the occasional episode in life's drama of pain" was the Thomas Hardy phrase that kept running through my mind.

When I became chairman, the sheriff of Albany County was John McNulty, a striking man with a square jaw and thick, straight black hair. He had an affable personality and had won his last election by an impressive margin. His deputy sheriffs took good care of the people of Albany—there were prompt responses to emergency calls, answers to teenage mischief, even help retrieving the occasional cat stuck in a tree—but they did not take good care of the county jail. There were fire hazards, poor food, substandard medical care, allegations of beatings that never got investigated by the sheriff, alleged financial mismanagement, and staffing so substandard that parts of the jail sometimes were left virtually unsupervised. We heard there was not even bedding on the steel bunks for some prisoners.

I started by visiting the jail myself and talking with McNulty, and it appeared that the allegations were broadly accurate. He was charming and persuasive when he said he had not given the jail the attention it needed and promised to do better. Staff went in after a week and reported absolutely no change. I asked them to write a full report and sent it to McNulty. No reply. I called and said the matter was serious. He promised to do better. Staff returned and reported no improvement, plus a few additional problems. I sent the report by a staff person marked Confidential to McNulty and the county executive and brought the matter before the full commission. I asked the other two commissioners to vote in favor of some level of censure if there were no improvements over the next thirty days. That seemed to me a minimum request. But they voted together, defeating my request, and said he should have more time—though they would not specify how much. In any case, they did not want to issue a public rebuke. I was stuck.

McNulty was running to become the next mayor of Albany. To do this, he would have to unseat the incumbent, Erastus Corning, in the Democratic primary. Corning had been mayor for a generation, dodging allegations of corruption with a patrician wave of his hand. This time he seemed perhaps to be nearing to the end of his political road.

Then came an event I still cannot explain. Someone leaked the commission report on the Albany County jail to the press, with the full list of McNulty's failings. The sheriff was furious and accused me of leaking it. I told him that I had taken special care not to make it public. The problem was not confidentiality; it was his jail. Was there anything in the report that was not true?

I then received a call from Erastus Corning, the man who was running against McNulty for mayor. Would I like to have lunch with him at the Orange Club, the fanciest in Albany? I knew the building and looked forward someday to seeing the historic interior, but told him that such a meeting, our first, had better come in the far distant future to avoid having people think that I was on Corning's side in the race. The conversation was brief.

Two days later, the Albany *Times Union* ran the story of McNulty's withdrawal from the primary race under the headline CHINLUND BAGS MCNULTY. I knew it was futile for me to try further to convince McNulty that I had only wanted to get the jail cleaned up.

I saw how the media can turn any issue into a political combat story. It was also typical of the way the commission "worked" in its official capacity, formally paralyzed by two-to-one votes against me. This was one case where progress was made in spite of that. It also made other sheriffs fearful of commission investigation.

When I met with other angry county executives and county boards and they tried to persuade me to back off from interfering with their jails, I explained that the commission standards were minimal. "How would you feel if your son or nephew were picked up drunk, taken to the county jail, and beaten by other inmates or officers; or if he failed to receive adequate medical attention; or even died in a fire because of conditions that could have been corrected?" I asked. That argument often was persuasive as conditions sometimes improved shortly afterward. But just as often, things returned to business as usual because budgets are voted annually, memories are short, and there is too little public appreciation for the problems of running a jail.

Soon after becoming chairman of the commission, I was invited to meet with the editorial board of the *New York Times*. It was a heady experience for me, a forty-two-year-old who had read the *Times* daily for thirty years, to be in the presence of people who had only been names on the masthead or op-ed page. The Olympians sat around a huge table offering elegant, intelligent, well-informed, solicitous questioning. It was disarming not to be fending off the media jackals who had interviewed me in the days before. Unlike the *New York Times*, the *Times Union* reporters had only wanted to know: Which prison was likely to blow up next?

The two hours of conversation went by rapidly, and I was pleased to get out of the meeting feeling I had answered their questions adequately. The *New York Times* editors were, it seemed to me, more than perfunctory in thanking me at the end and wishing me well. I did have a twinge of concern when a couple of them hinted that they wondered whether the lions would find me tasty. But that was only a vague shadow. I didn't yet know who the lions might be.

In the middle of the wide-ranging questions, the subject of parole had come up. I said, "Parole is functioning heroically under very tough conditions. Caseloads are too big and growing. The state has not provided commensurate funds to provide staff for parole in a way that would match the growth of the numbers of prisoners being paroled. Some offices are a shambles—too few people are doing amazing work to hold things together where twice the staff, or more, is needed."

I also said that all the talk of abolishing parole was bad for the morale of parole officers, that in fact, the idea of releasing inmates to the community *without supervision was* a terrible idea. The talk about flat sentences and getting tough on crime would mean that inmates would complete their whole sentence and be released entirely without or with only a very short time of good professional supervision.

I read the resulting article in the *New York Times* on the way to Albany in the morning and was pleased that it was accurate in every respect. It was even unexciting in a way that reflected my thinking that good criminal justice was just simply very hard work.

But on my way through the lobby of my Albany office building, my eye caught a banner headline in the Albany *Times Union*, running across the top of the front page: CHAIRMAN CALLS PAROLE A SHAMBLES. I thought, *Wow, who could be insulting parole like that?* They were referring to me! The article completely distorted my supportive remarks.

I went upstairs and called Ed Hammock, then the chairman of the Board of Parole. I explained what had happened, and he accepted my explanation and apology. But he did urge me to stay away from the Division of Parole for a while. He told me that all his staff were very upset about the Albany *Times Union* article and probably would not listen to my explanation.

Officers were not very understanding either. One day, when I signed in at the front gate of the prison at Great Meadow, one officer turned to another and said, "The enemy is here." Then he said to me, "Just sign in as the Enemy." He was only half-joking. I tried to explain that I was there as much for his protection as for the protection of prisoners. He was not persuaded.

At one point in 1976, the correction officers themselves went on strike in all the prisons for sixteen days over pay, staffing levels, and jurisdictional issues. It was at this time that I got the clumps of earth thrown at me as I crossed a field, which I described in the opening passage of this book. I was determined that the commission play a positive role, walking a fine line between siding with the strikers and siding with the DOCS central office. I tried to do so by emphasizing the role of the commission to work for safe, humane conditions inside prisons and jails. Part of that goal would be achieved by having enough staff, adequately paid, so that maximum programming, all day and all week, could be implemented. Walking the corridors with all inmates locked in during the strike, I felt we were a long way from maximum programming.

One night during the adventure, I slept on the floor in the commission offices in Albany, along with my wife and young son. Cell phones had not yet been invented, and it seemed prudent to stay near my office phone. It was an immensely stressful time, and they seemed to feel better when we were all together.

The settlement of the strike seemed favorable to the staff, but bitter feelings among officers continued for years afterward.

One of the most difficult and heart-wrenching jobs of the commission was investigating individual inmate complaints of assaults on the special housing units (the Box). It was painful because I knew that the inmates themselves were the hard cases, combative even when there was nothing to be gained. Most of them, but by no means all, were primarily interested in hurting staff either physically or getting them in trouble by reporting them. On the other hand, some who staffed the special housing units also enjoyed a physical fight and were capable of provoking one. So sorting out complaints was a challenge.

At the unit in Dannemora, we had many reports of abuse, but great trouble determining who was to blame, officers or inmates? And then, which ones in particular? I went myself, talked with staff and inmates, but got nowhere. Staff said everything was fine. Inmates were incoherent with rage—at least partly, I imagined, from past hurricanes in their lives before prison.

Finally, I decided to go and meet with a couple of the inmates one at a time in a room on the unit. I chose a name, Hernandez, at random. The officer went to bring Hernandez and soon returned with a very well-muscled, brooding man shackled hand and foot. I remember his triangular face, like Submariner Man in the old comic books.

I asked that the leg irons and shackles be removed, and the officer asked if I was sure I wanted that. He told me this was a very violent inmate and finally asked if I would take full responsibility for being left alone. I said I would, so he called for two other officers, who removed the irons. Hernandez stretched, and I reached my hand across the table to introduce myself. For a long time, he looked at my hand, then looked in my eyes and finally, slowly reached out his hand to take mine.

We sat down and had a long conversation, haltingly, because my Spanish was then intermediate and he had no English. He seemed like one led into the sun after being a long time in a cave. He blinked partly from incomprehension and partly from the surreal quality of the meeting with me. He spoke of past and present assaults in a way that was impossible for me to sort out into a coherent narrative. He twisted and turned with a restlessness I had not experienced before, like a coiled spring that could be easily released. When we concluded our conversation, he shook my hand and walked backward out of the room. I asked the officers to let me sit there a while alone.

It was a foolish thing for me to have done. He could easily have been a person unable to cross the line of trust. There are some people who have been so brutalized by life that their humanity is buried, almost unreachable, under a mountain of rage. I believe the mountain can be moved for many not organically damaged. But it would take thousands of hours of conversations with the same patient people.

My conversation with Hernandez solved nothing for me. However, the attitude of the officers running the special housing unit (SHU) let me know that there was something wrong. We continued to investigate and ultimately persuaded the DOCS to install a videotape, which ran on a one-week cycle. Whenever there was trouble, the video was to be preserved. The officers were furious, and in the early days, it "malfunctioned" often. Then they began to get used to it, and the sergeant in charge retired. Twenty-five years later, in 2003, I returned to the unit to visit those confined to death row and was surprised to find the video still there—and still working. When I asked about it, the sergeant in command smiled and said, "Oh yes. We not only use it, we're adding more cameras and updating this one. It's our best friend in court."

When I asked if things had changed from twenty-five years ago, he said, "Completely. Back then, we went to the stick. Now I go to the pen." That was his way of saying that inmates had been beaten in the past with batons (nightsticks) by himself and other officers, but that now, he writes them up, and they eventually go to an even heavier level of security, locked in for twenty-three hours. I realize that "the pen" can be very cruel also and have no doubt that it has been abused, but there does seem to be an improvement. Bureaucratic brutality is not as satisfying to a troubled heart as physical violence.

I remember back then watching a tape of an incident between an officer and an inmate, each of whom felt justified by the video evidence. The officer had taken the inmate's arm and had seen this action as "barely touching him." The inmate experienced it as an assault. The truth probably lay somewhere in between. No one likes feeling pushed around, but many inmates are especially phobic to touch and fly into a rage if someone even bumps them accidentally or even puts a hand on their shoulder, On the other hand, officers feel a need to assert their authority and think they should be able to touch inmates with impunity. What I saw was the unnecessary touch by the officer and the unnecessary assault by the prisoner in response. The officer was cautioned not to touch an inmate who was already moving in the right direction, and the inmate was written up for an unprovoked assault.

The special housing unit is surely a tough place to do time, even today. I believe the commission made it a little better because we were watching and because of our investigations. One sergeant was forced to retire after our investigation of repeated assaults on inmates. That was a specific help, and the reverberations were useful.

We worked at it, but excessive use of force will always be a problem in any prison. The borderline between too little and too much is crossed and recrossed daily.

One of my opportunities as chairman of the commission was to visit prisons in other states, as well as some of the federal prisons. There, I meditated on the meaning of silence. I visited institutions in fourteen other states and was impressed that they were sometimes doing better at prerelease and other medium-security work than we were. But in maximum-security, I found the silence sometimes to be devastating; they had gone too far.

For example, in 1978, I visited Columbia, South Carolina, to see a prison that had been built in 1850 (now mercifully demolished). There were five tiers, and I went to the top one. The catwalk bounced like the end of a diving board. The plumbing was dysfunctional, the lighting dim. The cells were seven feet by five feet with a ceiling just six feet high—and there were *two inmates* in each one. Yet with over a thousand inmates housed around a central courtyard, it was mostly silent. The whole space was managed at night by just two officers.

I met one officer who had worked the night shift—a quiet, intelligent, sad African American. He said he continued in his job because he needed it to support his wife and children. He showed me their pictures proudly and told me he was glad to be on the day shift now because he could be with his family in the evenings. And he said the night silence was especially awful. He just waited for the screams—from nightmares, from rapes, from "regular assaults," and from people just letting off tension. He said he felt like screaming himself. I asked what he did if he heard someone scream. He paused, then said softly, with pain, "They don't scream long." The silence of the night was filled with pain.

The event made me think about the issue of rape in prison. When I started visiting inside in 1963, there is no question that it was a problem. Sometimes with the collusion of staff, sometimes taking advantage of a dark place in the halls; it was a piece of prison life. Perhaps it was not as serious as in some other states, but it was there. Then over the years, it seemed to me to be disappearing as a cause of concern. So I started, in about 1992, privately asking people in reentry whether they saw it as a problem. They had nothing to be gained by telling me anything but the truth as they experienced it. Long-term formerly incarcerated people said that it had been a serious matter in the beginning of their time in prison (1970s and 1980s), but that in recent years, it was virtually nonexistent. That is a tribute to the vigilance of staff and improvement of programs. Rape can be stopped as a part of prison life. The federal legislation being considered as this book is written is much needed; it can be solved. A prison sentence should not and need not include the punishment of rape.

I also visited an exemplary minimum-security prison in Iowa, under the direction of Bernie Vogelgesang. They were doing a good job of helping with jobs and housing—way ahead of New York State.

While there, I went to the central office and asked to visit a maximum-security prison. I got as far as the deputy commissioner—a serious, concerned African American. He was evasive until he satisfied himself that I was not there to do an exposé. Then he said, "There is no need for you to go. It's a terrible place. We have several homicides every year. The place is understaffed. There is a 40 percent annual turnover of officer staff. It's a complete disaster." I did not visit.

When I went to California, I got to San Quentin, where an officer had just been killed by an unidentified prisoner. The word was that he looked like another officer who was hated by the inmates. So inmates were all locked in, going in continuous relays of fifty to the mess halls. Most had TV in their cells (unlike in New York State), but on normal days, there were no officers on the flats, mingling with prisoners as in New York. Instead, they tried to maintain safety with rifles from a catwalk inaccessible to inmates.

Staff told me of a recent murder: members of a gang had surrounded a stray member of another gang. An officer on the catwalk fired warning shots with rubber bullets, but the gang closed in and stabbed the stray. When the central office prosecuted the gang members, the case was thrown out because the officer had no corroborating witnesses!

I was discovering that prisons *can* be as bad as they are portrayed in the movies. The cap on my education came at the California prison at Chino, where they had a unit for gay and transvestite prisoners. The warden walked me through with several officers, but the murmurs of approval of my appearance made me feel like raw meat. There were prisoners with heavy makeup; loud, foul mouths; and huge breasts spilling out of brassieres. The warden let me know they were not only exotic, but also vicious; it would have been unsafe for me to be alone with them. There was no silence in Chino.

On the long trip home, I lived with my own silence and a new appreciation of the New York system. At that time, there were still individual cells for almost all maximum-security inmates. Walking down a corridor by day or by night when prisoners were all locked in was an experience of mostly silence. They sometimes called out to me, and that broke the silence. There certainly were some blocks that were noisy with arguments, ranting, or just wordless screams; but they were the exception—nothing like I saw at that time in California.

It all made me feel even more appreciative of the quiet and peace in my own home. Sometimes I was struck, even to tears, by seeing my gentle wife and my little vulnerable son James that they could be living on the same planet with the hard world of prisons.

Things were still tough in New York. Benjamin Ward was the commissioner of the Department of Correctional Services. He had the responsibility of actually running the prisons. I was only the watchdog, chairman of the Commission of Correction. He was no fan of mine. Appointed by Governor Carey in March 1975, Ward was the first African American commissioner of prisons. He had a police background, having risen through the ranks in New York City. He was opposed to the very existence of the commission; he did not want anyone policing him! He was a big bear of a man, brilliant, a fierce leader, asthmatic (like me), with a huge temper. He was also committed to changing the prisons, especially to recruiting more African American staff; he just did not want anyone telling him how to do it.

I quite unintentionally increased his wrath when I secretly, and foolishly, scheduled a middle-of-the-night visit to Great Meadow prison. I went without even telling my own staff. I was interested in inspecting the infirmary, about which we had received rumors of incompetence and unnecessarily painful treatment. To make matters worse, I took with me Fred Dicker, then a reporter for the Albany *Times Union*. I naively hoped that this legitimate involvement of a member of the press might improve my relationships with media people.

I presented myself with proper identification at 3:00 AM. The gate officer was flabbergasted; fear and anger crossed his face. He called his superior officers for guidance and was told I had to be admitted. As I moved deeper into the prison, passing through one electronically controlled gate after another, I could hear the phones ringing ahead of me. I wondered if people were being told to let me through or warned that I was coming so that they would be awake.

When we got to the infirmary, the nervous staff was ready to show me around. We talked about the work; they answered specific questions about the care. They wanted to accompany me as we moved to visit with the prisoners, but accepted my request to let us interview the prisoners alone. The whole process revealed that the infirmary was actually functioning fairly well. The inmate complaints seemed to be much like those about any hospital on the outside.

By the time I returned to Albany, it was time to go to the office. I called Commissioner Ward and left a message, informing him of what I had done and how good Great Meadow seemed to be, a positive report.

The story hit the papers that afternoon and basically said that I was doing my job by visiting as I did and that the prison system was also doing its job by providing minimally adequate medical care. It was favorable to both the commission and the prison system.

Commissioner Ward was furious. He called me in a rage and denounced my actions in such a nonstop torrent that I could not successfully call his attention to the positive nature of the story. That exacerbated the turbulence of our relationship.

The strain later became public over an issue often misunderstood by the public: prison construction. Before 1978, the system had grown at the net rate of about one thousand prisoners per year for ten years; then it jumped to two thousand a year. Even with new construction, the system was now about 10 percent over capacity, and further overcrowding would increase the dangers of violence.

In January 1978, I asked to see the budget proposal for the state prisons for the new fiscal year. Commissioner Ward refused. I insisted. We went back and forth until Governor Carey released it to the public as part of the budget for the whole state. There was virtually no money allocated for prison construction. Commissioner Ward would not take my calls, and finally, I went public with my concern.

I was quoted in the press the next day. "'Prisons are ten percent overcrowded,' says chairman of Commission." I was at a cabinet meeting with Governor Carey when an aide handed him my quote. He stared at me down the long table, a severe look in his eye. "Chinlund, did you say this?"

"Yes, Governor, I did."

"Is it true?"

"Yes, Governor, it is."

Later in the day, the governor's aide came to see me to explain that the state could be sued because of *my* having made the overcrowding statement. I explained that I realized the problem, but that it was my job to tell the truth, and the governor would best be served by my doing that. It hurt to say that, but that was the problem: no one wanted to draw the line because it was an expensive, unpopular truth. If you pass the tough laws, you have to build and staff more prisons.

It was true also that I advocated construction of new prisons to relieve overcrowding—a controversial position. Then as now, the public was inclined to shrug off overcrowding reports. People would grouse, "I'm overcrowded in my own home! Why shouldn't those guys be overcrowded too?" On the other hand, many legislators wanted to look tough to their constituents and advocate more prisons. And for upstate legislators, new prisons delivered jobs in construction and staffing. As the years passed, legislators competed to win contracts for the building of new prisons in their jurisdictions.

My liberal friends saw this position as my greatest failing. They wanted me to use the authority of my office not only to block the creation of more prisons, but also to close some of the existing ones. I agreed with them that we should *send* fewer people to prison and that we should *release* more people from prison. We should do more to create a society in which fewer crimes are committed, and we should pass laws in which there are more appropriate alternatives to prison for those who are convicted of certain crimes. My critics closed their ears when I tried to explain that simply closing one prison or seeking to block funds for new prisons would be useless or worse unless the laws and court/parole practices changed. We had to have fewer going in or more coming out before we had fewer prisons. It was for all these reasons that I ultimately stated publicly that I believed the absence of capital funding for new prisons in the 1979 budget was a mistake.

Again, Ward was in a rage. He telephoned, saying that his capital budget was not the business of the commission and that I was a meddlesome nuisance adding to his already-considerable burdens. He justified his zero-growth plan by saying that the baby boom had passed and that there were many fewer people growing into the age group that committed crimes. I replied that I thought the numbers of those committing crimes did not seem to be diminishing even though the overall population figures were going down. By that I meant that the numbers of people with poor education, poor work histories, and families involved heavily with drugs were not dropping by any apparent measure.

His anger not assuaged, Ward called a press conference and denounced me as "an incompetent racist." He had assumed I was referring to African Americans when I described the group committing crimes. Governor Carey refused to take sides; he said it was "a useful, interesting debate." The Albany papers ran a cartoon of Ward and me shooting at each other over the head of Carey in a foxhole, who was saying, "This is the way the system is supposed to work." When I declined to reply further, having said what I felt I needed to say, there was another cartoon of me in a prison cell with Ward making me eat my words from a bowl handed to me between the bars.

My hopes for working with the Department of Correctional Services to institute serious prison reform seemed very unlikely to be fulfilled. I was miserable.

It is no comfort to me that I was more accurate in my prison population predictions than I had imagined. In fact, the system grew by more than 2,000 per year—from 21,000 in 1978 to 72,000 in 2000. That is the equivalent of adding one maximum-security prison per year. The number of prisoners has been since reduced to 62,000 in 2009. Six prisons have been closed. More prisons are scheduled for closing in late 2009.

Chapter Nine

Network Communities at Last

I had been working for a while at the commission when I shared with my quiet, astute deputy, Jim Ryan, a wish that I had kept postponing: my desire to carry forward my old group work with inmates. He encouraged me to proceed in spite of the indifference and antagonism then prevalent in the system. Furthermore, he thought Cherie Clark, our director of training, shared my determination to go a step beyond the commission's mandate and help create positive communities inside state prisons.

Cherie had designed, managed, and sometimes taught classes herself at the training academy for deputy sheriffs of the county jails—a scene heavily charged with antagonism. Among other things, she intervened to stop trainers from teaching trainees off-color lyrics that were chanted during marching drills, and she added real substance to the classes on prison philosophy and practice. She humanized the whole process so that officers were trained to elicit cooperation from inmates by coming to a mutual agreement with them—not by brute force. She was a no-nonsense person who realized that physical intervention was sometimes inevitable, but she always worked for negotiated agreement.

Jim Ryan arranged a lunch for me, Cherie, and himself on April Fools' Day 1977. We got right into it and found ourselves discussing a plan for starting "monasteries" and "ashrams" inside prison.

I told Cherie and Jim of my own love for the cloisters of monasteries and the freedom that seemed to flow from the discipline there. If the monks could be free within the confines of the cloistered life, why could not inmates be free within the walls of prison? We knew only a small number of staff (especially superintendents) who might be interested, but that small number could have a significant impact on the life of the rest of the institution and the system as a whole. Some prisons even had gothic motifs in the archways and courtyards that had stressed the transformational hopes of the system at the turn of the last century even though it coexisted with its own gruesome brutality. There is even a complete cloister at the center of Woodbourne prison! There were times when I wanted to spend a month or two inside, as a "prisoner," to try to pull the idea into reality.

We dreamed of creating separate Protestant and Catholic monasteries, a Jewish kibbutz, a Hindu ashram, a Muslim mosque, and a Buddhist monastery. Buddhism had become popular at this time, partly due to Zen literature like D. T. Suzuki's *Manual of Zen Buddhism* and various books by Alan Watts, such as *The Way of Zen* and *The Spirit of Zen*. It was a discipline particularly well suited to prison life. Having experienced the vitality of the Protestant/Catholic monastery at Taizé, I believed that it should be possible to launch a prison parallel to that. I imagined prisoners singing regular Protestant hymns (as they already did in the regular services) as well as Taizé music. The Catholics might learn to do Gregorian chant, with ample time to bring their singing to perfection. The Buddhists would learn the chants of Tibet; the Jews would be trained as cantors, rattling the walls with the deep notes. The Koran, itself believed to be the incarnation of Allah, could be chanted as it is from the minarets. We were really dreaming big-time.

Obviously, the first step was to meet with Commissioner Ward, but we quickly agreed that there was no way that I personally could do that. However, Cherie had become a friend of William Gard, deputy commissioner for Security. Bill Gard had come up through the ranks, was widely respected by the line staff, knew the problems, and could be relied upon to block any foolish new ideas. If Gard approved of a plan, it would stand an excellent chance of being implemented.

Cherie had already conferred extensively with Bill Gard about training issues, and they saw eye to eye on the need to improve all levels of classes at the training academy. So when she came to him to discuss a new idea, he gave her maximum attention. He was an ascetic-looking thin man with a close-cropped head of white hair who spoke quietly and with great authority. He *looked* like the prior of a monastery!

Cherie discussed the plan with him, and to our surprise, Gard was immediately attracted to it. He saw it as a way to restore officers to their old role (as he thought) of counselors, in the days before counselors went on payroll as separate staff. But the idea hit a roadblock when it came to the Muslims. There was no problem with the faith of Islam, as such. Bill Gard was familiar with the positive force the Sunni Muslims had been in the prisons over the years. They preached pride, peace, and a commitment to self-improvement. Most dramatically, they had played a heroic role in the light of the flickering torches of D yard in Attica, before the tragedy. There were prisoners in that yard who wanted to kill the hostages one at a time until their demands were met. The Muslims were the majority group that persuaded the others not to kill anyone. They were ready to die to protect the lives of innocent people, a role that they believed to be an injunction of the Koran. Their positive leadership has never been properly appreciated by the general public. They reminded the others that the very word *Islam* means "peace," and that only Allah has a time for every person to die. The more literal meaning of *Islam* is "yielding" or "surrender," as in giving oneself utterly to God.

But some other Muslims were different. After the slaughter of prisoners and hostages by the New York state troopers at Attica and the brutality indiscriminately shown to all surviving inmates, some Shiite Muslims preached, with understandable persuasiveness, a message of hatred and vengeance. To Bill Gard, the thought of this sect gathering every day, all day, was explosively unwise.

This was only the most dramatic example of the divisions within every faith group. And it was one of the reasons the faith-based part of our plan never even was proposed. It quickly became evident that it would not be possible to create faith communities inside, because each faith has groups within itself that create, or seem to create, separations from others. Whether it is the saved and the damned or God's Chosen People or contrasts between "the faithful" and "the infidels," faith communities almost seem doomed to be divisive. The joy of being "us" and feeling strong in our solidarity becomes distorted into condemnation of "them."

We wanted above all that the inmate members see themselves as peacemakers, individuals who would be recognized by all prisoners as large-minded people who could help inmates get along better with each other and get along with staff, as much as possible, regardless of their faith commitments. Or better, that their faith commitments would inspire them to be radically open to respect every human being regardless of faith allegiance.

It was hard for me to leave behind my monastic ideal. The vision of prisoners praying and singing together still seems possible. However, the nature of faith communities on the outside probably must change before such a vision can be implemented inside. For example, simply saying "Jesus Christ" can irritate or infuriate people who have been abused by fundamentalist zealots. The same is true of the Sunni/Shiite split in the Muslim community and (though less so all the time) the Protestant/Catholic divisions. Religion often continues to be more of a wall than a bridge.

When I was recruited, years later, by Chuck Colson's group (it has had several names), I said I would help if they would abandon their commitment to the dualistic theology of the saved and the damned. I explained the potential for violence when a person claiming to be Christian tells another person that he or she is "going to hell" because they have not accepted Jesus in a way that the Christian approves. It is a way of thinking that is the opposite of the ideals of the Network Community.

I still wish there could have been a way to implement the monastic ideal. However, many conditions are needed to create a monastic community: superhuman commitment by the participants; a prior of surpassing gifts as the leader, administrator, bookkeeper, confessor, and peacemaker; an economy that supports such a community; an accepted rule (like the Benedictine Rule) that has been proven and gives the new community momentum. None of these existed in prison.

So we shifted the plan. We named it the Network Community and adopted the Network forms of meeting. It had no specific faith reference, though the spirituality of the basic idea came shining through. Such a community could be initiated in every prison, one by one, starting in maximum-security. Participating inmates would live on their own units. They would be people of any faith or no faith, encouraged to share informal mentoring in math, English, Spanish, philosophy, law, history, or any other subject they knew something about. They were expected to encourage and challenge each other to be better people. They would go to regular programs and have regular work assignments with the rest of the prisoners.

Gard accomplished all this by calling Network a "security program" to be staffed by the officers. That was a startling oxymoron in the minds of staff. Program and Security normally fought with each other: program people wanted officers to deliver inmates to "their" programs while officers wanted minimum movement, minimum paperwork, and minimum opportunities for trouble. Network aspired to break this tension by having the new units be run by officers who were committed to making Network beneficial to the life of the whole prison. Bill Gard himself took pride in having "helped inmates onto the right path," as he put it (though one cannot help but wonder how the prisoners would tell the story). Whatever the truth, it did seem possible that back then, when there seemed to be more respect for authority, there might well be a significant minority of inmates who responded to an officer who counseled them like a good Dutch uncle. Now that seemed quite unlikely; we needed to create a community in which the prisoners largely helped each other. Gard persuaded Commissioner Ward to make a commitment to explore the idea with a handful of superintendents.

Cherie again played a crucial role in persuading Professor Hans Toch of the State University in Albany to work with us to organize a conference with the subject "Therapeutic Community Inside Prison." Because of his stature, we drew together luminaries from all over the world to Albany to meet and talk about the dream. Maxwell Jones, psychiatrist and pioneer of mental health treatment, was the keynote speaker. It was a success and added momentum to the dream.

In the spring of 1978, one of the first prisons we decided to visit was Clinton, with 2,400 prisoners. At the time, it was the biggest in the system. It had a reputation for being tough and racist, but at least it was clear and predictable. Many inmates preferred it to other prisons because they knew where they stood. Once you knew the routine, you could usually stay out of trouble.

The superintendent, a strong chunky man named Gene LeFevre, had actually been one of the three commissioners on the original Commission of Correction with Herman Schwartz, but had resigned to get back home to the North Country. He also was said to be too far, philosophically, from Schwartz. But I had always known him to be a fair, steady, thoughtful person. He remembered Cherie favorably from his commission days and welcomed us both to visit.

To house our "security program," I asked to see the worst housing units in the prison. Our idea was that we preferred the smallest cells with the poorest ventilation, plumbing, and everything else so that prisoners would be unlikely to apply for entry into the Network Community with the sole purpose of improving their housing. We wanted them to apply only so that they could learn to live better lives. In the months that followed, we softened that policy somewhat, but it was helpful to have started that way.

After some discussion in the superintendent's office, the three of us—Cherie, LeFevre and I—went to look at the space. The prison is on a steep hill, requiring everyone to go up and down the stairs all the time. We went through corridors and up stairs and finally encountered a whole company of inmates. They were then still required to be silent in the halls at all times in that prison, and they were absolutely quiet as we walked past. The space indeed had the smallest cells, had not been recently painted, and suffered, more than other units, from cold in winter and heat in summer. But Clinton, unfortunately, was not one of the first three prisons chosen. It was just too far from Albany for us to be able to nurture the program. However, it was added later and became one of only three prisons to survive the big shutdown, which came ten years later for budgetary reasons.

The three chosen were Bedford Hills (maximum-security), Mid-Orange (medium-security), and Hudson (also medium-security) partly because of the receptivity of the individual superintendents. I wanted to start the Network units in three places at once because if even one was successful, the other two would feel more compelled to make it work. If we started only one and it failed, critics could easily say the program itself just did not work. Cherie set in motion the first of the training Network sessions, which were to be the cornerstone of her fine later career, still flourishing at the time of this writing.

With Cherie as the trainer and Gard as the key opening access to the system, Network was launched in 1979.

There was a heavy tide of antagonism against the program. One officer who volunteered to work with the Network program found a diaper and a baby bottle taped to his locker with a note, "For your sweet inmates." Others were more directly confrontational; fellow officers questioned the manhood of the volunteers, called them traitors.

What was so threatening about the Network program? Beyond change to a system with longtime rules about how things were to be done, it may have been the premise that all participants were equal as human beings—even officers.

We were clearly expecting virtually all prisoners to be released eventually, but from the beginning, I wanted Network to be powerfully useful to those who still had many years, or even life, inside ahead of them. I hoped that they would bring stability to the groups. What needed to be done? The list was similar to those I had made for other programs.

For one thing, it cannot be overemphasized that prisoners feel they are "not worth bothering about," and until that changes, little else of a transformational nature can occur. Even small achievements lead to a higher sense of self, which in turn leads to more commitment, then to another achievement, as in growth from child to adult.

A prisoner must believe deep inside that he or she is defined by the present and the future, not simply by past criminal behavior. That is a mammoth challenge.

And in order to succeed on the outside, prisoners must begin immediately to think about jobs, housing, new friends, and reconnecting with family, rather than waiting until the end of their sentence. They also need to think about the nature of process (instead of thinking only in quick fix terms): reexamining their faith, continuing their education, finding new hobbies, and facing the reality of the crimes they committed.

The early start-up experience was positive. Some of the best officers volunteered. The best incarcerated people wanted to join up. The whole world of the Department of Correctional Services was watching, and many hoped for success. Some officers liked the idea of working on a single unit, instead of moving around the institution as they normally did. Many incarcerated people wanted to flee the unpredictable violence of life on a regular prison unit. They wanted a gang, but a positive, nonviolent one.

From the beginning, 5 percent or 10 percent of the population at Bedford, Hudson, and Mid-Orange were positive about the idea, so there was no problem filling units of fifty to seventy-five almost instantly. Inmates were happy to have a setting in which they could "learn to be square." And since they had their own units, no longer did they have to worry about instantly mixing back in with the hardened general population, as in the early days of the Network meetings.

The comparison with monasteries in the Middle Ages seems clear. A man coming home from his fields to find his wife raped and dead, his children gone or killed, and the house looted and burned down was a man who might well turn to the monastery as a place relatively safe and sane, attractive as a refuge from the violence of outside life. The scenario happened countless times.

For those living in our inner cities, the ravages of street life make even this extreme comparison legitimate. Life seems so hard, especially on release: no money, no job or even a work record, a poor education, weak family ties, often not even a place to live. So the prison/monastery begins to look good to some when compared to the streets. Similarly, anxious prisoners who find life in the general prison population chaotic and frightening are attracted to volunteer to be on a Network unit in order to have a safer and more-orderly life.

Training the incarcerated people to be leaders of their peers was a crucial part of Network success. The structure of leadership was derived from the classic therapeutic communities on the outside. Daytop and Phoenix House were the two strongest. I visited both and learned from them. They expected ex-addicts to be firmly in control of each piece of the program. Though I found them to be somewhat rigid, I respected greatly the transformational power of their work.

Inclined to be too harsh on other prisoners, inmate leaders needed to learn to be encouraging and balanced. Network administrators (usually former officers) trained the inmate leaders. However, prisoners were expected, under supervision, to take full responsibility for the program itself, recruiting new members, screening for admission, calling and running the meetings, supporting each other and challenging each other, encouraging studying and reading, monitoring for cleanliness, and keeping the unit reasonably quiet.

It was because of good peer leadership that Network units quickly became the cleanest and most peaceful in the prison. At the same time, officers continued to take ultimate responsibility. They had the authority even to close the unit and start the program with a new group if a negative culture became too strong inside the unit. That has happened only once, but the option was always explicitly there.

Reflecting the ideals of the monastery, we wanted to make it possible for inmates to leave the program or to be asked to leave with a minimum of ceremony or disruption. This was not a simple request. They would have to be moved to another cell on another unit; in a system where every cell is taken, that is a major challenge. We wanted to be able, honestly, to say, "No one flunks Network." Someone could leave "because he needed more time and experience to be ready for the challenges of the program."

It worked out just as we had hoped. Prisoners sometimes left and then returned to the Network unit, weeks or months later, often to be particularly positive community members. In fact, one reason some individuals chose to leave was because they needed to return to their old scene to be sure they really wanted to "square up." Sometimes, though, they were so disruptive the community as a whole requested that they go, with encouragement to return as soon as they could settle down.

The original way of structuring the Network housing units held up well over the first years: two officers were assigned in a typical cell block floor. One was secure inside a mini-command post (often called the bubble) from which he/she could telephone for help from the rest of the prison and, in a maximum-security prison, control the individual electronic gates on the cells. The other was the "roving officer," the person who talked more with inmates, checked cells, checked the showers and, in general, kept track of the unit's mood. The roving officer monitored the group meetings.

New Network units were started in one prison after another, between four and six added each year. At the peak of the Network activity, in 1983, there were twenty-six prisons with Network units. Even when Network was "closed down" due to the budget crisis, two prisons continued, with some of the best staff in the system remaining as Network officers rather than go on to other jobs because they felt that they were really doing something valuable. All their gifts as people and their skills as professionals were called into service to maintain a high level of life in the communities.

The Network meetings every day brought—and still bring—the small revelations that are the threads that make the fabric of a life. Here are some of the things inmates said in the group meetings:

"I realize that I had actually bawled out my woman for buying me the wrong sneakers! I apologized and thanked her for staying by me."

"My son wrote back saying he was glad to hear from me. Up until then, I had felt so guilty that I went years without writing him. Now I'm going to write him every week."

"I always thought I was stupid. Now I'm in prison, and I have nothing to do but read, so I've been studying and getting good grades. I'm learning! It's amazing."

"When I told Tony I was sorry for putting him down, I thought he would lose respect for me. Now I feel more like a man, to be able to say I am sorry. I've done a lot of bad stuff I need to say I am sorry about."

"My mother broke down when she visited last time. I wrote her thanking her for sticking with me through all my craziness. She said I never in my whole life had thanked her before. I felt great."

"I helped John pass his math test. He thought he should give me something in return. I told him no, just do the same for somebody else someday."

These phrases might sound too good to be true. But for these inmates, they were real and constituted significant personal achievements. Our dream had come true. The Network units, at their best, really did seem to be a little bit like monastic communities within the prisons. It was not just that they were spotlessly clean as with a well-run monastery. The cleanliness was a sign of devotion to the life of the unit. Like Benedictines washing the dishes to the glory of God (as Benedict commands in rule 81 of the Benedictine Rule), Network inmates mostly seemed glad to take their turns at cleaning.

And their study took place throughout the day, as in a monastery where it is expected that the monks will study as part of every day along with prayer and work. The prisoners were encouraged to read anything they could find, just to improve their vocabularies, their speed of reading, and their store of information.

Prayer was never a formal part of the program, but in some individual units, it was stronger than in others. There was almost never a spoken prayer in the whole group. But especially in the Fishkill unit, under the inspired leadership of a local minister named Ron Perry, there was a strong open sense of the presence of a higher power. Ron was an active Christian minister of a church in Beacon and found the church and Network to be a complementary ministry. Men and women often referred to *praying* when they described how they dealt with a belligerent officer or fellow inmate or how they maintained their positive attitude.

The Network units were also like monasteries in that small irritations took on large proportions. In a monastery, one might hear, "I can't stand it when Brother Ambrose picks his nose" or "Brother Timothy needs to bathe more often." The Network equivalents were more like "Who always leaves his towel on the shower floor?" and "Who is the one who misses the butt can with his cigarette?" (back when smoking was allowed in prison—it is not anymore). Such gripes were luxuries in an environment where issues previously had been true life-or-death matters.

Most of all, the Network units became like monasteries in the sense that they had an ordered direction. The prisoners felt that they were going somewhere. Even though, to outsiders, they may have seemed only to be going in circles, as with the walk around the cloister ambulatory, their lives were in fact often more purposeful than the rat race of outside society.

The most important part of the success of Network was the training directed by Cherie Clark. Starting as one-week long, it grew to two and finally five weeks and was as intense as it was long. The participants were all officers who volunteered for it. They were divided into teams and stayed at the training site except for weekends. They came to know each other in unprecedented depth in order to be prepared for the demanding nature of the work. Racism, macho problems, difficulties with authorities, substance abuse—all went under the lights for review. At graduations, people were weeping. Wives said things like "Thank you all for giving me a brand-new, wonderful husband!" Even today, staff will go out of their way to talk with me about how much they still appreciate those wonderful, life-giving training weeks.

In 1981, Network was introduced as part of the state's new Shock Camps. The Shock Camp program offered a young person convicted of a nonviolent crime a shortened sentence if he or she agreed to participate in a rigorous physical, mental, and emotional discipline, much like a military boot camp. Cherie Clark was central to the initial planning, training, and ongoing life of the camps. They emphasized calisthenics, drills, and long runs at dawn over the hills. The Network meetings became the heart of the camps, which are still operating with success today.

The camps were organized into cabins, established according to the month of the person's arrival (first-month platoon, second-month platoon, etc.). A group stayed together until they were paroled together after the sixth month. If anyone failed to be an active program member, they would be sent to a regular prison where they would not be eligible for parole until the end of their regular minimum sentence, usually a total of three years.

The Network meetings in the Shock Camps were even more intense than the ones in regular prison. Though the groups were together only six months, they always kept the same members as the days went on. This was unlike prison, where people were released when their individual dates came up. In Shock Camp, the group bond and commitment was life-giving.

I visited one five-month dorm at a moment of great tension. The men had come through almost five months of tough life together. The physical rigors were more than matched by the emotional challenges of the group meetings. They were about to start the regular platoon meeting. Everyone stood at rigid parade rest. The group leader, choking back tears, said, "Before we start the regular meeting, I just want you guys to be able to say anything you want about Joe being sent back [to regular prison] this morning."

Silence except for some snuffling. The specks of dust drifted in shafts of afternoon sun.

"I tried talking with Joe last week. He was a wreck. I tried . . ."

"Joe could've done it if he had just let us help him more."

Then finally, "Joe is never gonna make it without us." Many were openly crying. It was several minutes before the regular meeting began, and the power of the removal of Joe continued to be expressed.

But even for those who made it through the six months, the transition process to life back in the community was overwhelmingly difficult. Now I felt surer than ever that a released individual who had gained personally from participating in the Network meetings, feeling comfortable with those forms and rituals, would be reassured to continue in the same forms of meeting after being returned home.

At a transition meeting at Calvary Church in Manhattan, I met one ex-Shock Camp inmate named Danny, who said, "It all seems like a dream. Even though I was only released eight months ago, I wonder if all that good stuff really happened. I'm sleeping on the floor again at my uncle's place. I mean, I'm grateful to him. There's a carpet on the floor, and I sleep on my stuff. The heat is good, so I am especially glad to have a place when it's cold. But he's still using drugs and selling drugs, and that's really tough." Danny could not save enough money to pay a month's rent and a month's security for his own place.

Formerly incarcerated people like Danny need not just a job and a place to live, but they also need new friends and, most of all, a reliable place to go to meet with people they trusted. That meant other people like themselves who were following a *process*, in a form of meeting they had learned to trust.

For these reasons, I had tried hard over the years to establish connections with the Division of Parole, with which I had been struggling all the way back to the 1960s. Commissioner Russell Oswald had made efforts in the 1960s to professionalize the supervision system as a service to the individuals on parole rather than its being only an extension of police supervision. Back then, it had been common practice for individuals on parole to report to their parole officers, show their pay stubs, and leave. They were typically questioned in a hostile, suspicious way by men who were sure that they were all committing new crimes. Oswald wanted the parole officers to turn the discussion to problem areas in the life of the released person and encourage them, in a professional way, to drop old destructive friendships, even old or new lovers, who were leading them back to a life of crime. Officers were now expected to help the formerly incarcerated people find jobs and places to live. This constituted a revolution in previous practice.

I wanted to make a small change in the system: to require that people released from Shock Camps, called AfterShockers, attend Network meetings on the outside. It was only after some conspicuous failures by people who had completed the regimen of the Shock Camps, who had seemed certain to succeed, in the first groups being released, that the authorities finally agreed. Some legislators and others were moved to tears when they met inmates at Shock Camp graduations and heard them describe their struggles. They knew the graduates were sincerely committed to a new life. When some of them failed and came back to regular prison, the authorities knew it was not because there was something seriously wrong with the camps. Something was missing in the *transition*.

So the state started a program called AfterShock, to be administered by the New York State Division of Parole. We applied for and were awarded a contract with the Division of Parole. Network had arrived on the outside.

In 1979, three years into my term as chairman of the Commission of Correction, there was a hostage-taking event, this time in Coxsackie, a prison near Albany. Eight staff members were being held by about a hundred prisoners in one cell block. They were barricaded in. The coup had taken place in the late afternoon, and all the key department brass came into the prison that night. That was done so that the inmates would not know who was there. The department would then be able to escalate slowly the level of administrative involvement as part of the negotiating process. Similarly, I went in then so that the prison officials could "play the commission card" if they felt that was useful.

We were all together in the office of the prison superintendent, Jack Czarnetski, and he went back and forth between us and the inmates as the negotiations proceeded. Some of the most out-of-control inmates were centrally involved, so the situation was tense. The strategy group was divided on the question of whether or not time was on our side. Some were fearful that one or two inmates could just lose it and "get revenge for Attica." We spent the night stretched out on Czarnetski's office floor. We were tired, anxious, and edgy.

Finally, almost twenty-four hours into the wait, Czarnetski came back from a meeting with the inmates and happily reported that eighty of the one hundred prisoners wanted to quit and had asked to be let out. The department officials were also happy and prepared to give the order to release the eighty.

I asked them to sit a moment and consider something: that the most positive inmates would leave, putting the process in the hands of the most negative twenty prisoners. That would change everything. Would it not be better to say that no one would be let out until they were all willing to come out? They agreed. Just twenty minutes later, the prisoners all asked to be released. The hostages came out unharmed.

The resolution came about in the same way that a Network meeting works: the positive energy of both groups, ours and the inmates', was given the opportunity to dominate. In my time on the commission, these high-pressure situations were unusual; one rarely witnessed miracles, but the results were favorable when the best came from everyone.

Progress was agonizingly slow. It seemed more obvious than ever that everyone would be served by better prison programs and improved parole supervision. That would lead to fewer crimes and fewer people in prison. Money saved. More safety. But it was almost impossible even to engage legislators in such terms. *Tough on crime* was a hypnotic term that carried the day.

Chapter Ten

Back on the Streets

Governor Carey asked me in 1981 to serve another term as chairman of the Commission of Correction, but it had been mostly a painful tour, and I could see nothing more that I might accomplish in that position. Five more years stretched before me like my own prison term, a road marked by frustration and misunderstanding. To be sure, the establishment of the Network program probably would not have been possible had I not had the dignity and authority conferred by my appointment. I had helped avert some fairly serious crises. But while Commissioner Ward and I shared the same philosophy at base, he always held me at an unnecessarily great distance. And my relationships with my two fellow commissioners were vexing. They were inclined to be much more lenient than I was toward prison officials and especially toward county sheriffs. They would outvote me two to one on most issues and seemed not amenable to negotiation.

So I declined the governor's request, and going out on my own again, I proposed to start a prisoner/family program. I wanted to write and field-test a curriculum designed to help prisoners reunite better with their families long before release and then on the outside.

When a person is incarcerated, after a year or so, the family often begins to forget him or her. Especially men over thirty who have more than one conviction—they are often written off by the family as hopeless. This is especially tragic because as prisoners age, they often become more able to see their families and recognize all that they have suffered because of the one in prison. And it too often happens that women of any age in prison are quickly abandoned by their husbands.

Fortunately, there are some incarcerated people who continue to enjoy the loyalty of spouses, children, and parents. Some of them are also the people who undertake major changes in their lives, either self-directed or helped by a variety of programs offered inside prison. When they actually do change, family members may be bewildered or startled by the end of familiar behavior. They may be confused and edgy about the stranger they are meeting on visits. In fact, some old girlfriends (and even some parents) look forward to the release of the incarcerated person as the time when the big money from his criminal activity will flow again for a while. However, many family members, the vast majority, welcome positive change; but they need help coping with it.

Many programs, especially Family Works—directed by Carol Shapiro, have properly emphasized the role of family in successful reentry in ways I wish we had in the early days of Network. Work with families will surely be a major part of reform work in the years ahead.

Any work that is ever done in the future will rest on the astonishing legacy of Sister Elaine Roulet. She had already started her amazing mission when I first started working in the system. With saintly, single-minded devotion, she worked to bring mothers in prison together with their children. She did so against the mindless tide of acid feelings in the general public against everything she tried to do. She succeeded in reorienting Bedford prison to that purpose; raised money for buses to bring the children and family members up to the prison; created a child-friendly place for them to visit, long before the liberalization of visiting rules elsewhere; and managed it all with almost unbelievable style and grace.

There are endless stories about her and her sense of humor. Once, when I visited her in her office on the unit for mentally ill women, one of them poked her head in to say hello. She had a big smile, clearly holding Sister Elaine in the greatest trust. When she moved back to the hall, Sister Elaine said, "She is such a sketch. She came in the other day and said, 'I have great news!'

"'What?' I asked.

"'I am having an affair with Frank Sinatra!'

"'Lucky you!' I said. 'I have great news too.'

"'What?' she said.

"'I am having an affair with the pope!'

"'Isn't it great?' she said. 'When you're crazy, you can say any damn thing you want!' And off she went, singing happily."

A big book could be written about Sister Elaine, not only for her work at Bedford prison, but also for her establishment of Providence House to help women with their transition back to society and the good care of their children.

I had learned from prisoners in the Network program that it had been valuable to them simply to know how to talk when visiting with family members. Prisoners, especially men, often sit in the visiting rooms in noticeable discomfort. They do not know what to say or do; and their wives, girlfriends, or mothers often come quickly to the end of their own conversational creativity. We addressed this in several ways: by getting the men to put themselves in the place of their visitors, by their learning to talk about feelings, and by their serious consideration of plans (instead of saying, "I never plan because it always gets messed up"). Those three initiatives gave a new world of discourse to the awkward visits. The men were surprised and pleased to be able to carry on what we would call a regular conversation for the first time in their lives.

My plan for the prisoner/family program was to meet first with prisoners in groups for ten sessions and hope that they would enlist their families, then meet with the mothers and wives separately for ten more sessions, and conclude with four sessions together.

The curriculum was designed to elicit the maximum participation and minimum lecturing. The points of focus were learning to listen, being able to put yourself in the place of the other, planning a schedule for a week, learning to budget money, and examining attitudes about the opposite sex.

Inmates volunteered—we gave preference to those in the Network program—but they had to have family members willing to participate who lived in the Albany area (since by that time, I was living there). We therefore drew from a small but adequate number. The program was approved, and in 1981, I became a staff of one.

Most inmates started with poor interpersonal skills, so learning to put themselves in the place of their wives sometimes came as a stunning revelation. One inmate I remember was shocked that he had scolded his wife for not bringing more money for him to spend in the commissary. He came to that moment of realization when I asked him to make a list of all the things she had to do to get ready to make the trip to visit him. It was a long and arduous set of tasks.

He apologized to her on her next visit, thoroughly amazing her; he had never apologized for anything in their years of marriage.

In fact, watching people learning to say "Please," "Thank you," and "I'm sorry" was very satisfying. Inmates sometimes found it hard just to say the *words*, with no attachment to content, in front of other inmates. They believed that they would "go soft" and become too vulnerable to manage life inside prison.

The important point is that they showed a capacity to change and grow. When they discovered that it took *more* courage to ask for help, ask for forgiveness, and express appreciation than it did to be a strong, silent, macho man, they were able to think of this as a new index of their level of manhood.

We had a good time. In one group session with prisoners, when I tried to unveil the ways men and women win arguments, I asked for them to role-play. Getting a male prisoner to take a female role was a major challenge. But we eased into it; and they were funny, exaggerating the teasing, cajoling, stormy silences, and the rest of the armamentarium of spousal warfare.

One such session took place in Great Meadow prison in Comstock. The facility had a well-earned reputation for being more gratuitously tough than some other places. Laughter from staff or prisoners was very rare. But the inmates were laughing at the role-playing. When one man, playing the wife, jumped into the lap of the "husband" and started blowing in "his" ear, the whole classroom exploded with laughter, continuing as the persuasion went on with verbal endearments. Tears were rolling down the faces of many of us, including the two officers who were in training with the purpose of eventually leading the program. Suddenly the door flew open, and two other officers looked in, their mouths open with disbelief at the scene of mirth in that house of pain.

The session on budget may have been of the most practical help. I asked them to say how much money they thought they would make in a year and took the *largest* reasonable amount suggested, rounded it off to a monthly figure, and wrote it at the top of the board. Then I asked how much they thought they would spend on each item of expense, using the *smallest* reasonable amount. Finally, we added the numbers and *always* came to expense totals well over twice the amount of income. They were amazed. No wonder many had had the feeling they had been tricked or conned by not having any money in their pockets when they felt they were spending very little. Then they were surprised when they got in trouble as they committed a crime to get more money. I gave them work sheets to take back to their cells and invited them to rework the material in ways that fit them specifically and to discuss the matter with their wives.

The obvious solutions were to raise the income or lower the expenses, but I always put the third alternative on the board: crime. Then I crossed it out. This training in joining the ranks of the middle class was well received, especially by the wives, who felt new waves of appreciation from their husbands.

Issues of fidelity were the most painful, husbands fearing the worst, wives despairing of convincing their men that they were not acting as the men would have acted if the roles were reversed. It healed people just to get the issue out and to recognize the confusion and sensitivity of the other side. The men faced the fact that they were more likely to be unfaithful than their wives, and the wives stopped trying to convince them that they were being true. But the issue never went away.

One man, Tom Anderson, white and handsome—he lost his wife to divorce while he was in prison, just before the family program started. He was short, intelligent, and quiet. When he was released, he quickly fell for a girl who was strikingly beautiful, a little taller than he. Tom asked if he could attend the prisoner/family meetings because he soon needed support in deciding how to respond to her provocative behavior. She insisted on wearing very short shorts and rolling her eyes at other men. When the men responded, she looked to Tom to "fight for her." It was amazing to see a piece of cultural behavior that just made no sense, except on some preverbal caveman level. Tom never got in fights in prison even though, because he was handsome and not tall, he was the stereotype of a likely victim of rape or some other assault. I met with the two of them and tried to help him persuade her to dress more conservatively, but she insisted on continuing her "dance." That kind of teasing by some women is a common problem for men trying to reenter society. Tom finally let her go, with great reluctance. That was a step toward maturity for Tom, but I was sad thinking of all those who, after years in prison, could not do what he had done.

The prisoner/family program lasted a year and a half. Unfortunately, it was never continued in New York State because even though the Department of Correctional Services wanted to keep it going, they believed that it cost too much money and was too ambitious in structure. However, the state of Virginia has started up its own program modeled on this one and expanded upon it.

Getting the program started had required me to log 52,000 miles in one year after raising money—and hopes. After training others to do the workshops in my place, I was greatly disappointed that it would not continue.

I had always intended to return to parish work, where I imagined I would be with a wider range of people. So I began to look for a parish and even dreamed that I might actually use some of the prison experiences from which I had learned much of personal value.

I hoped that I could somehow share my discovery of the healing Body of Christ in the groups in prison, explain the importance of caring about people in prisons, and communicate my own joy in being useful to people who needed to believe more in themselves.

Trinity Church in comfortable Southport, Connecticut, was looking for a rector. They had fired the last one, a man I had never met. Some had wanted to keep the rector and were angry at those who had "won." I met some wonderful parishioners who wanted to heal the division in the church. I believe passionately in the healing process and also believed that a parish could be a grand healing community, a variation on a Network unit. When the position was offered to me, I eagerly accepted.

I was glad that I was able to help bring the two factions closer together. We raised money to build two little churches in Ecuador and adopted a parish with financial difficulties in Bridgeport, Connecticut. Trinity became a happier place. But for me, some of the greatest satisfaction resulted from a pilgrimage to South Africa.

I had met Michael Cork, headmaster of Saint Barnabas School in Soweto, outside Johannesburg, while he was fundraising in the suburbs of New York City. He invited me to come to be an honorary chaplain in the school. This was to be a three-week visit, and it occurred during the depth of the apartheid horror. Saint Barnabas was a multiracial boarding school that flaunted the laws and customs opposed to the mixing of races. Cork himself was an extraordinarily brave white man whose life, or at least his freedom, was at risk daily.

So I flew to Johannesburg in May of 1985. It was an experience that has nourished me ever since. There I saw the faith of people of both races who lived at a depth of patience and hope that I have never experienced before or since, although meeting heroic people in Palestine in 2009 was a parallel inspiration. They were, in effect, prisoners in their own country; and yet I have never met human beings more free and alive.

Among many other giants, I met Joseph Seremane, whose daughter attended Saint Barnabas. As a young man, he was committed to nonviolent change. His mother had raised him as a Christian, but he was hearing God invoked everywhere, especially by the Dutch Reformed Church, as the One who justifies apartheid and violence against blacks. Like many of our own young adults, he rejected his parents' faith. He consciously stopped believing in God.

Because of his increasing activism, he was arrested and went to prison on Robben Island for six years. This could have killed him, but instead, he used the time to make himself tougher and more sophisticated. He told me that being with Nelson Mandela was a particular inspiration. When he was released, he continued to work with those seeking the vote for all peoples of South Africa, and he continued to be committed to nonviolence. Then he was detained again by the police, without charges. That was the worst because you had no idea of when, if ever, you would be released—and because torture was routine. The police wanted names of coworkers. He refused. He was beaten, hog-tied, punched, and kicked. "There was more," he said, "that I wouldn't even tell my wife."

After a long irregular time of such torture, he felt he was going to die. He could no longer feel the pain. He said to me, "It was as if I was separated from my own body. The kicks were faraway from me. And then I said to myself, 'Joseph, you're going to die.' And then suddenly I felt God was there. It sounds impossible, but I was still so rebellious that I still argued. I said, 'You are not there, God.' God didn't argue with me, but he said, very clearly, 'Joe, I gave you life. Only I can give you life. These men could take it away, but they are not going to take away your life, Joe. You will go on living.' I was not sure whether to be happy or sad that I would go on living. Then suddenly I realized the police had stopped beating me. They untied me. Then the captain came in. He swung his fist at me, but it was as if I was protected by a shield. He shook his fist in my face and said, 'I had decided that today was your day. Either we break you or we kill you. And here you are, still alive.' Then he said some more angry things, and he left.

"That was the beginning of my new life. When I got back to my cell, the guard came and said he wanted to bring me a book. I couldn't believe it. He had been very hard with me, always. I argued with him: I reminded him that he could get in trouble bringing me a book. He said he had been praying for me every night with his wife. Now he wanted to help, and he was willing to take the chance. He brought me many books. It was as if he was my friend. It was a miracle. Then everything was quiet. I stayed in silence for a long time."

Then they let Joe go. He had thought about his wife the whole time and planned to kiss her when he saw her, "a big kiss, a very big kiss!" When he saw her, he ran to her. "But she put out her hand, and she said, 'Wait! Before we kiss, we must give thanks to God because I have been praying for you with the other women, every night.' Now she had been like me, Father, she did not believe in God, but somehow God helped her begin. He told her I would live and come back to her." They gave thanks to God, then gave each other a very big kiss. Joseph had been made strong in the silence.

Silence came to me in a new way when I went to the prison where Nelson Mandela himself was still confined. He had been moved from Robben Island to Pollsmoor, a much less-severe setting. I was denied permission to visit him, so instead, I drove around and around the outer perimeter one night, praying for the great man locked behind the walls, which were bathed in an incongruously soft honey gold light.

Silence came in quite another way in a second prison I visited in South Africa. Perhaps as a consolation for being denied permission to visit Mandela, I was granted approval to go to the maximum-security prison called Leeuwkop. Upon my arrival, I was escorted by a man in shining high boots, the colonel who ran the place.

My visit to Leeuwkop was unforgettable. It was a maximum-security prison holding 5,300 black men. That is twice the size of the largest prison in New York State. It was out in the country, in an arid area not too far from Cape Town. The colonel had a hard, desperate face and a high, shrill voice, which he used all the time, especially when addressing prisoners. Those confined were technically there for regular crimes; but it was an open secret at the time, 1985, that many were in prison for trying, often very modestly, to organize people to improve their conditions of life.

Though many were straight political prisoners at Leeuwkop, I soon felt that they were brothers of some I had known in New York City, confined because they had acted in frustration against a world that seemed only to torment them.

The colonel walked through the corridors, a guard on each side, loudly describing what we were seeing. He moved as if he carried a swagger stick. The officials proudly told me that they were fully in compliance with the UN Charter on Prisons. The cells were small, the dormitories overcrowded, and the atmosphere filled with the tension that comes from terror and homicidal anger.

In the clinic, which was very clean, every bed was filled. Inmates were lying down in blue bathrobes. Most of them were on their backs, staring at the ceiling. Those who could stand did so by their beds. The colonel loudly explained that they were "all malingerers," but in his generosity, he allowed them to be treated. He then yelled to them, "This is your big chance. Our visitor comes from the United States of America. You have many complaints. Now is your opportunity to voice them!" There was total silence.

We moved on, at my request, to the isolation unit of the prison. It surrounded a cement courtyard, perhaps thirty feet by fifty feet. The walls went up three stories, solid concrete except for metal roll-down doors, but curiously, these were only on the first story. I had never seen a prison like that in my life. The colonel bellowed a command, and all the doors rolled up. In each doorway stood a man, heavily shackled hand and foot, the hand shackles bolted to thick leather belts, which were themselves locked. Hands together, each man held an ID card in front of him.

We approached the first man. The colonel asked him his name, and the man mumbled a reply. The colonel screamed, "What is your crime?"

The man was silent, and this infuriated the colonel. He looked at the man's ID, called him by name, and the man softly said, "Fighting." The colonel laughed, referring to the violence that erupted in the townships. "They are always fighting. They are very violent people."

At this point, I was able to look past the people locked up in prisons and see that the cells behind them were about eight square feet, but the ceilings went all the way up the three stories. The walls were smooth. Food was lowered from above. Ventilation came from above. Chamber pots were raised full and lowered empty by inmates from elsewhere in the prison. It was like being thrown to the bottom of a well.

I describe all this as background to having the privilege of looking into the eyes of each man as we went along, finally in silence, around the courtyard.

I was by then fifty-three years old and had considerable experience of prisons and inmates. However, never, before or since, have I had an experience of silence to compare with that one. I felt as if I was gazing deep into the "well of life" as I looked into those eyes. The men looked at me without hatred or bitterness. They were alone, so they did not exhibit the tension and anger I had seen in the dorms. Dignity and profound peace seemed to flow out of them. It was as if the strange giant cement tubes in which they were confined were connected to the core of the earth. Their massive strength of spirit and their seeming roots in some cosmic serenity were in total contrast to the hysteria of my guide.

The eyes of all those men come back to me even today in times of silence. They seemed to have come to trust in God or the primordial ocean of life at a depth I doubt I will ever reach. I am not sure I want to reach that depth because the voyage usually comes at the price of great suffering. But I will always feel grateful for the privilege of looking into the window of those eyes. I asked the colonel if I could go to the bathroom, locked myself in and wept.

Soon after, in 1986, I heard that the Network program had been abolished in New York State! A budget crisis had led the commissioner to order that all the Network administrators revert to their prior civil service positions (correction officers) and thereby save the state hundreds of thousands of dollars. I felt quite helpless, far away in Connecticut, to protest; and I doubted my protest would have helped even if I had been closer to the scene. It was heartbreaking to know that all that hard work, Cherie Clark's wonderful training, was all for nothing. The Network administrators were hazed pretty harshly by other officers who had never liked Network and saw this betrayal by the state as a way to get back at their "high-minded" colleagues. Those who tried to keep the program going inside were vilified as "scabs."

In May 1988, I went on a pilgrimage to try to discern what I should do next in my life. I visited several monasteries in Europe and kept their hours of prayers. I went back to Taizé, where I had been as a teenager. I went to Solesmes, near the Loire, south of Paris, home of Gregorian chant, and to La Pierre-qui-Vire, in central France, attending the prayers at 2:00 AM and 6:00 AM, including the singing of many psalms. It was hard getting up in the middle of the night, going back to bed, and getting up again. The effect on me was the intended one, to emphasize my consciousness of my radical dependence on God, eyes fuzzy, unkempt, disoriented, and stumbling from my room along dark corridors to the dimly lit church where fifty monks were assembled.

I felt a little as I imagined some prisoners must feel: fighting for control, wanting to leave the hard frame of the prayer services, and just wandering the soft countryside. But I believed it was good for me to surrender to the exacting schedule, to give up my control. If it was too difficult for me to give up control, I who was entirely free to sleep late or just leave the monastery and go elsewhere, how much harder would it be for a prisoner to give up control when he had no option to leave?

Nevertheless, when I returned to the USA, I felt like a water bug, darting over the surface of life. I wanted to plunge down deep into the dark depths or high into the sky. I did not think I could do that as a parish priest in the Southport, Connecticut, setting, worrying about raising the money to paint the church, running the stewardship campaign, smoothing over the feelings of someone who felt he had been disregarded by a member of my vestry. I felt called to help people who were suffering. There certainly were parishioners who were suffering, had great difficulty admitting their pain. They wanted me to bless their comfortable lives and pray that nothing would change. When I preached about life being a river of constant change and how we needed to learn to swim well, they did not like it.

Also, finally, in August 1988, I was homesick for my hometown of New York City, for its amalgam of different races and classes, and for the opportunity to help people transform their lives in a setting that seemed to fit my vocation.

I was ready to go to a parish in a poor area of New York City and live in a tenement apartment, if necessary. I had done that before, happily. I was in touch with the old wish to give up my life, perhaps in the literal sense, to follow wherever God might lead. It seemed especially true at that time that such a commitment might involve danger, could even be life threatening.

But once again, a life of apostolic simplicity eluded me. I accepted a call to be executive director of what was then known as the Episcopal Mission Society (EMS) of the Diocese of New York, now Episcopal Social Services. The Mission, as its workers called it, had been created by Saint Michael's Parish in 1831. Back then, its focus was to give charitable aid to prisoners in the newly constructed jail called the Tombs, to poor people suffering on the back ward of Bellevue Hospital, and to mental patients in Blooming Dale Asylum, on what is now Roosevelt Island. The Mission, soon after, added a concern for the many children who were homeless on the streets of New York City.

By August of 1988, when I began working at EMS, we served foster children, developmentally disabled adults, and the elderly; we also provided support to several chaplains in hospitals and one in a prison.

At the same time, I moved as quickly as possible to reestablish the Network program in the New York State prisons. It had flourished from its inception in 1979 until 1986, when as noted, the fiscal crisis that year had forced severe cuts in all state budgets. Saving $500,000 by requiring all Network administrators to return to their former positions and eliminating training costs had been too great a temptation. All the units were closed, with the exception of those at Fishkill and Clinton, where administrators continued to work on the units even though they were paid only their regular salaries as officers.

I tried without success to persuade Commissioner Thomas Coughlin and then his successor, Phil Coombs, to bring Network back. Speaking of the way it had been before, without full-time Network administrators, one Fishkill officer told me, "It was really better, in a way. We had come to be doing too much for the inmates. This change put more responsibility back on the inmates where it belongs."

However, the Episcopal Mission Society, as a private agency, was free to provide Network meetings inside New York City for people on parole. In 1989, we started on Thursday nights at Calvary Church on Gramercy Park. It is a tribute to the clergy who led that parish at that time, Tom Pike and Steve Garmey, that the meetings have continued from 1989 to the time of this writing. Gramercy Park is an elegant, historic neighborhood, and I am sure that some neighbors have protested the presence of up to one hundred people convicted of serious crimes, taking their smoking breaks on the sidewalk next to the gated park. But those complaints have never reached my ears.

I finally got funding in 1989 to hold Network meetings outside prison, as part of a transition program for those in AfterShock. A budget from the Division of Parole of $170,000 was approved, and we started transition work with people who had been in Network upstate and also others released on parole. I was thrilled. This was a little consolation for the drastic reduction of the in-prison part of the program upstate.

There were three sections to the AfterShock program: work, sobriety, and resocialization. Most AfterShockers had no job. Former inmates were assigned to a project run by a contractor called Wildcat Inc. At the time, Wildcat did an excellent job, offering well-supervised work projects like sandblasting walls, demolishing old buildings, and cleaning up empty lots. They also did some Sheetrocking, plastering, and painting. In keeping with the Network idea, AfterShockers themselves were trained to become supervisors. A thousand AfterShockers went through the training each year.

The part of AfterShock designed to help inmates remain sober and drug free was also well conceived. All the AfterShockers had abused drugs in some way, and the temptation to return to drugs was strong and constant. So another group, Fellowship Inc., was awarded a contract to provide drug counseling and to refer the AfterShockers to Narcotics Anonymous or Alcoholics Anonymous meetings. After considerable debate, these twelve-step programs agreed to modify their traditional policy protecting anonymity and take attendance for Fellowship. Failure to attend meant that one might be sent back upstate to prison.

AfterShockers, both men and women, also had to attend Network meetings once each week, in the evening. Many seemed happy to come—especially when they encountered several members of their old platoons. They arrived covered with plaster dust, wearing their work boots. They complained about how hard they worked and how low the pay was; but they were clearly proud, underneath, that they were able to work that hard and maintain some continuity with the old solidarity they had experienced in the Shock Camps.

They often asked for permission to "do cadence" during the break. They would line up in platoon form and chant as they marched in place, just as they had in the camps. The inventiveness of the one leading the chant was much on display, a preview of the best of rap, which was about to come (it was then 1989), and an echo of the old prison toasts, which had a long oral tradition. "Here's to King Heroin" was the beginning of many a toast in the drug culture of the 1960s; and it continued, in new forms, into the 1990s.

Tony, an AfterShock graduate, came to a meeting two nights before Valentine's Day. He said, "I have never been clean *and* free on Valentine's Day in the five years my woman has been with me. She never used drugs and always wanted me to stop. Now here I am, and I don't have any money for a Valentine's Day present for her. I've got to get her a big present. I'm gonna have to *do something*."

I was leading the group that evening, as I did occasionally because I continued to enjoy it. The group looked at me, expecting me to intervene. I said, "It's your group. Tony needs feedback from you, not me." One man told him, "You are an idiot! She wants *you*, clean and free, outside prison. She doesn't want a big box of candy or a fancy sweater and you in the joint. Go tell her, *I* am your Valentine's Day present!"

Tony asked every single member of the group to respond to him, and they all said essentially the same thing. It was as if he was eating food, storing up energy for his decision and subsequent action. When they were through, he said, "I'm gonna do it! I'm gonna do just like you said!" He looked a bit grim, clearly reflecting the challenge of thinking that *he* would be enough. I thought of my own friends and myself, wondering if we would have the courage to say, "I am enough without the present."

The next week, Tony came back, and I was surprised at how relieved I felt that he had returned. I had been more pessimistic than I had recognized. He was ecstatic. Even before the formal group began, he was bubbling to his friends. "I done just like you said. And she *loved* it. And it was great *afterward* too!"

It was a wonderful time in my life, a fulfillment of the years of trying to put the two pieces together: Network units inside the prisons and Network reentry groups in the community outside. It was a powerful connection, and visitors to the program were invariably moved by the energy and hope throbbing in the room.

I continue to believe that even though Network outside prison served hundreds, not thousands of people on parole, it made a significant addition to the regular work of the Division of Parole. Many men and women were able to live crime-free lives because of those Network meetings.

It was a common experience for a man or a woman to struggle to his/her feet at the end of a meeting and say, "Coming here tonight was the last thing I wanted to do. I was ready to stay home and just suffer the consequences. But this is just what I needed. Thank you all!"

Every time there is a newspaper headline saying, PAROLEE COMMITS NEW CRIME, there are cries to abolish parole. But actually, what we need to do is strengthen the parole system. People on parole used to be returned to prison on the whim of their parole officer, for any technical violation; but now, in part due to the need to deal with prison overcrowding, things have changed. Now it is necessary for a person on parole to commit a new crime or come very close to it in order for a judge to authorize a return to prison. A parolee with "dirty urine," who refuses to show up for job interviews, who changes residence without permission should be returned to prison, at least for a short time, before being released again. In the long run, this would lead to the incarceration of fewer individuals because they would be confined for a few weekends or a few weeks instead of committing new crimes that would lead to jail for many more years. There should be a way to return a person on the verge of a new crime for such short periods instead of the heavy reimprisonment now required for people deemed to be in violation of the conditions of their parole.

The problems of transition are so numerous and deep that I hope someday there will be a place formerly incarcerated people can go for help at many hours of the day or night, as with AA. At Episcopal Social Services, we conduct four evening meetings for formerly incarcerated people on different days of the week. Especially in New York City, of course, there are AA meetings in the morning, afternoon, and evening, and there is a hotline. Formerly incarcerated people could use a similar set of opportunities. The present twelve-step programs have been lifesaving for millions, but most people out of prison need an even more personal connection to someone who understands their particular reentry problems. Most lack the self-esteem to seek out a twelve-step sponsor and maintain the obligations that such a relationship requires.

In 1993, a new governor was elected for the state of New York, George Pataki, and our contract with the Division of Parole was abruptly canceled. Much to my dismay. Our program cost only $170,000, and we worked with a thousand people released from the camps every year. For $170 per AfterShocker, we were a major resource in keeping people crime free, saving the state the costs of arresting, convicting, and incarcerating more people.

However, my determination to keep providing help for those who needed Network continued stronger than ever. Reason might have seemed to be saying that it was time to quit, but this seemed to be a challenge beyond my own choosing.

I appealed to Senator Roy Goodman, an old friend of my father. And I reached out to Dale Volker, chairman of the Correction Committee of the Senate. Senator Goodman came back with the message: "He thinks that you are a party hack. Only a party hack would ever have been appointed to the Commission of Correction." I asked them to carry the message back that I was, in fact, embarrassed that I had not contributed money and time to Governor Carey's campaigns, but in fact had given virtually nothing. The message came back: "He does not believe you. He thinks you must be a party hack." No renewal of contract.

But I could not stop. Momentum came from people who believed in the program. We continued with only one worker, Joe Santana, paid for with private funds, with formerly incarcerated people coming by word of mouth. Finally, we were unable even to pay him, and he remained on a volunteer basis. Joe had been in Network at Sing Sing, and he believed the program had saved his life.

Equally amazing, certainly more unexpected, was the devotion of two unlikely volunteers, Roger and Marty Gilbert. He, Roger, a retired engineer businessman, and she, Marty, a retired schoolteacher, visited the program at my invitation and loved it. Since they were national leaders of the Marriage Encounter program, they knew plenty about group process and personal transformation.

The amazing thing was that they continued to be a part of the program almost every week for ten years! They would insist that they did it for the benefits it gave them as individuals and as a couple. I believe them, partly because the same is true of me. But they contributed greatly, sometimes leading their own small groups, extending the process to wives and mothers of group members, and adding to the sense of seriousness of the meetings by their presence.

One of the incidental delights of the program has been the vision of these two aristocratic, well-educated white friends moving with comfort and to the benefit of all among a group that, according to conventional wisdom, would reject them.

We were hanging on to Network by a thread when unexpected help arrived. A new commissioner of the prison system, Glenn S. Goord, was appointed. I wrote to him, making my case for the restoration of Network and asking to see him.

Much to my amazement, Commissioner Goord agreed. Earlier in his career, he had been appointed to run the first prison, an annex of Eastern prison in Napanoch, New York, which was entirely a therapeutic community for inmates of all ages. It was not a Shock Camp, so inmates could stay longer than six months. It was more strict than a Network unit, but it was similar, and Goord was sympathetic to Network. Enough time had elapsed for some of the old anger (about the abolition of the program) to subside; officers were again willing to help.

Then an even bigger miracle occurred. Out of the blue, I received a call from Joe Cruickshank, then the director of the Clark Foundation. Would I be interested in coming to his office to discuss putting together a transition program that would move prisoners to the community in a more effective way than current practice? I could not wait! I met with Cruickshank and others at his office in 1997, and the result was a $200,000 grant for the first year of what became a five-year $1,000,000 undertaking. Joe understood the complexity of the endeavor and the necessity to do more than offer a quick solution to prisoners upon release. He embraced the plan, which called for the creation of Network units in upstate prisons to prepare inmates to come to work-release facilities in New York City and attend Network meetings on the outside. It would even include some long-term incarcerated individuals.

That was 1998. For the first time since the program had been designed, in 1979, full implementation was finally possible. Prior to that time, the program had flourished magnificently *inside* from 1979 to 1985, then inside and outside, and as part of the Shock program from 1989 to 1993, but it had still been unavailable to nonaddicts and to long-term inmates. Now we could reach back into maximum-security, involve prisoners who still faced many years inside, who could structure their whole lives in prison around the Network program. Then as they became eligible for medium-security, they could continue in the prison to which they were transferred. Finally, they would go to minimum-security, work release, and the same forms of meeting on the outside. At last, the Network could provide the stabilizing gyroscope through the challenges of each change.

Network's good fortune continued when Chuck Hamilton became director of the Clark Foundation. He is the one who sustained the Clark commitment, persuading the board to maintain the funding level at $200,000 per year. He then became a wise counselor to the program, helping me strategize through new steps.

I recruited two excellent graduates of the old AfterShock program. Ed Jones was an ex-addict now working as manager of a single-room occupancy hotel, handling the many daily difficulties associated with that work. He did so with a combination of tact, patience, firmness, good humor, and a deep faith in God. He had been the director of our small Network program on the outside. Yolanda Johnson agreed to become codirector.

At the time I recruited her, she was working at an employment agency concentrating on ex-prisoner job placements. Yolanda's story also illustrated the alchemy of character change—for her, as with many others, it had been a combination of being held still, plus her own courage, brains, and love. Pregnant when she was arrested for possessing a small amount of drugs, she had her baby in prison and signed up for Shock. It was difficult for her to take orders, and so she was ordered by an officer to carry a pile of rocks from one place to another—then ordered to move them all back. She refused even though she was told that disobedience meant that she would be returned to regular prison to complete her three-year sentence. She still refused. As a last step, before "going back," she was taken to a room with a big sign on one wall that said Think. She faced the sign for three hours. She remembers it as her turning point. She had time to calm down. She had time to remember her son. She had time to reflect on the poor rewards she had reaped so far for being the toughest woman in the class, on the block, in the prison.

She continues to be restless when things do not go well, but she has managed to be a good mother to her son (with major help from her own mother), to work for Network, and to complete her BA. She is electric, excelling in her capacity to bring energy to a meeting. Yolanda and Ed were effective in establishing or reestablishing the Network program in seven upstate prisons.

It is not easy for men and women to go back inside. Neither Ed nor Yolanda had been incarcerated for long, so long-term inmates were sometimes tempted to say, "You don't know what it's like to do real time." There are some officers and counselors, even superintendents, who find it impossible to forget that these staff had been prisoners.

We talked long about these issues before Ed and Yolanda started, and they clearly understood the precariousness of their situation. They knew they could be yanked at any time and that there would be no appeal, that they must walk the fine line every day, continuing to do the work rather than advocating for administrative change. When shown disrespect, they must persevere.

As expected, getting started again was not easy. The support of Commissioner Goord was crucial. It was usually clear, when talking with a couple of superintendents, that they were only cooperating because of the commissioner's insistence. Most, however, seemed genuinely cooperative. With all their responsibilities, it was to their credit that they took the time and trouble to figure out all the complicated logistics and other staff/space questions that come with the implementation of a Network unit.

On the negative side, one of the pendulums moved again in New York State, and work release was almost eliminated by Governor Pataki. He made this dramatic reduction in work release because of his apprehension about crimes that might be committed by individuals still technically on inmate status. Once there were seven thousand prisoners at any one time moving through this crucially important reentry from upstate prison to full release into the community. At the time of this writing, there are only five hundred. That has greatly reduced the pool of inmates from which we can draw for our Network meetings on the outside—at least for now.

When the funding from the Clark Foundation ran its course, we once again faced the end of the Network program. I reached out to Senator Dale Volker, chairman of the Correction Committee of the Senate. It was an act of desperation. He had been the leader of the fight to restore capital punishment in New York State. I had cochaired the Committee to Abolish Capital Punishment in 1963. There had been no executions since then. Dale and I had good long talks. He decided to help Network with grants of $100,000 each year until the funds were no longer available to him. Episcopal Social Services heroically made up the difference, the majority of the program costs. The Moore Foundation, an anonymous benefactor, and other individual gifts were also crucially important.

The director of the Network program since 2002 has been Anne Williams, born in Scotland; taught seven years in Padua, Italy; and moved to America at age twenty-four. She earned her BA in English and psychology, then an MA in comparative literature, and a job as director of a job training program. She trained staff for agencies for the developmentally disabled, and eventually, Network got her. She has been superb—directing staff and watching the budget, writing grant requests, negotiating the complexities of communicating with various DOCS personnel. Most of all, she is utterly dedicated to the work, a lioness of devotion. She lives upstate, so the actual work of supervision of the prison program is more accessible to her. At the time of this writing, the program is thriving. Anne Williams is the best Director Network has ever had.

Sam Waterston, the actor most famous for his work on *Law and Order* as DA McCoy, did us the great honor in 2004 of visiting two

Network meetings in prison. Both prisons were all buzzing before we arrived, with staff finding reasons to be in the lobby as he came through. The meetings were regular meetings, the men seriously involved with the different parts. One man, about to be released, said that he was very excited to be on the verge of freedom, but said that he was anxious about leaving friends who were "closer to him than anyone on the outside." He was not sure how well he would manage. At the end, the men asked Waterston if he had any comments. He said, "I am very impressed with you all. And I am particularly impressed that I can sit in a room with thirty men for two hours as they give their full attention to trying to make sense out of life. You are so intense! It has been a privilege to be here with you all." Of course, the men were moved, and they often ask about him and want me to send their regards and their appreciation for his coming.

To work on this book, I went one weekend on retreat and talked with Sister Mary Christobel at the Community of the Holy Spirit in New York City. I told her about the subject of my writing, in which I was comparing prisons and monasteries, and said I thought that the biggest difference was that it was necessary to be a fairly strong, healthy person to enter the disciplined life of a religious order, whereas prisoners often started out in need of basic transformation. I said I believed that the transformation would, ideally, be lifelong, implying that it would not be so in a religious order. I asked whether she felt that nuns were already transformed, prior to coming into a semicloistered world. Eyes twinkling, she said spontaneously, "Oh no. Maybe partly. But transformation is a lifelong process!"

Chapter Eleven

Holding Still: The Breaking Point

Prison is sometimes called a school for crime, a dehumanizing place in which prisoners are simply made worse. Indeed that is true in many cases. There are new articles and books being published all the time now, trying to measure the degree to which prisons are harmful or helpful. The topic is one of staggering complexity because the variables are endless. The factors of age, racism, classism, economic changes, job opportunities, cultural shifts, fund availability for staff—all endless. The debate will go on.

But it is my experience that at some point during their incarceration, many people in prison *turn* and begin the process of self-transformation. I call this the breaking point, and I have seen it come for many people in many ways.

One unit at Bedford Hills, the women's prison, was designated to be a Network unit. That meant that all the women on that unit were offered a choice. They could ask to be transferred to a regular unit. Or they could choose to remain, see what life was like on a Network unit, and either leave later or continue as regular members of Network. We explained all that in detail to the women who had assembled in the day room. They asked questions, and we answered.

I then went into the dormitory section to meet those who had chosen not to attend the meeting, to do what I could to minimize any feelings of antagonism they might have about this change in their lives. Moving from one cubicle to another may seem like a small change; but for men and women inside, especially women, it seems quite shattering. They have managed to make this little, tiny space their own. A few photos on the wall, clothes put away, letters in a particular place—it is their small circle of free choice. And it may be shared with another person! So "giving it up" can seem like a cataclysmic thrust into the unknown. I wanted to do what I could to minimize that impact.

My first stop was the cubicle immediately on my right. It was a double cubicle occupied by Selma Price. I started to introduce myself to Ms. Price, as she was called by everyone, who was a mountain of furious flesh, weighing well over four hundred pounds and seeming to be over six feet tall. Before I could even say my name, she said, "I know who you are! You can take your fucking Network program and shove it up your miserable white ass!" She then continued to lay me out with an anger I had never experienced before. It was not just that she used every cussword in the book; she was inventive, even artistic in her use of language. I have some perspective on the encounter now, but at the time, I was really afraid that she was about to hurt me physically. She was so heavy that she had to move with a walker, which may have saved my life.

I managed to say that I hoped that she would change her mind about the Network program, and moved on to the next cubicle. I found out later that her mother had "put her in the street" at the age of twelve and had been her pimp until she ran away from "home" to live as best she could in the street. She was serving twenty-five years to life. Her crime was the grisly murder of a man who had abused her and cheated her in drug deals. She had suffocated him in a trunk where she had locked him up. That act was believable as the climax of a life of helpless rage.

The cubicle normally assigned to an inmate was too small for her, so Superintendent Elaine Lord had removed one partition between two cubicles and had given her a double cubicle where she could move around with comparative ease. That was an unprecedented concession to her condition.

Months went by, and I heard that she was diagnosed with diabetes, had begun to lose weight and to attend meetings. I was told that she seemed to be calming down somewhat.

I returned for another meeting and went to the day room, waiting for the women to assemble. Ms. Price was already out there, the first, with her walker, seated and looking composed, noticeably thinner but still way over three hundred pounds. Mindful of our first meeting, I gingerly took a place near her, saying a cautious hello, then faced the same way she was facing. I was startled to hear her say softly, "Good morning, Father Chinlund."

"Good morning, Ms. Price?" (Silence.)

Hesitantly and very softly, she said, "Father Chinlund, are there things that you hope to do before you die?" For a second, I thought that she was referring to the fact that she was about to kill me.

"Why, Ms. Price, what an interesting question! Yes, there sure are lots of things I hope to do before I die. What about you?"

"Oh yes, Father Chinlund," she replied again warmly and gently. "There are lots of things I hope to do too."

"Would you tell me one or two of them?"

"It's a long story. I remember when I was a little girl. All I remember is sunshine and running in the grass. I was a good little runner. And there were flowers, and I was very happy. And I was a good girl, and then—I don't know what happened, but everything got dark. There were always clouds and nighttime. And then the people were very mean to me. They did awful things to me. And then I got heavy, and they were more mean. And then I did bad things, very bad things." She started to cry. "For the first time in my whole life, since I was a little girl, people have been nice to me since I became part of Network. People don't tease me because I am heavy. And I notice the sun again, like today." She let out a sigh. "So I hope someday I might get out even just for a little while, even a few days before I die, to be in the sun on the outside and maybe see a little girl . . . running." She began to cry again. And so did I. Selma Price had reached her own breaking point.

During the Network meeting, Ms. Price participated appropriately, and then she said to everyone, "I just want to thank all the women in the Network Community. I know that I was real mean a few months ago. I been mean for almost as long as I remember. But you all treated me so kindly. You never teased me about being—heavy. Little by little you helped me to relax. Now there ain't no place on earth that I would rather be than right here on this unit."

She continued to live there and began to read voraciously. I asked more about her and discovered that she eventually got to Shakespeare and loved looking up new words and really understanding the text. Finally, she was too sick to remain and had to be moved to the hospital so that her diabetes could be watched. I visited her there and found her shrunken, weighing under three hundred pounds and quite bent over. She had a room of her own in the hospital and seemed to be well treated. We had a long visit, and I reminded her of our first and second meetings, telling her what I remembered of those conversations. "Yes," she said, "you got it just right." Smiling broadly, she said, "I guess I am going to be running around in the grass in heaven because I can barely walk now. That's all right. These years since Network have been the best years of my life. Right here in prison." And she beamed.

Selma died on August 4, 2009 surrounded by people who loved her. Once hated and feared inside, she had become transformed. She gave the Network program all of the credit. Her funeral was attended by many, both staff and incarcerated friends. I believe she is running free in the grass.

Quite often, as with Ms. Price, the opportunity to receive education provides the breaking point. I remember sitting with fourteen women around a table in Bedford Hills in 1998, talking about all that college meant to them. Black, white, and Latina—their love of life and learning shone as brightly as their intelligence. One spoke of having been suicidally depressed before starting in the school program, entering in the college program, and then being devastated when the axe fell, in 1994, on the college program (it had been financed by Federal Pell grants and NYS Tuition Assistance Program grants—both cancelled by the Gingrich Congress of 1994 and the New York State Pataki administration of the same period). After speaking with shining eyes about her life, she summed it up by saying, "Once, I only had a yesterday, and it was horrible. Now, I have a today and a tomorrow." Her words were more than a rhetorical flourish. They reflected her.

The person who made a lot of this happen was Benay Rubenstein, an energetic, optimistic woman with huge brown eyes and beautiful wavy white hair. She worked with many others to revive the college program with private funds, her brains and dedication enlisting many to the cause. When it became possible to recruit her for the Network program in 2002, I reached out for her, and she began our College Initiative, clearing the way for both men and women who had been in prison to enter regular college work after they were released. In the beginning, she was especially helpful with women she had known inside, making it possible for them to finish and earn their degrees.

I was worried that it would be too difficult for people newly released from prisons to juggle home, work, *and* college; but Benay never wavered. Instead of college being an extra burden, it became an added incentive. The men and women in the program had a higher sense of themselves; and their families were willing, even eager, to help with money and babysitting. "Now he [or she] is really going someplace!" people would say.

The admissions office at the City University of New York was especially receptive because Episcopal Social Services was clearing the way: collecting transcripts from previous schools, paying the application and transcript fees, and securing financial aid. Most of all, Benay was always right there, encouraging former prisoners when the going got tough. The results were obviously good for everyone.

Chuck Hamilton, at the Clark Foundation, recognized that this was the next step-up for the prison program. He persuaded the Clark board to give our College Initiative a life, just as he had for the Network program. It was all because of the wise help of Chuck Hamilton that the College Initiative thrived and grew to the point where it was possible to shift from ESS to become part of the world of the City University of New York. It is now a vibrant part of the strong new national attention being given to formerly incarcerated people's reentry into mainstream society. At last!

Benay helped me recruit Max Kenner, an energetic and savvy young man who was still in his senior year at Bard College. Largely on his own, he had recruited fellow students to go into Eastern Correctional Facility in Napanoch, New York, to tutor inmates at any educational level. I was amazed at his multiple accomplishments: he got permission from Bard to take students inside prison and work with "dangerous prisoners," he got permission from the authorities in the prison to allow men and women of college age to come inside even though one or more might have been troublemakers, he had begun to recruit faculty to go inside and teach real college classes and get Bard credits, and he had sustained the work over two years. I was very impressed. He managed to do all that in spite of the opposition of Governor Pataki to having college-level work going on in prison even if there were no state money supporting it. Bedford got away with it on the condition that there be no publicity about the work. I was delighted to recruit him for ESS staff and encourage him to keep on going. He did that with exceptional skill, and the Bard Prison Initiative now has a hundred students with a dozen faculty members going inside. President Leon Botstein is a vigorous and passionate advocate for the program, speaking with his customary eloquence at the commencement ceremonies inside Eastern; then in a second prison, Woodbourne; now a third, for women, Bayview. I was honored to receive from his hand the first John Dewey Award, now given annually to those who have contributed to the development of the college program in prison.

It is a scandal that federal and state funding for college inside was stopped in 1994, but it has been a joy to participate in its resumption. Hopefully, soon, there will be state funding to supplement the pioneering work of Bard College.

Many men and women confined to prison have voluntarily said, "Going to prison was the best thing that could have happened to me. I could barely read when I got sent upstate. I went through Adult Basic Education and then I got my General Education Diploma, and now I am ready for college. None of that would have happened if I had not been held still. I was prevented from going on with the crazy way I was living my life."

The first time I heard someone speak like this was decades ago; the speaker was a big strong black man with a little gray hair. He did not care who heard him say it. He said it happily and without apology. More recently there was an overweight white woman with shining eyes at a meeting at Calvary Church. She used the same words and then explained, "My husband was a compulsive gambler. I worked in a bank. I started 'borrowing' money to pay his debts. No excuse. It was entirely my fault. In prison, I got a handle on all that. My responsibility. I got divorced. Never going to do anything illegal again. I will have a hard time getting a job doing what I know: handling money. I know that. So I will get some other job. I will live on what I make. I will see my children, now all grown. I have stayed close to them." She was radiant with excitement about the new bright life ahead of her. It never would have happened without her accepting the limitations of her life in confinement.

The progress of a man who was called D by everyone exemplifies the way one person was held still long enough to discover gifts and strength that he did not know he had. And it took him a long time. Finally, he was able to make the commitment to change his life, to use effective programs to take giant steps, and now to inspire other incarcerated people.

I first met D in 1999, at an Interfaith Center retreat for people working inside prison, when he was looking for a job. We worked together for four years at Episcopal Social Services, where he helped, with great imagination, some of our most challenging foster care children, as well as worked in the prison/reentry program.

D had been a wild twenty-five-year-old who as a boy had literally fought his way to and from the grocery store every day. Then he became a drug addict. It all culminated on the day he went with a partner to rob a tavern. A customer standing at the bar started to plead, then argue, then fight. D shot and killed the man.

He was sentenced to twenty-five years to life and went to prison in 1973—an angry, high-energy youth struggling against the consequences of his own bad decisions.

For years he was a desperado inside prison. His name was Desmond, but everyone called him D and had better not call him anything else. With his broad shoulders, athletic build, and reckless anger, "nobody messed with D," he says. A hard look was almost always sufficient, but he still had many fights.

It was boring for him, finally, inside state prison. The food was always the same; the walls were the same; the staff turned over but, even they, seemed the same. So at the age of thirty, he tried out for basketball. He had played no sports prior to this. He was an instant star. When his nose was broken badly in a game, it was not properly set, and D has gone through the rest of his life looking like a black Lorenzo de' Medici.

Undeterred, he started to play football, a game he also had never attempted before. His coach, who taught him the game, was one of the first men he had ever respected. An older man on the staff, he simply commanded respect by his manner. He said, "If you want to play, you must do what I say." D experienced the satisfaction of training, discipline, and teamwork. "When the coach said to put your face in the mud, I put my face in the mud," D told me. "It was fun, we were putting something together. I played well, found satisfaction in being a member of a team," even if his own star role was not always brighter than everyone else's. He could break up fights, encourage teammates after a bungled play, and enjoy the game in spite of being in prison "forever," as it seemed to him then. It is regrettable that contact sports are no longer permitted inside.

Buoyed by his newly discovered skills, personal and athletic, D found the courage to test his academic ability. He had dropped out of high school, but had managed to learn more than he realized in his occasional visits to the classroom. Still, he was surprised to find that his GED (General Education Diploma) score placed him within reach of success. He would not ever say he was stupid, but he had never thought he could be a player in the academic arena.

He had been in prison, by then, for seven years. It was 1980. He had eighteen years to go to the end of his minimum sentence. He was thirty-two years old and could not imagine being fifty. He felt as if he would spend the rest of his life there. He was certainly being held still.

But a new idea of freedom began to come to him. There was a day, alone in his cell, when he realized that he had been changing for a while without knowing it. He found himself saying, "I am free. I am going to do what is good for me and not what others expect. I am my own man. I am free."

Many others in prison, criminal or not, have made the same decision when they were able to accept the fact that they would be locked up for a long time. For some, it has been the beginning of a lifetime of learning. Having found, perhaps for the first time, that it is possible to be transported, in reading, to Africa, Mexico, or Spain, to new ways of thinking with Plato, Descartes, and Marx, they have sought and achieved their freedom through books. For some, reading is only a distraction, a way of passing time; but for others, books are the beginning of a new life.

With new confidence, D set his sights on college. At that time, college courses were still offered directly by the state in prison—a policy unfortunately abolished in 1994. It is a good policy because only a very few prisoners who take college courses commit new crimes.

D chose to study psychology "because I always was sizing people up, wanting to know what made them tick, and I thought that studying psychology would be a way of adding to the street wisdom I already had." He was amazed, again, at the ease with which he handled the academic challenges, keeping his own counsel about which teachers and which books were useful and which were not. He continued in classes, studied hard, and eventually earned a BA in psychology. In the process, he found himself helping other inmates with their own academic progress. Some were illiterate, ashamed to reveal it, and adept at hiding it. But they were surprised to find that they were not embarrassed to tell D and ask for his help.

As is the practice in New York State, D was transferred from one prison to another—part of a policy to keep negative connections from forming and to reduce inmate violence. But this constant moving also often causes disruptions in education programs and family connections. D took it as an opportunity to meet new positive inmates, to learn about the ways different prisons are run and the different cultures that inmates form inside prisons.

He decided to take courses toward a second bachelor's degree, this time in social work. As he continued his studies, he encountered the Alternatives to Violence Program (AVP). In 1975, a group of Quakers led by a retired schoolteacher named Larry Apsey developed a set of exercises to help inmates recognize the choices that led them to violence and the alternatives that were now possible. The founders were gifted in their ability to help inmates come to their own conclusions. As good Friends, they did not preach. The Quakers have been involved in prison reform since the 1800s, and this program may be their best contribution. AVP has been implemented all over New York State and in other states.

D was a natural. He has a gift for creating new experiential learning forms. He quickly became one of the leaders of the AVP and was glad to realize that many of the steps constituted progress he had already made. He was encouraged to discover that his reputation for being tough now seemed to be to his advantage in his new role. In the slow merry-go-round of inmate transfers, he began to encounter inmates he had known years before when he had not yet begun his self-transformation. Some dismissed him as a sellout (though rarely to his face) and continued in their old ways. Others were intrigued and made themselves available to his further counsel, some enrolling in AVP.

So D came along at a time when the prisons were relatively more ready to respond to his self-transformation than they had been before. Nevertheless, it continued to be a gigantic challenge.

D continued to grow every year he was inside. He learned sign language at Eastern prison and was able to help deaf inmates in spite of their mistrust of hearing people. (For some strange reason, in my experience, deaf inmates seem more inclined to be more suspicious than blind inmates, but D successfully crossed the line with many.)

On Christmas Eve in 1996, in Sing Sing, where D was then an inmate, a Muslim prisoner killed a Christian prisoner, allegedly for wearing a cross. The mother of the dead man, who had given him the cross, arrived with Christmas gifts before she learned what had happened. One can imagine the scene. The prison was filled with tension in anticipation of a revenge killing of the Muslim. Two days later, it was AVP recognition day; and D, initially unwilling, was persuaded to be recognized in the ceremony. It seemed that the smallest spark could cause a bonfire. The AVP coordinator from the outside asked D if he would ask the inmates to turn in their weapons. Inmates always have weapons; the best that staff can do is to keep searching, try to keep them at a minimum. D could not let the ceremony end without recognizing the potential disaster hanging over them all. But he felt it was unrealistic to ask them to turn in their weapons.

Instead, he called for the beginning of something he called Peace Week. Everyone needed time to cool off, he said. He asked the victim's people and the murderer's people to observe a no-fighting time.

That week, no one was killed. The week was extended to a month, and finally, the heat cooled.

That momentous event has led to an annual Violence Awareness Week at Sing Sing, a time when there are visiting speakers, including, formerly incarcerated people. And there are special events, as one would expect of AVP, when everyone present participates in learning exercises.

D eventually sought entry into the masters of divinity course initiated by the New York Theological Seminary under the leadership of the Reverend George "Bill" W. Webber. Bill, out of his experience as one of the founders and ongoing leaders of the East Harlem Protestant Parish, was challenged by a prison chaplain, Rev. Ed Muller, to reach out to those who had been missing from the streets of East Harlem because they were in prison. Believing that many of them seemed to be people who had transformed themselves in prison and had developed a strong faith in God, he asked, "Why not offer them the same opportunity as those on the outside?" In the post-Attica period, there was so much openness to trying new programs that the DOCS leadership was willing to try even this, which at other times would have seemed just another crazy idea.

As a result, under Bill's leadership, other new classes and vocational training were begun and expanded, especially at Attica and the other maximum-security prisons. The master of divinity course, begun in 1980, was demanding. People in prison, required to have earned a BA already, were gathered from all over the state to Sing Sing to live for one year on the same unit, creating a community of challenge and encouragement. Protestants, Catholics, Muslims, and Jews were all admitted. I believe that there was even a Buddhist in one of the classes I taught. Graduates went back to the prisons they came from to continue their ministries in any way that seemed best to them and the individual institution.

D went to Sing Sing in 1996 for his year of academic training, and he did very well there. He was not planning on seeking ordination to be a minister in a church, but he wanted to continue his ministry both inside and, maybe eventually, outside as a layperson. In 1998, D was transferred to Eastern Correctional Facility, in Napanoch, New York, when he only had a few years left in his twenty-five-year minimum sentence. He had the routine interviews by the institutional parole staff to prepare his folder to go before the Board of Parole. Typically, in 1998, any prisoner with a record of a homicide, like D, would be denied parole. "Nature of the crime" was the explanation routinely given. That answer is understandably accepted by the general public, who rarely see a transformation from wild man to normal citizen, and especially not to heroic leader.

The day came for D's first parole board hearing. He went, eager to present himself as best he could, but fully cognizant that his parole probably would be denied; and he would have to wait another two years and then maybe many more two-year "hits" after that. After all, the dead man in the tavern was never going to be released to return to *his* family.

And then there was an extraordinary event. The superintendent of Eastern, David Miller, asked to appear before the Board of Parole. He spoke of D's outstanding record, said he had never known his equal in his thirty years of work in the prison system, and pleaded with the board to grant him parole. No mention was made of the fact that it had taken him seven years inside to begin to wake up and appreciate his own gifts. The board released D at that first appearance.

He had been out several months when we met, and I hired him as a group leader with Network as quickly as I could. He then added positions with our foster care work, helping our young people keep out of gangs and make good decisions early in life—hard decisions about choosing good friends, continuing to study, and taking responsibility for their actions.

He has also gone back to Sing Sing to work in Network and to visit each year's group of students for the master's program. When I return with him to any prison, it is an amazing experience to walk the paths between buildings. Voices call out of the shadows, hardly daring to believe: "Hey, is that D? Yes, it's D! Hey, D, are you all right?" I turn and look, barely able sometimes, to see the speaker. D will turn and recognize the one in the dark place, call him by name, and ask, "Are you still doing stuff [AVP, education, growing your character]?" And the prisoner will say, with varying degrees of strength, "Yeah, I'm still doing stuff" or "I'm going to the next workshop" or "I'm a leader now." They crowd around him, dropping their shields of bravado like children around a champion athlete, as if they hope by being close to him, they will get some magical transfer of his gentle power, his graceful authority and, most of all, his inner freedom.

It was a challenging transition to move out from that hero worship to life on the outside, where people did not know the mythical D. It may have been the mightiest part of his self-transformation to accept that and start working with people with AIDS, most of whom did not know him. He had to start over and make a new reputation as an unusually sensitive, charismatic, and wise helper of people trying to find their way in life.

There are many young people like D, who, for various reasons, need to be held still, confined, perhaps for years, until they transform themselves into the people they had it in themselves to be all along. Right now, we do not effectively distinguish, although we could, between those who become worse and those who become extraordinarily better inside prison.

There are tens of thousands of inmates who experience the "breaking." Some people become disabled by the breaking. They are not broken in a positive way; they are crushed. Others break and discover spirit and brains they never knew were there.

For many people in prison, that happens even without any specially good program inside; simply being held still—the very impossibility of escaping—has brought them to the breaking of their wildness and rebelliousness. It is impossible to know, statistically, how many people experience what one inmate, Douglas Dennis (editor of *The Angolite*, the best prisoners' publication in the world), has called "criminal menopause" and many others refer to as the "aging-out" process. The testosterone count is lower, the dreams are more realistic, so the disappointments do not seem so cataclysmic. That happens inside and outside prison, and it is not exactly the same thing as breaking; it is more like wearing out.

The challenge is finding a way to break the wildness and still keep the spirit alive so these people can fight effectively against injustice and oppression and, most of all, so they can continue to grow and blossom as human beings.

David Ward, an inmate whom I met in the MDiv program at Sing Sing in 1999, told me one day, "I realized one night, as I lay in my cell, that I either had to *walk* or die. I felt God was telling me to *walk*. He was saying that if I would walk, he would walk with me. I have never been afraid from that time on!"

The idea of "breaking," or surrender, is close to that of kenosis or self-emptying, which has as its principal reference the passage from Saint Paul's Letter to the Philippians (2:6-8): "And counting not equality with God a thing to be grasped, Jesus humbled [emptied] himself by becoming human, even unto the death on the cross."

One might think of two contrasting movements in a modern dance. In one, the dancer sweeps imaginary things toward the body, grasping and clutching. In the kenosis, the dancer's hands and arms help an imaginary flow outward, toward others, giving everything away.

Breaking may be also described as the process of controlling the wish to have revenge, instead of reacting violently to a real or imagined hurt—a process that brings a certain vulnerability.

In prison, the vulnerability of being open and acknowledging feelings can be fatal if it is not grounded in courage. Sometimes that courage comes from feeling that there is nothing more to lose. "I am in prison. I have gone down a long way. I am at the end of one road. So I am no longer going to strive to please anyone or achieve anything. I am free, standing on a rock at the bottom of the world. I am empty. My freedom is in my emptiness." That was what I saw in the eyes of those men in the bottoms of their well-like cells in South Africa. That kind of kenosis contains great strength.

It is similar to the courage some have found in coming close to death. On the battlefield or in a hospital bed, while facing that possibility even if only for hours or days, a person can change forever.

At one point, I was suffering from a mysterious stomach ailment. I was in the hospital and felt as if I were dying and surprised myself by saying, "I have looked death in the face, and I am no longer afraid. I know that my achievements will not be a shield against death. I am empty. I am ready to live as one peacefully emptied, given to God in this life and the next." Ultimately, the ailment was cured, but I never would have had those moments had I known for sure that I was going to get better.

There is a prison version of my hospital experience. The knowledge that death will come can be used to form the "yard eye"—the way you look at people in the prison yard so that they will not mess with you. Prisoners at this point say to themselves, "I know that I am going to die. Maybe soon. I would rather go with my head up. I am ready to fight as hard as I can with anyone who challenges me." But looking at your own death can also be the deepest way to form the "cell eye"—the way to look at who you really are when you are locked in your cell, able to be completely yourself, for better or worse, protected by the bars. I have only heard those terms spoken, never written, so I sometimes wonder if people mean the *yard I* and the *cell I* struggles.

On the outside, of course, we have our own version of that challenge, sorting out the difference between our working selves, all dressed up, with offices and telecommunications, as against our domestic selves, sometimes naked, sometimes identified by our little children as "making really big smelly poops." Even people who live in the free world have, of course, our own breaking points when the public, working self yields to the satisfactions of family life, and high-powered jobs are turned down in order to maintain family life.

I believe that the large number of people who come to the breaking point in prison constitute a significant percentage of the prison population. When they are engaged in that transformation, in Network units or elsewhere, the whole life of the prison shifts in a small but significant way.

People inside who have lived through the suffering and fear of prison have much to teach those of us who have lived only on the outside. We outsiders are all under the thrall of pyrotechnic distractions, but people inside are not distracted by these things until they are released to the freedom they have yearned for and have made into a fantasy life. Before that release, there are many who have learned to be centered, undistracted—like wise men, mystics, monks. Any prison usually has a few who stand out. Some are following a specific religious path. Others are simply full of excitement about life.

That was true of Jerome Washington, another man I met who had been convicted of a violent crime and had reached a breaking point that allowed him to turn himself completely around. While I was on the New York State Commission of Correction, he had written to me for help after composing material for the prison newspaper that was deemed over the line, and he had been silenced by the superintendent.

Washington had become a Buddhist. He meditated long and well, and he became spiritually indestructible. He went beyond pain. He had a small quiet following, and there were others who admired him from a distance. He was not tall, muscular, or imposing. Like D, he was one of those who managed to be "free" inside prison. His mystic ascent did not prevent him from struggling against the needless harshness of life inside. On the contrary, he was gifted as a writer and eventually published a book called *Light in the Yard* and a short book of poems, *Crow Boy*, dedicated to his *sangha*, his Buddhist group in prison. They are meditative books, but they are also taxonomies of the horrors of life inside prison. After he was released in 1986, Washington went on to be a professional writer, traveling the world. When he came out, our paths crossed. He reminded me, smiling gently, that while I was chairman of the Commission of Correction and he was a prisoner in Auburn prison, I was of no help to him.

We talked; he forgave me, and I ultimately recruited him to help our foster care youngsters at Episcopal Social Services to learn to write poetry. The result was another book, written by the foster care group home girls, called *Up From Down There*, which ESS published privately. Their voices are lean and clear, crying out their teenage disappointments and telling of pain deeper than teenagers should ever have to bear. Washington helped them manage their solitude, as de facto orphans, out of the strength he had learned in his own prison solitude.

I also encountered David Hernandez, a burly man with a strong chest and steady blue eyes. He had been involved in the drug world early in life. But he was also a serious student of the martial arts. Before getting in trouble with the law, he had studied a martial art called Ketsugen Karate. He came to see himself as a "warrior and a fighter committed to protecting my family and neighbors in the best way I knew." He told me that he had reached the point where "in my small world, I was a hero." He was even appointed an auxiliary police officer by the Twenty-third Precinct in New York City. But he slid over into working both sides of the street and was present when a drug dealer was killed by an associate. The man had approached the victim with the gun hidden under his coat. David knew what was about to happen. He feels he could have prevented the murder. Convicted along with the actual killer, he served fourteen years inside.

David Hernandez had made great progress toward becoming a full human being before slipping into the drug culture. His family supported him inside, and he was able to qualify for entrance into the college work offered inside by the State University of New York at New Paltz. It was a higher quality of academic work than he had ever experienced before. He says, "In learning, I found freedom."

He remembers one class as a particular turning point, perhaps his breaking point. His sociology professor, David Matlin, initiated a discussion about machismo, trying to expose the truth about a word that prisoners think of positively, as meaning "combative in some masculine way." Matlin defined machismo as having the courage to be patient, persistent, even forgiving and caring. David Hernandez struggled with the new definition, fighting against the opposite perspective on his whole approach to life. He concluded that he needed more than martial arts to be a real man.

When he yielded and saw masculinity in a new way, he became a more serious student, recognizing that gaining knowledge was a new discipline, similar to the one he had embraced as a participant in the martial arts programs. "I experienced knowledge as power," he told me. "For the first time in my life, I could discuss ideas, explore the unknown, and think about the future."

He was released in 2001 and has been employed as a case manager and treatment counselor in a halfway house for released prisoners. He is also a student enrolled in the master's degree program in the Wagner School of Public Administration at NYU. He is living with his mother until he graduates, finds a better job, and has a realistic opportunity to start a family.

There are many thousands of others who have transformed their lives. They have achieved personal change in spite of obstacles created by other inmates and by the other conditions of confinement. Their faces reveal a centered peacefulness, which contrasts dramatically with their hard faces of years ago.

I have never forgotten the mug shots I saw when I was superintendent of Taconic. These photos of the inmates were taken at the time of their arrest and entry into the prison system. Repeatedly, even for inmates who were serving terms as short as three years, the contrast of their appearance in the mug shots and in their faces when I saw them in the flesh was astonishing. Instead of looking angry, desperate, or sullen, they now looked focused, serious, even vulnerable.

D insists that he is not unique, and he is correct. Many have come through the furnace of prison life with graceful patience, thoughtfulness, and courage. To see their faces is to see the vulnerability and quality of character that have made them good friends, sons and daughters, wives and husbands, mothers and fathers, and grandmothers and grandfathers. They came to their breaking point, and then they started a new life.

But it is also true that many have not come through prison so well. They have never reached a breaking point, and they perhaps never will. I admit that my work generally has put me in direct contact with the best, but a significant number of prisoners, unfortunately, are not ready for parole. Their emotional handicaps have remained or have even deepened.

One man looked like Santa's helper—cheerful, with wispy white hair and a German accent. He was Gustave Abitz, and he fixed the tiles on my office floor when I was superintendent of Taconic Correctional Facility. He whistled and hummed quietly as he worked. Curious, I looked at his record and saw that he was serving a sentence of twenty-five years to life and had been denied parole many times. He had come home, a soldier in the U.S. Army after World War II, to find his wife in the arms of another man. He killed them both. His young daughter had witnessed the double murder and testified to the truth in court. When I asked him what he would do if he were released on parole, the twinkles disappeared; his face became red and contorted. He choked out the words, "I will find my daughter, and I will kill her!" Santa's Helper was only one of many prisoners I have met who are clearly eager to commit new crimes on release. He seemed to be one who should never be paroled.

I inquired recently about him and found that he actually had been paroled years later and died on the outside without committing any new crimes. His daughter may have died before him, or he may have been terminally ill on release.

Then there was Teddy Stollman, a handsome green-eyed man who was very quick to understand the program and participated well. One day, the participants started to speak about exactly what happened on the day of committing the crime for which they were incarcerated.

Teddy said that he had bought new shoes with the money from his first paycheck. He loved those shoes. On the day in question, it was raining. He did not want to go to work and ruin his new shoes. So he stayed home and called his social worker, with whom he was intimately involved. She came over, and they had a disagreement after which he stabbed her twenty-nine times. He made no attempt to run away.

Teddy said, "It all happened because it was raining." Once again, I was amazed at the depth of the problems: that he could commit such a brutal crime at all and that he really could identify the problem in such a superficial way. It was hard to imagine him being released on parole, but he was, many years later. Then more years after that, I saw him on the inside again. He looked at me and shrugged. We talked; and he said, in effect, that he belonged inside. "I just can't handle it out there."

Another man I met was a paraplegic. While locked up in Clinton in 1979, he had gained the attention of a woman I never met, and she had written to me, taking up his cause with persuasive fervor. She claimed that he was being deprived of visits, commissary, religious services, and access to the law library. Furthermore, she claimed that he said he was subject to mistreatment by the other prisoners because he was white.

It sounded a bit exaggerated, but I decided to find out for myself on a trip to Clinton. Clinton is built on a hill, like Sing Sing, so there are endless stairs to climb to go anywhere inside. Confining a paraplegic there seemed like a bad joke. My man was on a top floor in a kind of unit for inmates needing special medical attention on a routine basis.

I found a balding, pudgy white man of about forty-five badly in need of a bath, almost rocking in his wheelchair as he spluttered with anger and racist invective. He did not want religious services; he was an atheist. I explained that I was the chairman of the Commission of Correction and that his friend had written to me out of concern for him. Could I help? That only produced another explosion of fury. I began to realize that he was primarily angry about being paraplegic—a condition that resulted from a gunfight in which he had killed the person who shot him. As he fumed, he revealed that he had been in other scrapes that could have left him in the same state or dead.

I thought that if I came back at the end of the day, he might calm down enough to let me know how I might help. But when I returned after making other visits, he was still enraged. It became clear that he was actually mentally ill. If staff insisted on bathing him, I learned, they were in for a fight. In short, I was unable to help him. With a minimum of tranquilizing medication, especially of the variety available today, he might calm down enough to begin to come to terms with the wreck of his life. Though he would probably never go on to be a healthy man, he might gain from improved mental health services inside the prisons. He was so unbalanced that I could have easily imagined him killing people from his wheelchair if he were ever released. Even I, the eternal optimist, do not easily imagine a breaking point for him.

As many as a fifth to a quarter of people in prison may be mentally ill. Much has been said in years past suggesting that prison provokes mental illness, but I do not believe the facts entirely support those claims. I believe most of these inmates were ill to begin with—a condition that may have contributed to their crimes. Others are simply marked by never-ending anger. Every new event seems to be grounds for fury. They are usually the young ones, swept into the system because they were unwanted at birth, scolded (even as very little children) for being "just like your father," furious that all doors appeared closed. Now in prison, feeling as if they have no power of choice, they believe they have nothing to lose. Holding them still deters them from crime on the outside, but it does not lead to a happy ending. It is finally impossible to tell which ones will make progress and which ones will remain stuck. Only time will tell. For now, there is much more that could be done for them inside.

There is no question that mentally ill people in prison have been poorly served for all the time I have worked in prison. They have been scapegoated by other prisoners and staff and have been shoved into special housing units (SHUs) out of sight. That is still true as this book is written.

However, there is new national attention being given to the problem. New York State tried to bring new money into the prisons during the Pataki years, but he rejected the efforts. Now finally, there is a new day for those in that terrible darkness.

The big change has come as a result of the tireless efforts of Assemblyman Jeffrion Aubry, chair of the Assembly Committee on Corrections, a champion of prison reform. He successfully steered legislation through the legislature to require New York State to provide mental health services for people in prison who are mentally ill. This has led to the transfer of all mentally ill prisoners to the prison in Marcy, New York. There they receive minimum care including group and individual therapy and appropriate medication. The cost associated with this change is great, but New Yorkers should be proud that the bedlam of the old system has been corrected, thanks to Jeff Aubry.

My additional hope is that there will be training for a whole new group of laypeople, including those who have been in prison themselves. They could visit in the supermax prisons and simply engage the prisoners in conversation. Most of the prisons are located far from urban centers where professional help is available. But laypeople, with good supervision, might be more useful than highly educated professionals who have difficulty engaging the trust of those who are bleeding emotionally from the beatings of society.

No consideration of "holding still" would be complete without some consideration of the prison cell itself. Each is individual, reflecting the occupant. Many call it "my house." So it is upsetting, sometimes devastating, for them to have their cells searched. The officers involved are sometimes not careful about the way they conduct searches, often simply trashing the cell. Prisoners say, "my cell got tossed," because that is a clear description of what has happened. When the whole world has shrunk to the dimensions of five-feet-by-nine-feet existence, the invasion of that space feels like an assault on the body of the occupant.

Therefore, the abandonment of the policy of limiting occupancy to one person in a cell—the norm since the nineteenth century—was a significant change in the New York State prison system. Before 1980, most people in prison were housed in single cells. During the year 2000, many were housed in cubicles in dormitories (many with double-decker bunks in the same cubicle); two in a regular cell; and now, finally, even two in an isolation cell! Spending twenty-four hours a day locked up with another human being leads to many problems, not the least being forced sexual activity.

It is true that many people in New York State prisons have been raped and/or sodomized by the person with whom they share a cell. No one will ever know how numerous those victims have been. And there is no way to overstate the horror experienced by those, smaller, weaker, less able to fight, when they are confronted by the person with whom they must share their living space, sometimes for 23 hours a day, sometimes 8' by 10' including the toilet and shower. Surely there are many men and women who have become broken people for no other primary reason than that they were locked up in a tiny space with an angry, unreasonable, muscular person who was not very bright and not interested in exploring the complexities of life.

By the summer of 2009, as more prisons were closing, it became possible to return to the old policy of housing only one person in a cell. For example, in Green Haven, 70% of men in cells were once again alone and could be at peace when the bars slammed shut.

This is a major step forward and it has received no publicity whatsoever. Tension inside, and the violence it produces, is reduced. More important, it is much more likely that men and women will be emotionally stable when they are released.

Special housing units are the ultimate in being held still: twenty-three hours of every day in the same cell with the same cell mate. Food is slid under the door. "Exercise" is allowed for one hour in an adjoining yard entirely enclosed by wire mesh fencing. Visits are extremely restricted, although books and radios are allowed. Every part of the cell, including the toilet, is visible for monitoring.

The Department of Correctional Services should be given credit for trying Years ago, in the first few moments of the initiations of the double cell policy to minimize the potential for violence by attempting to match two people in a cell with as much consent as possible. I heard of one man who was taken to the special housing unit and moved from one cell to another; there happened to be only one inmate assigned to a cell at the time. Each was asked if he was willing to have the new people in prison live in that cell. The one already there looked at the new man; may have recognized him; but knew that if he did not accept this man, the next one might simply be imposed on him and might be even less acceptable. This is routine administrative procedure, a way to minimize the potential for brutality between two men locked in together.

The other side of the argument about two-in-a-cell is the occasional story of people in prison who have been self-isolating all their lives, loners who have finally lashed out to commit the crimes, which have gotten them in jail. They have been forced, in a double cell, to connect in some way with the human being with whom they share their tiny space. The potential for suicide goes down. Even if prisoner A cares nothing for prisoner B, he is likely to intervene if B is preparing to hang himself. A's motives could not only include some residual fellow feeling, but also concern that he might be accused of murdering B and trying to make it look like a suicide. (I know of no such examples directly.)

Nevertheless, the potential for self-transformation, my ongoing concern, may be diminished when two people are locked in a space, which is not even big enough for one. Instead of engaging in useful introspection, each must spend considerable time in conversation and trying to manage life with another compromised person. The benefits of silence: reading, praying, and meditating are much harder to achieve.

There has been much appropriate criticism of the overuse of special housing units. Sometimes people in prison request protective custody (PC) in SHUs because they fear for their own safety if they live in the regular prison population. Staff usually question prisoners making such a request because once someone goes to PC, that tag stays on for the rest of his/her time in prison. Other prisoners learn that they were in PC. They lose program opportunities, the availability of visits diminishes, and there is no way for them to participate in regular religious worship. So it is important that prisoners weigh the relative values of the PC choice.

By far the greatest numbers in SHU are there for problems of violence. For decades, there have been no "dark cells" with light so minimal that it is impossible to tell if it is day or night. Plastic shields are bolted on the cell bars of prisoners who throw urine or feces on passing personnel.

With good behavior, the shields are removed. Many new SHU cells have solid steel doors with slots at the base for passing food trays in and out, slots for locking handcuffs, and small windows for conversation with staff. For some, this kind of confinement causes mental illness or exacerbates the pathology that previously existed.

The solution to this problem is elusive, but there are definite improvements possible.

The steel doors should at least be replaced by open bars. If the prisoners throw feces or other things, the open bars can be covered with plastic. No sound security purpose is served by forcing the solid steel doors on everyone in SHU.

There is no question in my mind that the regular maximum-security prisons of New York State are much safer now than they were in the turbulence of the 1970s and 1980s. When I go inside with visitors, men and women, without exception, say that they "feel totally safe, never had a moment of fear." That safety seems to be not only the result of greatly expanded family visiting, somewhat increased programming (with the tragic exception of college, which was withdrawn in 1994), but also the availability of SHU cells in greater numbers, leading to the removal of the most violent prisoners from "general population."

It is possible to be released from SHU even after being given a long sentence to that prison-within-a-prison. I know this not only as stated Department of Correctional Services policy, but also directly from inmates.

One man in particular was Pedro Hernandez, whom I met at Eastern Correctional Facility while I was participating in an Alternatives to Violence weekend. Slim, with wavy black hair, he was a particularly notorious gang member. Pedro had been arrested, tried, convicted, and sentenced to twenty-five years to life, with each part of the process trumpeted in the press. So he arrived in prison at the age of twenty-two already infamous. He immediately plunged into organizing gang activity, was warned, keep-locked, and finally involved in a bloody, nearly fatal assault on another inmate. He was sentenced to five years in SHU.

Pedro came to himself after two months. "Nothing like that had ever happened to me," he told me. "I was just *stuck* in the fucking cell! No gang around me. No one to organize. That was new. I had my guys in the street. I had them on Rikers Island. I had them in the receiving prison where I was processed into the state system. And I had them big time when I finally landed where I was going to do my twenty-five years to life. I was busy organizing my guys in the yard. Then we had the big fight. Really bloody. It was bad. They sentenced me to the upstate maxi-maxi for five years. My cell mate was not a bad guy, but I was really pissed. I yelled a lot. Nobody answered. I shit on the food tray. Officer said, 'Don't do that stuff, you'll be here your whole five years.' He didn't sound like such a bad guy, but I cussed him out. Then it was all quiet again except for guys in other cells cussing *me* out. I was almost literally banging my head against the wall.

"Two months later, I woke up and said to myself, 'It's over. I want to be back out there. I'm through with gangs. I'm tired.' It wasn't about God. I was just through. So I started trying to talk to the guys who were putting my food trays in. Said I was sorry I had shitted on the trays and sorry about the mess. I asked for books. Talked with a counselor. They let me out after nine months of my five-year bid. And I have stuck to it pretty good. I still hate this fucking place and all the police, but I'm really into AVP." He is a facilitator of the Alternatives to Violence Program, having gone through all three levels. "And it works. I still feel like tearing it up, hurting guys. I can feel it behind my eyes. AVP helped me discover that. When that happens, I'd better split, or I'll be back in the box for another five years, and this time, they won't give me no nine-month break."

Pedro is still clearly an angry young man, but he has had his first long experience of sobriety, free of the drunkenness of unchecked fury. It is also his first experience of being required not to participate in gang activity, even in prison. He likes it. He is surprised and pleased to discover that he could have a successful life in the "square" world. It remains to be seen how he will react to the intoxications of life on the outside, but that is still two decades away.

Ironically, the *New Yorker* published an article about special housing on March 30, 2009, which almost undercuts its own thesis. Atul Gawande tells of Robert Felton, who was a "force of mayhem" since he was a child, first arrested at age eleven for theft. He has a terrible temper, committed a bloody assault, and went to Illinois State prison for fifteen years. He soon landed in isolation and began to hallucinate. He became psychotic and tried suicide twice. Finally, he was given a new lawyer who took an interest in him and brought him books. "That small amount of contact was a lifeline." The lawyer helped him get a GED and paralegal training. He began to advocate for himself, writing various politicians and attracting the interest of Senator Paul Simon, who appealed to the director of the State Department of Corrections, Donald Snyder Jr., who denied all the appeals. Finally, Felton was readmitted to general population in anticipation of his eventual statutory release on July 12, 2005. As one might expect, he had a terrible time adjusting to life on the outside, but refrained from crime and lived with his mother. He found a succession of jobs and began to settle down, fell in love, got married, and had two children. Then his car died, and he lost his job. He was finally arrested for breaking in to a car dealership and stealing a car. He is back in prison for seven years.

The strange twist to the story is that the director of prisons, Donald Snyder, was arrested and convicted of taking $50,000 in illegal kickbacks. He was sent to prison for two years. When I asked Felton whether he would let Snyder out of solitary confinement if Snyder were sent there, I quoted Felton as saying, "I'd let him out. I wouldn't wish solitary confinement on anybody. Not even him." So Felton, after all the torture he endured, has come out a more humane person than the one who had been in charge of the prison system. The resilience of the human system is beyond measure. This is meant in no way to justify one day of the brutality that Felton endured. It is only to emphasize that the heart of a person can come through terrible trials intact.

Though SHU has surely been a road to the nightmare of mental illness for some, it has been turned into a useful tool for self-transformation for others.

The books about anger management that are provided to supermax prisoners are written for about a seventh-grade reading level, which many SHU prisoners have not achieved. Also, the prisoners really need to talk with someone about their reactions to the books, and there are not enough counselors in the current staffing pattern.

It is fair to say that outright despair probably afflicts well over half the population—deep, seemingly intractable depression. Inmates pull it around themselves like a cloak to protect them from the pain of facing new paths; to protect them from feelings of love, which they believe only leads to new pain; to protect them from faith and the agony of not understanding why God seems so far away; to protect them from the pain of uncertain hope and the hard work that must come when you follow a dream. These people drag through the days and nights, doing what they are told. Many stay out of trouble and even "succeed" when they are released on parole by drifting from homelessness to a single room, leaning on family and friends, drinking cheap wine, and holding low-level jobs that require much less of them than their best potential.

Then there are those who are living testaments to the harshness of evil, the cruelty that one human being can inflict on another. One of the times I saw this was at the routine beginning of a Four-Part Meeting. It was in the early days of Network implementation at the prison on Mount McGregor, near Albany. There was one new prisoner in the group—pale blue eyes, about thirty, a weight lifter. He may have been put in the group by officers who were not in favor of the Network program.

When in the first part of the Four-Part Meeting, it was his turn to share a self-affirmation, he said, "I am a terrific lover. When I get a woman . . ." He then began, with hardness in his face, to describe a rape. I stopped him, saying that this was to be a time of sharing a positive experience.

"This is positive. I feel good about doing this."

"It does not sound as if there was any love involved."

"You said only that we should share something we feel good about doing, for which we take responsibility."

"How about choosing something you did this past week?"

"You let other guys talk about things they did years ago. So after I tear her blouse open—I like the tearing part—"

"No, I am not going to let you continue."

"Then you are full of shit! And this whole fucking Network is full of shit."

"I'm going to ask you to leave."

I then asked the officer in the corridor to take the man back to his housing unit. I did not want to change the frame of the meeting (so consistently valuable) and involve the other inmates in an exchange with him, partly because the new man was white and almost all the others were black and Latino. It could easily have escalated into a physical confrontation that would have erupted either in the group or outside in the yard with racially divided sides.

I have thought often of that moment and of the stunning cruelty in the new man's face. He clearly was ready for violence, was used to it, and expected to continue with violent behavior even if it meant great physical pain or death.

Reflecting on this incident and on similar ones, I feel sometimes as if I am opening a heavy, grimy steel window on a vast room of horror. Criminals and victims are writhing together, since today's victims can so easily become tomorrow's monsters.

I do not believe in a literal hell after death, but there are indeed prison inmates who are almost certainly living in hells of their own making here on earth.

Not all are, however. There are people like D and many more who have reached a breaking point. In life, there is sometimes an exit from hell, but it does require leaving behind one's old life. We need to open the door to exit from hell and to do all we can to guide people to it. We can do much more than we now do to provide humane care. The hundreds of thousands who have gone from our mental health hospitals to our prisons deserve much more than the revolving door we currently offer.

Chapter Twelve

Revenge and the Theology of Prison

Revenge is a problem that visits us all. I remember Scotty McDougal, a wired and wiry black man in our sheltered workshop in Exodus House in East Harlem. He was an ex-addict who had committed numerous street crimes, as well as several burglaries. He was doing well in the program, and we had high hopes for his success. He finally graduated to a job unsupported by the program and started saving money for a better apartment.

One day, Scotty came crashing through our office door, almost knocking it off its hinges. "They cracked my crib [burglarized my home] and stole all my money! They should be killed!" he ranted. When he settled down enough to call the police—a unique experience for him—he launched into an impassioned plea for using the death penalty for those convicted of burglary. "Damn! I worked *hard* for that money!" He sailed on, oblivious of the fact that he was justifying his own execution. Scotty later disappeared, and I fear he may have sunk under the waves of his homicidal vengefulness.

As odd as it may sound, I recognize myself in Scotty's desire for revenge. I remember walking with my children in the park one day when half a dozen teenagers came suddenly over the brow of a hill on their bikes, headed for my two little ones. I raced to protect the children, and the teenagers swerved and skidded, narrowly avoiding them. I picked up one of the bikes, waved it over my head, and yelled, "I'll take you all on!" I must have looked fierce, as they all rode anxiously away. I was trembling with fury. I have been burglarized and felt helpless and angry. I am sure that I would go into a murderous rage if anyone hurt or killed anyone in my family. Even imagining this makes my heart race. I am ready for violence. It is a reflex; vengeance is a personal wish that comes to many crime victims. Turning the other cheek is possible only if the offense is small or the spiritual discipline is great.

Where do we find such discipline? Some profoundly spiritual people have found it in the monastery. Others have found it in prison.

One place I encountered the wish for revenge was in court where I have gone three or four times in my life, to give character witness testimony for a person accused of a crime. The victim looked at me angrily as I said kind things about the person on trial. One woman in particular, Maria Perez, was sure that the young man who had been arrested was the one who had stolen her pocketbook in a lightning-quick mugging at night. She glowered at me as I told of John "Peewee" Bowie's devotion to his wife and two children, his regular work habits at the church, and the high regard that the neighborhood had for him. The point was that her money was gone, and perhaps worse, she was now frightened in the streets around her home. She would have voted for capital punishment for Mr. Bowie.

The criminal justice system was created, in part, to hold us back from acting on our wish for revenge—the wish you and I have felt when someone has robbed us, hurt us, or killed a child. The system makes our response to illegal aggression a matter of public, rather than individual, concern. It protects us from the potential for escalating violence. In effect, it protects us from ourselves.

As a moral improvement on state-sponsored vengeance, Western society has combined the notion of punishment for criminals with the ideal of preventing criminals from committing further crimes by incapacitating them behind bars, deterring crimes by others through this example, and unfortunately—often as an afterthought—of correcting or rehabilitating the criminals while they are locked up.

Even the most conservative among us would surely agree that the fact the state spends more on prisons than it does on education is not acceptable. That finally changed in 2007. I hope that we will spend much more on programs inside prison; the additional money will lead to great savings by reducing the numbers of prisoners who would commit new crimes and return.

The issue is not only about money; it is about our identity as a people. We want everyone to have a fair chance at a good life. It is now national rhetoric that we must "leave no child behind." There may be limits to that wish, but at the root, most of us want all people to have reasonable opportunities in life. A more flexible criminal justice system is part of that dream: tougher, more realistic, less expensive, and, in the end, providing greater safety for us citizens.

Prison plays only a part in that system, but it is the most polarizing part. People generally take one of two extreme positions: more criminals should be put in prison for longer terms, or most prisons should be closed, because only a small number of criminals require confinement. People take these positions with emotion, based on personal experience as victims, or from television, or, on the other side, as relatives of criminals or as criminals themselves.

One might say that ideas about God are a big part of the problem. "'Vengeance is mine,' saith the Lord. 'I will repay.'" This phrase from the Bible (Romans 12:19 and thirty-seven references in the Old Testament) seems to enthrone the very idea of revenge. If God does it, people say, then why not us? Are we not acting for God?

Actually, I believe that God was saying, "Vengeance is *mine*," meaning mine *alone*. Not yours, you little human beings. Hands off. "Let him who is without sin cast the first stone" (John 8:7). "Judge not, lest ye be judged" (Matthew 7:1). That is why we make our attempt at diverting individual revenge by assigning it to the state as surrogate for a higher power. And that is why we have to try to use that power to do better than little individuals would do and closer to what God would do even though we do it imperfectly.

T. Richard Snyder, in his fine book *The Protestant Ethic and the Spirit of Punishment*, points out that while a person is guilty if he has committed a crime, there must also be a context in which his crime was committed. The responsibility for guilt must be shared in part by the family, the neighborhood, the nation.

Tyrone Brown, the young man I met early in my career who had robbed a gas station to get money to take out his new girlfriend, had gone to a dysfunctional school. He lived in poor housing and was surrounded by images in ads, sitcoms, and soap operas glorifying an opulent life that he would never be able to afford. Worse, these images implied that he was not really a *man* unless he could buy the ingredients of that life. In many ways, society set him up to commit the crime. Then it punished him for committing it.

There is a chilling account of just such a culture crime in Ralph Ellison's book *Invisible Man*. Ellison describes the capture of an African American man by white men in a racist town. They strip their victim down to his shorts, keeping him tied up and standing. They then confront him with a pretty white naked woman who cavorts around in front of him until he begins to have an erection, visible under his shorts. They then beat him horribly for "lusting after white women."

We do the same thing today when we elevate materialism as the ultimate good and then make it impossible for people to live the "good" life we dangle in front of them. It is impossible because we shortchange public education, refuse to subsidize new housing, or fail to offer employment to anyone willing to work hard. This makes us complicit in, though not literally guilty of, the resulting crimes. *We* are the people (mostly white, mostly male) in Ellison's circle of tormentors. We need a scapegoat for our own sins. The ancient Hebrews attached signs of sins (written or otherwise symbolic) to a goat and then drove the animal into the wilderness. The scapegoat carried the burden of the sins away. The goat was sometimes killed and burned, another way of "consuming" the sins. Prison is the wilderness into which we send our scapegoats now. We make them pay the whole price for our stunted public policies.

I believe that we overuse prison in part because of the basic theology underlying our culture. Though we are an extraordinarily diverse nation, with the widest range of beliefs drawing significant numbers of adherents, a vast majority believes in a god called "he." We believe that he has certain expectations of us all, and that if we let him, he will help us to achieve those ideals. We believe in a life after death, and that when death comes, he will reward those who achieve the ideals and punish those who do not.

I reject that. However, the laws of this land reflect, in various ways, that basic theology. Dividing humans after death into two groups—the saved and the damned—encourages us to make exactly the same division here on earth.

When some ask, "How can a merciful god send anyone to hell?" The orthodox answer has been that God is just, and that in the name of justice, there must be such a division. But I believe that God is *truly* merciful—that we will all ultimately be united in God. His will is that we all be together in him and that finally, somehow, his will shall prevail.

How does that square with justice? The answer is that God's justice is higher than ours. God's justice is restorative. He will heal those who have been abused; when abused people abuse others, God will understand and find a way to bring them all into his bosom. When people robbed of opportunities in life turn to robbing others, God will restore both the robbers and the robbed. Even when a person takes the life of another, I believe those two people will ultimately face God together and be drawn to his heart in reconciliation. This belief has come from my exposure to hundreds of prisoners who, like the hit man George Beeks, were abused as children, people who were incapable of making decisions because of the way they were raised. George tried hard, but his father's brutality and the limits on opportunities after his release finally led him back to drugs. If George could speak from the grave, I believe he would say, "I had no choice." And I believe that is the truth. People like him learned to hit in reaction to the hits of others or to keep others at bay. They learned to rob because they themselves were robbed. I believe God will embrace them with the love they always wanted and could never find.

People have challenged me on this position, and in response, I have made a study of all the New Testament texts referring to life after death. I divided them into three lists: first, a group of texts that clearly suggest that some people ultimately will be separated from God; second, a group that seems clearly to say that all people will ultimately be reconciled in God; and third, the passages that seem ambiguous.

I conclude that the first group is Mideastern hyperbole. Jesus is trying to get our attention to take seriously what he is saying. He is not angry about what we think of as regular crimes. What he seems angry about are greed and hypocrisy. Those are the sins that draw him out to speak dualistically of sheep and goats; the rich man with the beggar at his gates; the whitewashed mausoleums and the den of snakes. Then in his calmer voice, he says, "Tax collectors and prostitutes will go into heaven *before* you" (Matthew 21:31), not that anyone will be excluded forever.

The teaching in the parables of the lost sheep, the lost coin, and the prodigal son would never have survived the process of choosing texts for the New Testament if they were not true sayings of Jesus. In the parable of the lost coin, the woman sweeps her house until she finds it. She can then rest; her treasure is complete. The parable of the lost sheep in particular emphasizes the importance of keeping the *whole* flock together. Ninety-nine are not enough. Go and find the lost lamb, and bring it back so that *all* are together. The prodigal son story is even more powerful because the one lost is human. The father says, "Of course I am celebrating, because we are now *all* together again."

But we hunger for vengeance, so we cling to the verses that seem to point to an ultimate division. The most powerful and most ironic is the parable of the sheep and the goats in Matthew 25. It is powerful because it seems so clear. The good ones are sheep and go to Jesus's right hand into joy. The bad ones are goats and go to his left into outer darkness, weeping and wailing. The assumption is that they are forever lost. The power of the simple clarity of that picture has overwhelmed Jesus's point even though he repeats it three times in the same verses. The picture is now repeated in countless churches, especially in the tympanum over the main doorway. It is pictorially perfect: Jesus high up, the saved sheep to his right, the damned goats to his left.

Why are those on the right hand saved? Only because, as Jesus says in the passage, they recognized Jesus in the faces of their fellow humans: "I was a stranger and you took me in; naked and you covered me; sick and you visited me; *I was in prison and you came to me*" (Matthew 25:36, italics added). Why are the people on the left hand damned? Not because of murder, rape, fraud, or theft, but because they failed to recognize Jesus in the faces of those from whom we instinctively turn away. We know how hard it is; we find it difficult to face even homeless beggars. How amazing that Jesus talks about people who are in prison! Most of the people in prison at the time would not have been political prisoners, for there were plenty of robbers and murderers in those days too. Jesus tells us that we should find *his face in their faces* or else be cast weeping into outer darkness. Who can stand? Not I. I am one of those who needs to do better, for there are plenty of prisoners in whose faces I utterly fail to see the face of Jesus. There are many people who beg in the street whom I avoid, much less really look at with a serious gaze, to find the face of Jesus.

So does that mean that we are all consigned to hell? No. I believe it means that Jesus, here and everywhere, is saying, "Look! Look at each other! Pay attention! Listen to the stories of each other's lives! Then join me when I look over the city and weep with me when I say, 'O Jerusalem, Jerusalem! O New York, New York! How I would have gathered you all as a hen gathers her chicks, and you would not'" (see Matthew 23:37). He pleads with us to open our hearts to *everyone* if we really expect him to open his right hand to us.

Instead, we yield to our hunger for revenge, which leads us to imprison too many people for too long. We create our own little heaven (freedom outside the prison walls) and hell (inside prison) right on earth. We do it all in the name of righteousness. We have long had the political will to build more prisons so that people can be punished. But for some reason, we do not yet have the political will to do the works that Jesus guides us to do: provide good public schooling, public housing, and jobs for all who work hard. All this would greatly reduce the amount of crime.

The problem of revenge is the failure to be clear about responsibility. The individual and society share responsibility for the actions of each person. Revenge puts all the responsibility on the individual, and that seems unfair. It is also wrong to put all the responsibility on society. To do so would be to rob individuals of the edge of their freedom. The answer, as always, is balance. We can do more to challenge anyone to live up to his/her highest potential, even in prison. We also must do vastly more to arrange our lives on earth in a way that enhances individual responsibility.

We cannot believe in a monster god who metes out utterly cruel punishments and still somehow trust God. I believe in a god we can trust.

Revenge is poison.

Chapter Thirteen

Prisons Are Being Transformed

I believe that we are entering a third phase of prison policy. The first phase was the rule from ancient history until about 1970. Prison operated as a place of punishment. Prisoners were locked up under dreadful conditions, and if reformers complained, they were told that these bad people had it coming. "Think of the victims." So flogging and cutting off hands were accepted. Food was disgusting. Rats were part of life. Medical care was almost nonexistent. Beatings, maimings, and brandings were included. Then, little by little, people came to recognize the humanity of the people who were locked up. Prison conditions began slowly to improve on humanitarian grounds. Charles Dickens was one of those bringing to light the appalling conditions, even in the "new silent system." The imposed silence was intended to be absolute. No exceptions—morning, noon, or night. The flogging was much diminished, but he wrote, "I hold this slow and daily tampering with the mysteries of the brain, to be immeasurably worse than any tortures of the body; and because its ghastly signs and tokens are not so palpable to the eye and sense of touch as scars upon the flesh; because its wounds are not upon the surface, and it extorts few cries that human ears can hear; therefore I the more denounce it, as a secret punishment which slumbering humanity is not roused up to stay" (from *American Notes*).

But slowly a slumbering humanity was roused up, and the worst excesses of the silent system were abolished. We still need to learn more about all that to change our supermax prisons into much more humane confinement.

So the second phase began, animated by the hope that those convicted of crimes could be "fixed" like a car or a recalcitrant child who just needed a good spanking. With good American optimism, we thought it should be simple: make prison disagreeable enough, and they will not want to be sent back. So there would be no more crime. It turned out to be much more complicated. They did come back, and often they did not seem to care. True desperadoes, they found it impossible to hope for a better life.

The momentum built up as the "lock 'em up and throw away the key" philosophy gripped the macho mentality. Prison populations soared across the country. The politicians of the less-populated areas of many states welcomed the opportunity to bring construction and stable jobs to their constituencies.

Prison programs even declined because they were labeled as being "soft on crime," which was political suicide for the legislative advocates.

Then it slowly became clear that a monster had been built: big prison systems that required huge amounts of money to build, maintain, and staff. You only create the fuel for riots when you try to run a prison with too few (or too poorly selected and inadequately trained) staff. Private entrepreneurs found that out when they decided to get into the prison business, refusing to believe that they could not run a prison efficiently and save a lot of money that would go to their shareholders. That experiment is still being tested, but it has long since been clear that it is not a big moneymaker. Excellent management only saves so much; then finally, you need lots of good staff to be aware of all that is going on inside and respond appropriately.

So we have entered phase 3. It is motivated by the philosophy that we must do everything possible to keep people from committing new crimes. Just being cruel does not work. And "just lock 'em up" does not work. There are three big parts to this phase 3.

First are the amazing new drug courts and youth courts. They are nothing less than a whole new way of administering criminal justice! It is significant that people who have not heard of it find it hard to believe that it exists *across the whole country*!

In one of these courts, the person who has committed the crime is brought together with the victim and the public defender, the district attorney, a social worker, and a judge. In the case of a street robbery, the mugger is confronted with the evidence of his/her guilt and required to listen to the one who was robbed, to hear the screams, and see the tears caused by the mugging. With the help of the social worker, the one who committed the crime acknowledges the pain that the crime has caused. He or she then agrees to a certain amount of money to be paid to the victim through the court to pay back the amount stolen and an additional amount for the suffering caused. If he or she fails to do that, then regular criminal justice takes over.

When the fabric of society is torn by a crime, we must do all that we can to mend the tear. We do that by caring for the victim and by giving the criminal the opportunity to make amends, to make the victim whole, as much as possible. Not by inflicting yet more pain, out of revenge, upon the one who committed the crime. That is another kind of justice: restorative justice. It turns not only to the law, but also to the actual people who are the victims and those who have committed the crimes, to see how new life and new commitments to justice and community healing might emerge from the pain of crime.

New courts have sprung up all over the country committed to this new kind of justice, willing to put rigid, automatic invocation of the law aside long enough to focus instead on the people. Prosecutors, instead of using victims to convict people accused of crimes, can turn to specially trained staff who work with both victims and those convicted of a crime to secure a deeper level of understanding of the torment that crime has caused, to bring about some mutually agreed restitution, and to plan for life ahead.

To be sure, there are many people whose crimes are too serious or too numerous to be treated this way. They must go to prison and be held still. But even there, restorative thinking still has a place. We can do more to provide opportunities there for people to face the crimes they have committed and the abuse they have caused so that they can face their victims (or the survivors) realistically and begin a new life.

Since both the alternatives of pure vengeance and premature forgiveness only lead to more violence and distortion, we are fortunate that there is this third alternative. Restorative justice has also been called progressive sanctions, intermediate sentencing, or community corrections. The best of these plans call for movement in and out of prison according to the demonstrated ability of the individual to manage a responsible life. The chief administrative judge of New York State, the Honorable Judith S. Kaye, has pioneered those efforts, now emerging as an effective alternative criminal justice system.

Having wrestled with the state bureaucracy a little myself, it seems miraculous that Judge Kaye was able to design the systems, introduce the ideas, lobby quietly for their implementation, train the staff, monitor for the highest quality of involvement of all participants, and then unobtrusively extend the work to more courts. Even after her retirement, the work goes on!

Someone who has been convicted of robbing a person on the street should certainly be regarded as having committed a serious crime. The best response is one that leads the person who committed the robbery never to rob again. And he should restore the money to the victim. That response is possible, and it is already working today.

Our criminal justice system is perceived as failing for many reasons, but mostly because the system puts almost all its focus on the criminal and almost none on the victim. Many victims feel cheated by a process that only uses them to achieve the conviction of the perpetrator. The perpetrator then goes to prison, and that is the "end" of the story. The victim gets nothing—not an apology from the offender, not a thank-you from the court or police, usually not even the restoration of their property. That victimizes the victim again. That is wrong. We can do better.

In the most extreme example, some of the families of murder victims have found ways, after years of work, to forgive the murderers. The murderers in turn discover depths of remorse, agony, and new life, which they had never dreamed possible. There are now a few formal programs to achieve such restorations, often called victim/offender mediation dialogue (VOMD).

Though the extreme cases of VOMD number only in the hundreds, there are many thousands now coming through the new drug courts and community courts in which people who have committed crimes are indeed helped to make financial restitution and to do community service as part of beginning a new life.

Though these new courts are achieving a new kind of justice, they won't work for everyone, and they are expensive to start up; but they are already saving lives, money, and pain.

A second part of the new phase we are in is the change coming in our prisons. We are being more sophisticated about which programs really work, really help people to stay out and lead crime-free lives.

We can do better, for very little money. Even a 5 percent increase in correctional budgets for more programs would reduce crime and, eventually, reduce imprisonment. It would be a small price to pay—and, in the end, would lead to paying less in prison costs.

As this is written, New York State experienced a decline in the number of inmates and recently closed six prisons, reducing the list in 2003 from 72 to 66, where it remains in 2007. The number of people in prison has dropped from over 72,000 to 63,000. That *finally* reflects the great drop in crime.

There will, of course, always be a need for prisons; but prisons need to be monitored closely. They must of course be run on a day-to-day basis with absolute authority by those in charge because otherwise, the desperate and angry people they house could quickly run wild, at great harm to each other and staff. But since absolute power corrupts, there must be someone with authority and monitoring responsibility over the prison officials; there must be constant checks and reviews of prison governance, from commissioners down to the lowest-paid employee who has direct contact with prisoners. Abuse can come suddenly and can grow quickly; so it is crucial that the monitoring agency have independence, sound judgment, and real power to act quickly. The Commission of Correction still exists, but it has a greatly reduced staff, making it almost impossible to do serious reviews of the work of all the prisons and jails of the state as it is required by law to do.

The media also play a determinative role. If they fail to report accurately on rumblings in the prisons or unfairly portray people in prison or staff as monsters, then legitimate grievances about bad conditions will not be heard. Then we will once again risk riots, hostage takings, and bloodshed. On a less dramatic level, we will simply fail to realize the potential for good that prisons carry.

Ultimately, of course, in order to make our prisons more effective instruments to improve public safety, the public must care about what happens inside our prisons. Without that caring, we will never have the political will to deal with the problems inside them. Without that caring, there will always be severe problems inside, no matter how meticulous the monitoring effort.

As a nation, we have a great history of generosity, and I believe we can extend that spirit to far more people. The basic changes needed are not necessarily new; we need only look back to some of the old-time reformers to see them and to reexamine the ideological foundations of modern imprisonment: deterrence, incapacitation, rehabilitation, punishment.

Imprisonment of people convicted of crimes is intended to be a deterrent to others who contemplate criminal action. Theoreticians base this idea on the belief that they themselves would not want to go to prison. So they reason that no one else wants to go to prison. Yet in fact, many prisoners have told me that on the outside, they were completely heedless of whether they went to prison; they were careening along without regard for any consequences.

After being inside, many have voluntarily said to me things like "Prison saved my life" or "Going to prison was the best thing that happened to me." Richard Speck, killer of eight nurses in a notorious crime spree in Chicago forty years ago, scrawled on the wall in their blood, "Stop me before I kill more." It has been my direct personal experience that hundreds of people who have been locked up have said basically the same thing, "I had to be stopped. I could not stop myself. I was too wild." But the *threat* did nothing; it was prison itself that did the service.

Incapacitation is the obvious corollary of being held still. In prison, people are indeed stopped from committing any more crimes, at least against individuals who are not in prison themselves. This obvious truth is part of what drives society to imprison more individuals for longer periods. We want to lock away the potential for trouble. Only a sense of basic fairness and justice keeps us from imposing even longer sentences for minor or impulsive crimes as a means of assuring ourselves that no one will ever trouble us again. The question then becomes, how long is enough?

That is a question for which rehabilitation should provide some of the answers. However, rehabilitation has been out of favor as a concept. It may have peaked in popularity in the 1970s, when the all-too-short tide of prison reform washed in, and states and the federal government were willing to spend a little money and energy exploring new ideas. Then Robert Martinson, a sociologist who studied dozens of rehabilitation programs, suggested that there was no proof that any of them were working. "Nothing works" was a catchphrase summarizing his article "What Works?" in a 1974 issue of the *Public Interest*. Unfortunately, "nothing works" was taken up as a defeatist truism. Martinson retracted that statement in more thorough studies he made in 1975, 1976, and 1979 and vehemently lamented ever having made it. Nevertheless, it has been embraced for over thirty years by those who want to save money—negligible amounts really—on programs and by those who were possessed by a fever for revenge against criminals. People who have never read an academic paper in their lives still quote Martinson and refuse to hear that he retracted his claim.

In fact, many programs, especially educational and vocational programs, do help people in prison transform themselves. When those individuals feel that they are changing themselves in fundamental ways, they are filled with hope. The word *rehabilitation*, as it has been used, implies an action *imposed* by an individual or program upon another ("We will rehabilitate you"). In fact, it is always and only the person who rehabilitates himself. The program or person opens doors, indicates a path, but the individual chooses (or not) to walk the indicated way. Many of us now use the word *transformation* instead of *rehabilitation*. It more clearly conveys the idea that the human being, not some outside force, is responsible for personal change.

Many studies also indicate that people who receive a college degree while serving prison time rarely commit repeat offenses. According to one by Michelle Fein, professor of social/personality psychology at the Graduate Center of the City University of New York, women who graduate from college inside Bedford Hills prison have a recidivist rate of 7.3 percent while those in New York State prisons who did not attend college have a rate of 29.9 percent. Similar studies of males who have been sentenced to prison show only slightly higher recidivism rates. Pride of accomplishment and new confidence in the abilities that the people did not know they had are more important than any particular knowledge or academic skill.

Punishment has been the dominant reason for prison. When someone commits a crime, people want that person found and hurt either by a fine or by prison. That is a feeling for revenge that we call normal in our culture, so it is difficult to imagine a day when the demand for revenge will be eliminated from the criminal justice system. However, as public understanding of criminal thinking grows, the intensity of the desire for revenge diminishes.

Revenge should not be the purpose of prisons. When revenge runs rampant, it always escalates the violence imposed for the perceived crime. That is how feuding groups—be they families, tribes, or nations—become so stuck in conflicts from which any exit becomes increasingly elusive.

At the same time, we want to stop the criminal activity as effectively as possible. The key word is *effectively*. This requires that we find a road between *vengeance*, with its high personal and fiscal price, and *forgiveness*, which produces equally little of value if given thoughtlessly and prematurely, before internal individual transformation has occurred.

I acknowledge that some people sometimes are just plain dangerous. It is only realistic to admit that many of them need to be held still for a long time so that they can focus over time on a new life and begin, if they will, to make the changes in their lives that the challenge of their crime requires.

But those of us who are on the outside also need some transforming. We can become more aware of our own wishes for revenge and for the desire to scapegoat others—and then make a rational choice to turn from those motivations to a higher and more practical wish: to have a safer society and a less expensive criminal justice system.

Unfortunately, events proceeded in the opposite direction from about 1970 to about 2000. Sentencing became ever more severe, and with that, the challenge of maintaining order on the inside has become ever greater. Boards of parole held many people in prison even until the expiration of their maximum sentences, which meant that they were more likely to be reckless inside because the hope of release seemed dim.

Programs were cut as the memory of Attica grew weak. Legislators have felt challenged by voters to answer the question, Why should criminals get a free college education while I have to pay ever more to put my law-abiding daughter through the State University of New

York? The answer is not to deny the one in prison, but to give the equivalent of the GI Bill to all Americans. Countless veterans received an education that they never would have otherwise achieved because college was offered free to them. The same can be true today for any American who qualifies. People are not so much angry at giving college to people in prison as they are frustrated by the costs of offering college to their own children.

Parole/reentry is the last part of the new phase of corrections development. The Board of Parole has been the fall guy for the media if a new crime is committed by a person on parole. That has made both the Board of Parole and the individual parole officers frightened about doing their jobs on a realistic, commonsense basis. They have been vilified unfairly over the past decades. In fact, parole should be greatly extended and parole staff increased. It should reach backward into the prison system to make early release possible by doing serious investigations of parole plans, and forward, making it possible to have a longer and more-supportive postrelease supervision period.

Early release would be less of a risk than it is now if a prisoner were offered some connection to continuing education, a "start-up" job, a bed with an address, and a network of peers to support him or her. One person, reading this passage in a draft, said, "I would like to have those same four things, and I never committed a crime!" He was quite correct. The same four things should be available to everyone. The connection to education would represent a challenge, the "start-up" job might be dirty and low paying, the bed would be in a dormitory, and the peers might be more challenging than fun, but it would be a real start to a new life for anyone.

Mental health services need to be greatly expanded to help people stabilize more quickly and completely on the outside. The same is true of drug treatment programs, which have been significantly expanded in other states. Abstinence inside prison is less of a challenge than abstinence on the outside.

Many people are returned to prison for violations of the conditions of their parole. The definitions of those violations vary widely from state to state and even within a single state. I believe that it is crucially important for the system to provide for such returns. The danger signs are clear to any experienced parole officer. However, there must be provision for flexibility in the length of time for such returns—as little as overnight, a week, or a month. A "wake-up call" can be useful as a newly released person tries to sort out his/her life. A return to prison for a long time for a small violation is poor public policy. It overcrowds our prisons and needlessly embitters those who are locked up.

I thought there could be no surprises for me after working in this field for over forty years, but I was surprised in 2003 by a new fact: conservative politicians across the USA were deciding that they must find new ways to save money in their state prison budgets. That meant that they had to think rigorously about how to keep released prisoners from *returning* to prison.

Recidivist rates vary from 30 percent to 70 percent depending on whether *recidivism* means rearrest or conviction for a new crime. Let us consider New York State and take the low figure. We release approximately 21,000 people from prison per year. If 30 percent return, that amounts to 6,300 coming back within three years for new crimes. At $25,000 per year, that adds up to $15,750,000 to the prison budget. If that figure could be cut even 10 percent with improved programs inside and outside prison, that would be an annual saving of $1,575,000. Some of that money would go to pay for the new programs and enlarged parole staffs, but over the years, the savings could be huge. And of course, there would be reduced costs of police, county jails, courts, and, most important, personal losses suffered by victims. I made this argument for years, along with many others, and finally it seems to be sinking in.

In the ebb and flow of public attitudes toward criminals, we have come a long way. People convicted of crimes are no longer maimed or thrown into wells to starve to death. We have long recognized that people in prison need meaningful activity every day. We are poised to embark on a whole new direction.

In New York State, that direction is gathering strength. Brian Fischer, former superintendent of Sing Sing, has been appointed to serve as the commissioner of the Department of Correctional Services. Fischer has the brains, experience, and progressive passion to be a superb commissioner. His appointment has been welcomed by staff and prisoners because of his reputation as a reasonable man, one who is willing to take risks (as demonstrated by his championing of college and the theatre program at Sing Sing) and who is also committed to doing the hard work required to minimize those risks.

So there are reasons to hope for a new chapter for prisons in our state. Commissioner Fischer has immediately reached out to the Board of Parole to initiate serious new kinds of cooperation.

And this phase 3 is well under way across the country. It will not just be a swing of the pendulum because the costs (fiscal and human) of returning to the old ways are simply too high. George Bush signed a bill (called the Second Chance, which was later called Act of 2007 when it became a law) with extraordinary bipartisan support offering federal money to states emphasizing reentry and programs to reduce recidivism. The tide has finally turned in the direction I prayed for over all the years of working inside and out!

My own life had been unexpectedly transformed on the occasion of my seventieth birthday, on December 23, 2003. After much thought, Caroline and I decided to celebrate it by going to Paris, taking my three children and one grandchild. We never had done anything like that before. We had a good time as a family and then went off on our own for three days. I had never been in Europe in the winter, and seeing the hills of Burgundy with a light dusting of snow was inspiring.

I had already written several drafts of this book, but I know it needed much more work. I had also written and rewritten a play about a widow and a widower, in their seventies, who fall in love and then have to face end-of-life problems. I had started another play about prison and the mystery of forgiveness. Both the plays and the book meant a lot to me. I also was enjoying painting more than ever—of the figure, landscapes, cloisters, and portraits. I had felt the wheel of life turning in a way I barely noticed when I turned sixty. There was not enough time left in my life, perhaps, to finish the book, the plays; to learn to paint much better; and to visit my children, two grandsons, and a granddaughter. I saw the possibility of retirement from being executive director of Episcopal Social Services. At first thought, I felt that I could not do it because I would miss the work in the prisons too much.

Then I realized that I could continue to visit in prison as a volunteer. I need not abandon the guys. They would know that I still cared about them and would continue to advocate for improved prison programs with the legislature, foundations, and private donors. Chills ran up my spine as I sat with Caroline at a good restaurant on New Year's Eve and the doors opened on a new life of freedom. I would not have to worry about balancing the budget, fighting with the legislatures of the city and the state for more money to maintain bare adequacy of programming for foster children. I would miss the satisfaction of resolving fights between staff members.

And so it has been. There was much more work to do on this book, but I finally had time to do it. I have worked as a member of the Actors Studio and in the HB Playwrights class on my plays and still hope someday to see them produced somewhere. Because of the first play, I have had to face more sharply the end-of-life decisions for me and Caroline. Could I give her the Pills if she were to have a permanently disabling stroke? Facing that has been life changing in itself. I have been glad that retirement has given me the hours and weeks to work on that play. And I have done lots more painting as well as giving a well-received talk on the connection between my faith and the painting of nude figures. Journeys to Iran and to Israel/Palestine have been new tumultuous experiences.

None of that would have been possible if I had not been able to continue visiting inside prison. "Going back inside" continues to be a necessary connection to some unexplained river of my life. I am touched by the respect that people in prison have expressed when I go back to see them. It seems helpful to them to know that I still believe in them, that I know that they can use their time in ways that are fulfilling for them, and that I continue to work with the forces of government to improve prison and parole practices. I have discussed this book with them, and they have encouraged me to tell it like it is.

If I have one regret, besides failing to emphasize family more, it is that I have never created a forum in which it would be routinely possible for people in prison to share with each other the real stories of crimes they have committed and other things they have done for which they feel wrenching remorse. I know that it would be a great relief to them if they could do that. Now they are trained by each other and by lawyers to "never admit nuthin' to nobody" because of possible future legal consequences, so their own perception of the past becomes covered with a murky veil. Way back, in the meetings in Green Haven, in the 1960s, we were all more open with each other. That happened because we all remained together in the same group for many months. They cried tears of pain, and I cried with them. I still think of going back, once a week, to the same prison and running a Four-Part Meeting. Maybe I will do that. I know that it would give me the same unique joy and satisfaction today that it gave me forty-five years ago.

A new day is dawning for the prisons in America. It will take new wisdom and determination on the part of our citizens. I hope and pray that the people of America will discover in ourselves the strength to turn away from vengeance. We continue to have terrible overcrowding in several states. Prisons vary greatly in their practices. Horror stories are still happening.

But we can choose to turn away from vengeance. We can focus on policies that will improve public safety. We can learn more from the best that some states are managing to do.

Most of all, we can learn from people in prison. We have the opportunity to recognize the satisfactions and blessings of our own self-transformations.

Appendix A

A Brief Overview of the
History of Prisons and Their Reformers

There have been many brave, wise men and women over the past two hundred and fifty years who have tried to make prison into productive engines of human transformation.

For much of Western history, prison was only an instrument of detention until some sort of trial and judgment took place. Following detention came the actual punishment—whipping, branding, exile, dunking, slavery, maiming, or execution.

One of the earliest mentions of prisons comes from the Middle Kingdom in Egypt (2050-1786 BC) and the book of Genesis, which describes the imprisonment of Joseph by the Egyptian authorities. However, prison was generally limited to confinement while waiting for some sort of punishment. The reference in Deuteronomy (19:16-21) calling for "a life for a life, an eye for an eye, tooth for a tooth, hand for a hand, foot for a foot" was experienced as an advance over more chaotic vendetta justice, in which uncontrolled revenge held sway, with resulting escalations in violence between aggrieved parties. Hebrew executions by stoning, decapitation, or strangulation were within the spirit of those primitive times.

The Athenian lawgiver Draco, around 620 BC, formulated a new law on homicide so severe that "draconian punishment" is the phrase even today for overly severe laws.

The Roman Empire refined the punishments decreed in the Twelve Tables (451 BC), the first written laws of Rome. A distinction was made between chaining (*vinculum*) and imprisonment (*career*). Chaining seems to have occurred in a public place, which made ridicule and worse torments possible. By the early second century BC, there seem to have been two levels of prison: a higher one for detention before trial, and a lower one of notable squalor, which also served as a place of execution.

Christians were routinely imprisoned before they were martyred. "Prison indeed ought to be employed for confining men, not for punishing them" is a phrase attributed to Ulpian, a Roman jurist in the early third century AD. It marks the end of the classical period of Roman law and speaks to the probability that conditions in all these prisons were harsh.

By the fourth century AD, edicts from the emperor began to show a concern for establishing minimal conditions for confinement. Constantine, soon after his conversion to Christianity and his military triumph in AD 312, decreed in the *Theodosian Code* that manacles of iron were to be used only for confinement and not for torture. Also, he said prisoners should "not suffer the darkness of an inner prison, locked into stocks or tightly chained, unattended to, unfed, suffering from heat or cold and filth, abused by jailers, or otherwise tortured while in prison."

In Europe, by the late sixteenth century, prison itself started being used as a punishment in and of itself, primarily for debtors. It is difficult to know what led to the change, but I wonder if repugnance over the physical brutality of other punishments had something to do with it. In these early prisons, young and old, male and female, were crowded together. No distinctions were made for mentally retarded or mentally ill prisoners. Conditions were horrific.

In 1704, Pope Clement XI built Saint Michael's prison in Rome, incorporating many features of monastic practice. It became one of the principal models for the development of prisons throughout the world.

Later in the eighteenth century, there came the first in a long new line of social reformers and thinkers to write on prisons. They opposed cruelty and capital punishment, promoted laws for the separation of the sexes, and succeeded temporarily in improving sanitation. Cesare Beccaria (1738-94) wrote his essay *On Crimes and Punishments* in 1764, generally recognized as the first thoughtful modern consideration of the topic. Prison reform could be said to start with his recognition that criminals could change. John Howard (1726-90) was appalled by the jail conditions he inherited when he became sheriff of Bedford, England. His campaign for improvement throughout England led to an act of Parliament improving sanitation and raising the pay of custodial staff. His *The State of Prisons in England and Wales* (1777) raised interest further, and he went on to study conditions in jails throughout Europe, finally dying of sickness contracted during his visit of prisons in Russia.

These reformers shared the vision that prison need not be only an expression of revenge, but also that it could have a restorative role for the prisoner, the victim, and society.

Father Andrew Slotnicki is a Carmelite who works in a California prison. He wrote in the Carmelite Newsletter in 2000, "My intent is to remind readers that the idea of the prison is neither hopeless nor cruel. It is a response to human weakness that has lost touch with the spiritual tradition that inaugurated it—a spiritual tradition whose insights are still the most humane and effective ones for righting what has gone wrong in the human heart."

In the United States, Quaker philosophy, which espouses a belief in the Divine Light in every human being, led to the founding of the old Walnut Street jail in Philadelphia, in the late eighteenth century. This was America's first penitentiary intended to be a place where criminals would be held still, read the Bible, and keep silence. But here the silence was carried to a virtually homicidal extreme where speaking was punished by flogging (sometimes fatal). Initially, prisoners were expected to keep the silence for their entire term. Since this kind of prison was a new alternative to flogging, maiming, or hanging, the prisoners did not complain much—or at least no record was kept of the complaints they did make. The minimal records did not show a dramatic reduction in criminal activity among those who were released. The institution also failed to satisfy those who wanted more bloody revenge against people who had committed crimes. There was less satisfaction in seeing them simply locked up.

A silent system was also instituted at Auburn prison, in Auburn, New York, in 1817. It was another innovative experiment. Prisoners were not to speak at all, at any time. If they lapsed, they were brutally punished. Each inmate had his own cell, but for some, the imposition of total silence was unbearable, and some people lost their minds before the policy was modified in 1820 to reasonable limits.

In 1829, a variation on the silent system model was instituted as the separate system, in the Eastern State Penitentiary in Cherry Hill, Pennsylvania. It consisted of solitary confinement day and night. Prisoners were fed in their cells and given Bibles to read. They worked as contract laborers during the day when not in their cells. Whipping continued for those who spoke. This was seen as reform at the time!

In all these discredited experiments, silence and stillness were the central features—grotesquely overdone—until the silence became a scream, the stillness a menace, instead of a blessed space that offered room to think and grow. But that does not discredit the idea of balanced silence and quiet, whether practiced in a modern prison or a monastery.

Alexander Maconochie, perhaps the most astonishing prison reformer ever, was born in Edinburgh in 1787. He came from a family of some wealth, received an excellent education, and was headed for a comfortable, successful life. But he was an adventurer with a career in the British Navy, where he saw action at sea, and was imprisoned himself. He went on to found the Royal Geographical Society. He finally was appointed by the British government to go to the island now known as Tasmania and reform the unspeakably cruel prison there. People arrived, sentenced to exile from Great Britain. The cat-o'-nine-tails was heavily used. Execution by public hanging was frequent. Men and women were sold as slaves.

For four years, Maconochie walked among the prisoners alone, without guards or arms, encouraged them to speak to him, stand up straight, look him in the eye, and say or ask what they would. Instead of whipping and hanging, Maconochie instituted the marks system by which prisoners could earn their freedom by good behavior. He caused two chapels to be built, initiated academic classes, had gardens planted, made music possible with instruments he bought in Sydney, offered theatrical events, and even grog, which was distributed once each week. All was going well—and it did not cost taxpayers anything extra because discipline problems were dramatically reduced.

Maconochie was eventually recalled because government authorities in Sydney and ultimately in England were outraged by what they saw as his being too lenient. But he returned to England and reported so eloquently on his work that he was reinstated. However, there was another wave of protest, and he was recalled again. He went on to become governor of Birmingham Prison, in England—a post from which he was recalled yet again. He kept getting recalled and reinstated because the government and the public could not make up their minds about what they wanted: revenge and blood, or correction and hope.

Even after he was relieved of his duties, Maconochie continued to be consulted at hearings on legislation and regulatory reform. In 1856, a select committee called him to testify. A committee member asked him what proportion of criminals he would say were incorrigible. Maconochie replied, "None at all—my experience leads me to say that there is no man utterly incorrigible. Treat him as a man and not as a dog. You cannot recover a man except by doing justice to the manly qualities, which he may have about him, and giving him an interest in developing them. I conceive that none is incorrigible where there is sanity, there may be some proportion, but very small."

Maconochie knew that prison management was a profession. It is complicated. The spirit of anyone who seeks prison reform may eventually be broken on the wheel of alternation between the public lust for revenge and the conscience of a society that knows we can do better. But Maconochie's spirit was not broken. He left a lasting legacy in many ideals of modern American prisons stated by the American Correction Association (a body of prison professionals who advocate for sound minimum standards), sometimes directly in Maconochie's own words.

One of his spiritual heirs was Howard Belding Gill, a contemporary of the more-famous Thomas Mott Osborne, warden of Sing Sing in the early twentieth century. Gill undertook an academic study on prison industries after his graduation from Harvard and was soon appointed superintendent of a new prison, the Norfolk State Prison Colony, west of Boston. Following Gill's design, it was lain out like a college campus with shops, classrooms, and dormitories. There was a cell block only for the more-recalcitrant people in the prison who could not "be trusted to live decorously within the [prison] wall," as Gill said.

The place was a success, but the Depression brought a reduction in funding. After four escapes, critics charged that Gill, like Maconochie, was pampering prisoners; and he was removed in 1934. He moved on to a variety of posts, but he stuck with his restorative ideals and concluded his career teaching in colleges in Washington DC, where he helped to shape a generation of prison administrators.

Of the many men who gained from Gill's work, the most famous was Malcolm X. It was at Norfolk a generation later that Malcolm educated himself. He had been convicted of pimping and drug possession in February 1946 and went first to Charleston prison in Massachusetts, where the toilet was a slop bucket in his cell. But with an eighth-grade education, Malcolm began taking correspondence courses in English and Latin and was transferred in 1948 to Norfolk. He was very tough and an instant leader. He developed an astigmatism from reading so much in the dim light in his cell. Yet of Norfolk, Malcolm X said in his *Autobiography* that it was "the most enlightened form of prison I had ever heard of." He described Norfolk as "an experimental rehabilitation jail where there were no bars, only walls, and the penal policies sounded almost too good to be true."

Malcolm X received the benefits of a prison that was well run, but many others have come through far more horrible ones and developed as humans nevertheless. These are people who, as soon as they encounter respect and see a path of hope, are ready to be fully alive.

There have been many other reformers. And there is a continuing need for more visionaries. But the trajectory is a hopeful one. We cannot go backward very far before the public is outraged and new progress becomes possible. Hopefully our progress can be more steady in the future. We have ample evidence to show that money spent on effective criminal justice will be saved in the prevention of future crimes.

Appendix B

On the Death Penalty

No discussion of crime, punishment, and prison would be complete without some reference to the death penalty. I have been opposed to it from my childhood, nurtured by Quaker teaching, which has always favored more humane and effective ways of responding to crime.

I was, with Martin Garbus, co-chair of the committee to abolish capital punishment in New York in 1963. We succeeded, and our vigil at the double execution of two prisoners (Flakes and Green are all I remember) helped get it done. They were the last ones in New York State. The practice was restored at the legal level under Governor Pataki, but that law has been overturned in court, and there seems to be no prospect in the near future that it will be reinstituted.

Capital crimes are all horrific; and each one, to varying degrees, leads to new calls for the death penalty.

It was May of 1998 when Stephen Simonetti drove past Cynthia Quinn jogging along the road. He stopped his car and pursued her. When he caught her, he raped her and stabbed her seventy-two times. She was a high school arts teacher and a mother of two children. She was thirty-two years old. In September of 1999, a jury in Long Island sentenced Simonetti to die.

When I visited Simonetti on death row in Clinton prison in Dannemora, New York, he was one of five incarcerated there. At the time, I knew little about his case; I was just interested in talking with him. I was interested in the conditions on death row. I found the five confined to their cells for twenty-three hours a day, all reading in adequate light, no one screaming in pain, no conversation between cells, though that was permitted.

Simonetti admitted his guilt. He wanted to die. He wanted the various lawyers defending him to back off and let the state go through with the execution. In taking that position, he was like many people who commit capital murder.

He was both homicidal and suicidal.

The two often go together. We read of people who shoot themselves after shooting other people. Still others do not have the level of mental illness to go through with the suicide, but are entirely reckless of their own lives by giving themselves up to the police, waiving their rights, making full confessions, and sometimes attempting suicide in their cells. All the men on death row were on perpetual suicide watch both by video surveillance and by direct observation by officers.

When I asked Simonetti why he was not fighting his case, he quite freely volunteered that he would do anything, indeed he would rather die than see his father take the stand in his son's defense. He did not explain further except to say that his father would weep, and he would literally rather die than have that happen.

I admit that, even after all these years, I was surprised that Simonetti appeared of average appearance and demeanor. He is white, of athletic build, a former hockey player, a big party guy, and addicted to alcohol and crack. He has a shock of black hair and a handsome face. He spoke softly to me, and though he was clearly emotionally involved in what he was saying, he seemed to be mentally healthy except for his extreme (suicidal) protectiveness toward his father.

The details of every case are unique. The important point is that the death penalty, on the books at the time Simonetti committed his crime, was no deterrent to him. Even after he cleared his head from booze and drugs, it was still no deterrent. On the contrary, the promise of being put to death may well have been, in the back of his mind, an attraction for him to go wildly, homicidally violent.

Many studies have been done about the death penalty, trying to determine whether it is a deterrent. The overwhelming evidence is the same in them all. The classic one by the Norwegian sociologist Thorsten Sellin compared similar states (Indiana and Illinois for example) during the periods when one had the death penalty and the other did not. There seemed to be a small percentage of higher incidences of capital murder in the states with the death penalty, but he argued that it was statistically insignificant. His point was that if there is no clear indication that it is a deterrent, then it should be abolished.

Since then, every nation in the world has abolished capital punishment except Iraq, Iran, Afghanistan, China, North Korea, Myanmar, and the United States of America.

I wish every citizen could visit death row. Not all the men confined there are as talkative and sociable as Stephen Simonetti. Some are sullen, deeply depressed, and uncommunicative. One looked at me in such an angry way that I was glad that the bars prevented him from attacking me.

However, *they were all entirely under control.* We have the power to do with them exactly what we choose. The idea of taking them, even the very angry ones, strapping them down, and killing them in cold blood is horrible. Officers who have the responsibility of carrying out the executions understandably report that this leads to nightmares, upsets their family life, and does not seem to square with their religious convictions. Most choose to request other assignments even after feeling rather matter-of-fact about the job in the beginning: "Someone's got to do it. They were convicted of gruesome crimes."

When I think of Cynthia Quinn's last minutes on earth and try to imagine her children and the rest of her family learning the news and the jury viewing the photographs of her mutilated body, it is easy to understand why some people favor the death penalty. The man committing that crime seems to have left the human race and should therefore be erased. But after meeting Stephen Simonetti, I cannot imagine his being strapped down and murdered as a justifiable act of the state.

In 1961, I went to see Judge Learned Hand to persuade him to appear at a meeting supporting the cause to abolish capital punishment. He said that he could not do that as a sitting judge. However, the cause was so important to him that he was in no hurry to end our conversation. "Father Chinlund, who do you think are the more bloodthirsty, men or women?"

I said I would not hazard a guess. "What do you think?" I asked.

"I believe that women are more bloodthirsty," he replied, waggling his gigantic eyebrows. "In my family, all the women favor capital punishment, and all the men are against it. The other day, I asked my daughter, Mary, how such a sweet, gentle person as she could possibly believe in capital punishment. And she said, 'Well, Daddy, some people are just garbage and should be thrown away.' So I said, 'Mary, one of these days, I am going to be just garbage myself. Are you going to throw me away?'" Judge Hand chuckled heartily. "She did not think that was the least bit funny!" He was serious about the death penalty and wished me good success with the campaign.

When the law authorizing the death penalty was overturned in 2006 by the New York State Court of Appeals, Simonetti and the others were released from death row into the regular population of Clinton prison. He has since been transferred to Sullivan prison. Simonetti seems now to have no wish to die, and it is my hope that he will find life inside to be better than he imagined it would be when I visited him. We correspond; I hope he will be willing to see me soon and let me encourage him to participate in a program in which he might help other inmates learn to read and write.

There are people who have been so brutalized by life that they should never be released from prison, but we should not brutalize ourselves by turning into the murderers they were and executing them, however "humane" the method might be.

Appendix C

Reforms in the New York State System since 1963

- Contact visits (in the visiting room with no separation between visitor and the person incarcerated)
- Conjugal visits (in a trailer with one or more family members, overnight without monitoring of any kind)
- Inmate liaison committee (established to help with the planning of family days and other events)
- Inmate grievance committee (established to provide a channel for inmate complaints to be considered; sometimes meaningless, often extremely helpful)
- Improved mail system (changed from the days when mail was sharply censored)
- Improved staff training (instead of being all "on-the-job training")
- Introduction of law libraries
- Recognition that working in prison is a professional undertaking
- Establishment of training for supervisors
- Introduction of the Network program
- Drug rehabilitation programs of several kinds including the dedication of a single cell block or dormitory to that purpose
- Introduction of college courses
- Accessibility to correspondence college courses

- Introduction of postcollege-level courses
- Introduction of theatre productions with incarcerated people doing the acting, directing, producing, and playwriting
- Introduction of computer training
- Widening of opportunities to create art of all kinds
- Introduction of business/commercial classes
- Alcoholics Anonymous meetings
- Gamblers Anonymous meetings
- Alternatives to Violence Programs
- Training of incarcerated people to be leaders of AVP
- Anger management programs
- Family reintegration programs
- Introduction (and withdrawal!) of various kinds of "good time" programs toward with the intention of early release

Index

N

Nehru, Jawahar, 82
network program, 96, 155, 164, 166, 173, 175, 181–83, 186, 210
New Yorker, 74, 209
New York State Commission of Correction, 9, 14, 119, 129, 144, 154, 162, 164, 179, 199–200, 203, 224
New York State Department of Correctional Services, 119
New York Times, 115, 138–39
Niebuhr, Reinhold, 30
nonviolence, 170, 194

O

On Crimes and Punishment (Beccaria), 235
Oswald, Russell, 114, 116–18, 121, 132, 161

P

parole, 12, 54, 74, 138–39, 147, 160–63, 176, 178–79, 196, 202, 227–31
Pasternak, Boris, 82
Perry, Rev. Ron, 159
Pirandello, Luigi, 10
Pope Clement XI, 234
positivity, 11
prayers, 21–24, 30, 36, 41, 62, 81, 90, 159, 174
premarital sex, 29
Price, Selma, 186–88
prisoners
  belligerence in, 57
  conjugal visits for, 133
  employment of, 112, 121–22, 126, 180, 183
  health of, 11, 15, 52, 75–76, 87, 123, 153, 204, 228
  recidivism among, 45, 64, 92, 178

reforms in, 190–91, 196–98
  relations with families by, 65, 164, 166–69
  solidarity among, 118
  sports among, 192
  strikes by, 15, 53, 133
  views of, 15, 36, 60, 63, 72, 201, 231
prisons, 11, 45, 129, 132, 146, 149, 191
  chaplains of, 175
  coed use of, 108
  colleges in, 11, 120, 189, 193, 226, 228
  comparisons with monasteries, 10, 156, 158
  crimes in, 49, 90, 143–44, 162, 194
  depictions of, 89, 144, 224
  designs of, 146, 150
  escapes from, 53
  faith communities in, 151
  as harmful, 48, 112, 140, 224
  as helpful, 9, 12, 45, 85, 215, 225–26
  history of, 233
  interracial staffing in, 56, 114, 119, 124, 133
  laws on, 172
  living conditions in, 10, 205
  management of, 209, 237
    separate system of, 236
    silent system of, 220, 236
  public interest in, 10–11, 93, 224
  reforms, contributions of Quakers to, 193
  reforms of, 17, 78, 86, 118–19, 141, 149, 152
  searches in, 205
  therapeutic communities in, 55, 63, 68–71, 77–78, 91–92, 153, 158–59, 162, 173
    ex-prisoners in, 54, 91
    opposition to, 186
    organization of, 58–59, 68, 77, 89, 156

LaVergne, TN USA
10 December 2009
166570LV00003B/145/P